T0243513

LEADING OUTSIDE
YOUR COMFORT ZONE

LEADING
OUTSIDE
YOUR
COMFORT
ZONE

The Surprising Psychology

of Resilience, Growth,

and Well-Being

D. CHRISTOPHER KAYES

STANFORD BUSINESS BOOKS
An Imprint of Stanford University Press
Stanford, California

Stanford University Press
Stanford, California

Special discounts for bulk quantities of Stanford Business Books are available to corporations, professional associations, and other organizations. For details and discount information, contact the special sales department of Stanford University Press by emailing sales@www.sup.org.

Printed in the United States of America on acid-free, archival-quality paper

Library of Congress Cataloging-in-Publication Data
Names: Kayes, D. Christopher, author.
Title: Leading outside your comfort zone : the surprising psychology of resilience, growth, and well-being / D. Christopher Kayes.
Description: Stanford, California : Stanford Business Books, an imprint of Stanford University Press, 2025. | Includes bibliographical references and index.
Identifiers: LCCN 2024009287 (print) | LCCN 2024009288 (ebook) | ISBN 9781503640528 (cloth) | ISBN 9781503641013 (ebook)
Subjects: LCSH: Leadership--Psychological aspects. | Resilience (Personality trait) | Well-being. | Management--Psychological aspects.
Classification: LCC HD57.7 .K394 2025 (print) | LCC HD57.7 (ebook) | DDC 658.4/092019--dc23/eng/20240514
LC record available at https://lccn.loc.gov/2024009287
LC ebook record available at https://lccn.loc.gov/2024009288

Cover design: Martyn Schmoll
Cover art: iStock

CONTENTS

Preface   vii

Introduction
Rising to the Outsized Demands of Leadership   1

SECTION I ▪ FOUNDATIONS OF LEADING

1 Moving Outside Your Comfort Zone as   15
a Source of Growth and Well-Being
Overcoming the Anxiety-Ridden Demands of Leadership

2 What Research Says About the Practice of Personal Resilience   30
Leading for Resilience, Growth, and Well-Being

3 Achieving Optimal Improvement   43
Through Learning and Performing
Moving Beyond the Unrealistic Expectations That Undermine Leading

4 Turning Adverse Events into Opportunities for Growth   57
Accepting Adverse Factors Beyond Your Control

SECTION II ▪ FUNDAMENTAL PROCESSES

5 Cultivating Novel Experiences   71
The Experiences That Count for Developing as a Leader

6 Accepting Unpleasant Emotions   86
Growth from Frustration and Other Painful Emotions

7 Implementing Learning Strategies   102
Five Strategies for Resilience and Growth

8 Motivating Yourself to Learn   115
The Psychology of Learning, Motivation, and Resilience

SECTION III ▪ APPLICATIONS

9 Keeping Focused   131
Overcoming Distractions or Why Staying Focused Is So Difficult

10 Leading Teams   147
Leading Through the Emotional Turmoil of Groups

11 Leading Organizations   161
Resilience, Growth, and Well-Being at Scale

12 Tiered Goal-Setting   177
Overcoming the Limits of Goal-Setting Through Tiered Goals

Conclusion
Pathways to Leading Beyond Your Comfort Zone   193
A Simple Formula for Leading: Move, Sleep, Learn

Epilogue   205

Notes on Methods   207

Notes   209

Index   233

PREFACE

Sheila's new role as team leader quickly turned to frustration. Many of her team members reported burnout and were ready to quit. She noticed turnover was increasing across the company, and the company struggled to hire qualified team members. The quest for talent was heating up. She saw growing unhappiness among her team. Leadership strategies that worked in the past were no longer effective.

Something needed to change. The company had focused on increasing performance through efficiencies for over a decade, which led to improving the top and bottom lines. This narrow focus put the company in a stronger financial position but left the team listless. Team members sought opportunities for personal growth. They wanted to improve their overall well-being so they could come to work energized to learn and perform. Company leaders needed something to increase retention and create a sense of connection to the company. Sheila looked for solutions.

Sheila's challenges are typical of the leaders I meet. Leaders want to support their teams and search for ways to address the demands of the changing workforce. They seek tools for moving outside their comfort zone and toward resilience, growth, and well-being.

The shift to resilience, growth, and well-being demands urgency. Consider the ongoing challenges at aerospace giant Boeing. In early 2024, a panel blew off a plane in mid-flight, exposing passengers to grave danger. Due to some luck, including the fact that the aircraft was still flying low and the quick action of the pilot crew, the plane landed safely. Only minor injuries were reported. However, the incident raised critical questions about airplane safety. Airline safety lapses usually involve many unforeseen events, but one factor began to stand out in this case. Several experts linked the accident to a potentially faulty manufacturing process. They suggested that at the heart of the manufacturing problem was a demotivated and inexperienced workforce. A complete analysis of the situation that led to the midair accident could take years, but one clear set of factors emerged: employee burnout, inexperience, poor morale, and fatigue contributed to the problem. When a workforce lacks a sense of well-being, it struggles with focus and attention to detail. This, unfortunately, results in errors and an inability to identify and respond to problems.[1]

Employee well-being and motivation can no longer be considered a luxury; leaders must consider how these factors impact the organization's short-term success and long-term viability. The situation encountered by Sheila and the morale problem at Boeing expose an essential insight about leading: leaders can no longer rest on old assumptions about employee well-being; they must embrace new approaches to leading and learn resilience themselves in the face of inevitable everyday adversities.

This book offers a path: leading today requires a new emphasis on resilience, growth, and well-being. This book provides the necessary tools to support leaders and their teams as they lead outside their comfort zones. Readers will find:

- Tools and pathways for overcoming common leadership challenges, threats, and frustrations
- Methods for cultivating a mindset to initiate, accelerate, and sustain learning
- Strategies—habits, actions, and attitudes—that support resilience, growth, and well-being
- Guidance on coaching for self-acceptance and managing unpleasant emotions in the midst of daily problem-solving and troubleshooting

LEADING OUTSIDE
YOUR COMFORT ZONE

INTRODUCTION

Rising to the Outsized Demands of Leadership

Leading in an age of anxiety is demanding. Existing leadership training is not adequate for the task. *Leading Outside Your Comfort Zone* provides a framework to help leaders learn and grow from experience in the face of adversity. This adversity-embracing approach helps organizations move beyond tired leadership models and instead focus on resilience, growth, and well-being. It provides a long-term solution that helps leaders find purpose and direction in their work. The strategies in this book will help leaders at all levels excel in the face of growing demands.

Leading Outside Your Comfort Zone emerges from research on the psychology of resilience, growth, and well-being. These areas have been largely overlooked by organizations, but their application to developing leaders can be transformative, both for leaders and for employees.

Your resilience, growth, and well-being are largely determined by your capacity for learning in the face of anxiety, doubt, or frustration. More than any other process, learning generates forward movement toward goals and emotional stability. Learning results in developing new neuroconnections, combating negative psychological states such as depression, and fostering personal and professional growth. Learning improves overall job satisfaction and well-being by fueling purpose, motivation, and social belonging. When leaders learn, they grow.[1]

Leading Outside Your Comfort Zone offers tools to address our contemporary leadership challenges. Workers report record levels of burnout, express a lack of

1

motivation toward work not seen in decades, and openly lament that their jobs lack a sense of purpose. Employees around the globe express a profound sense of loneliness in their lives and at work, and stress levels have reached unprecedented levels. Well-being and motivation are spiraling downward. These trends pose significant challenges to leaders.[2]

Too many remedies offered to leaders provide short-term relief without addressing the underlying problem. This book offers a novel solution: reverse the downward spiral in worker motivation and well-being by learning to lead outside your comfort zone. In the process, you will build resilience and support growth and well-being for both you and your team.

AWAKEN YOUR NATURAL DESIRE TO LEARN

Early insights into the nature of learning and growth came from the psychologist Lev Vygotsky. He proposed we learn when we push ourselves out of our immediate comfort zone. To paraphrase Vygotsky, moving outside a comfort zone awakens our natural learning abilities. When a student becomes interested in a topic, the pressure of learning becomes a source of positive stress. Likewise, a leader who takes on a challenging project becomes motivated and engaged. For Vygotsky, this was the purpose of personal growth: we learn not by seeking comfort but by moving outside of our comfort zone.[3]

To awaken our natural learning ability, Vygotsky introduced the "zone of proximal development," which describes the optimal learning situation. I call this the "learning zone" for short. Learning occurs as we seek to resolve tensions, solve problems, and respond to challenges. We enter the learning zone when we experience just the right amount of tension to activate learning and growth but not so much stress that we recoil into unproductive anxiety. Moving too far beyond your comfort zone shuts down both learning and performing.

Leading Outside Your Comfort Zone outlines three critical zones or experiences associated with leading as depicted in figure 0.1.

1. The comfort zone. Leaders' work is easy here, and they experience pleasant emotions and success. Despite its pleasantness, the comfort zone lacks the necessary tensions that encourage learning. It is also "the complacency zone," as improvement often stagnates.

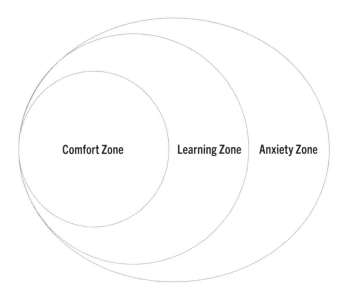

FIGURE 0.1 The Comfort, Learning, and Anxiety Zones

2. The learning zone. Leaders move outside their comfort zone and experience the tensions associated with learning and growing. Stress feels manageable as learning and productivity improve. The tensions inherent in learning are optimized.

3. The anxiety zone. Leaders move beyond the learning zone to a place where too much stress inhibits improvement. Emotions become overwhelming, learning and performance suffer, and productivity declines.

We all have an optimal learning zone. This is where you thrive, learn, grow, and improve. The challenge: this book will help you find your optimal learning zone . . . if you're willing to lead outside your comfort zone.

WHO SHOULD READ THIS BOOK

Leading outside your comfort zone has a dual purpose: helping yourself and others. First, lead yourself. The book will start by asking you to evaluate how prior experiences have shaped you as a person and a leader. You will identify how mentors and role models have influenced you and how you have integrated their values into your leadership. This will help you learn to rely on your values in difficult times and exercise judgment regularly. Good leaders develop the confidence to make decisions and act amid ambiguity and uncertainty about the consequences.

You will also help others as they move outside their comfort zone. The book will give you strategies, skills, and support systems for teaching resilient values to others. As a leader, you will play multiple roles, including coach, consultant, mentor, role model, and sometimes final decision-maker. Those who will benefit from this book include:

- Leaders interested in improving their performance, especially when facing the daily frustrations, stresses, and challenges of management

- Leaders concerned about their well-being and that of their employees

- Individual contributors seeking to assume a leadership role

- Emerging leaders seeking to build their resilience in the face of everyday frustrations and challenges

Others who will also benefit from reading this book include:

- Human resource and education professionals who want to increase their knowledge and capacity to improve the performance-driven well-being of others

- Coaches of all types seeking new tools to develop themselves and others

- Internal and external consultants conducting leadership development efforts

- Instructors and facilitators supporting leadership development

- Researchers seeking a better understanding of how to measure and study resilience

- Managers leading change in their organization

THE FIVE OUTSIZED PSYCHOLOGICAL DEMANDS OF LEADING

Leading has never been easy, but today, leaders face outsized psychological demands. Fortunately, leaders can draw on evidence-based solutions. The psychological demands leaders face include:

Demand 1: Leaders Avoid or Overreact to Unpleasant Emotions

The single biggest challenge that leaders face arises from unpleasant emotions. Unpleasant emotions lead to negative consequences if not adequately addressed. Procrastination, avoidance of conflict, and anxiety emerge. These result in poor performance and poor mental health. If unpleasant emotions are allowed to linger for too long or suppressed, the result is burnout, chronic stress, and disengagement. Too many leaders fail to realize their full contribution as leaders because they suffer at the hands of their unpleasant emotions.

Solution: Build Positive Emotional Engagement with Your Work and Your Team

Building positive engagement means generating curiosity, interest, and excitement. Building positive emotional engagement draws on the power of learning, generating positive feelings and a sense of purpose and growth. When positively engaged, leaders build resilience to navigate the complex emotional territory beyond their comfort zone.

This does not mean acting cheerful when you feel bad. The term *toxic positivity* has emerged to describe how you may be doing more harm than good if you suppress negative emotions and fake a positive attitude. Instead, building positive emotions facilitates finding and reengaging excitement, pursuing genuine interests, and enjoying learning. Don't ignore unpleasant emotions, learn from them.

Demand 2: Leaders Stay in Their Comfort Zone

When leaders stay in their comfort zone, they fail to reap the rewards that lie beyond. They turn to old methods and rely on existing skills. But following old patterns can be disastrous. When you're leading outside your comfort zone, old patterns and solutions no longer work. Complacency will fail you.

Solution: Be More Creative in How You Solve Problems

Leaders must seek new ways to learn and grow to overcome complacency. Being creative means taking chances and accepting new approaches to solve problems. The critical factor is resilience, the ability to continue learning despite short-term setbacks. Resilience requires self-awareness and the confidence to move forward in the face of frustration, fear, and anxiety. Leading outside your comfort zone can motivate you to seek new answers and push you to new areas of understanding. Approaching problems with creativity means being comfortable with challenges and accepting the positive role that unpleasant emotions play in creating the tensions necessary for learning and growth.

Demand 3: Leaders Overemphasize Performance—at the Expense of Growth

One reason leaders remain hesitant to be creative is the fear of failure. Focusing on performance and avoiding failure is the norm in the leadership playing field. Performance means demonstrating skills with ease and consistency. But when leaders stay in the comfort zone of their current performance, they can overlook the need to develop new or refine old skills. Some leadership skills may be innate, but most are learned.

An overemphasis on performance leads to performance plateaus. This can be disastrous when demands increase or situations change. Over time, when leaders focus too much on performing, they become risk-averse and fail to grow.

Solution: Build a Learning Identity

Long-term success in a competitive environment requires a learning identity— the courage to focus on improvement, progress, and change. A learning identity requires accepting short-term setbacks as a natural part of success and an inevitable part of leading. Responding to peaks and valleys in performance becomes natural while leading. A learning identity involves accepting setbacks as temporary. Leaders with a strong learning identity show confidence in their ability to progress even during the worst times.

Demand 4: Leaders Become Rigid Due to Fear, Anxiety, and Frustration

Leading necessitates putting yourself into new, challenging situations and constantly developing and refining your skills. Meeting new challenges involves uncomfortable emotions like fear, anxiety, and frustration. Leading outside your comfort zone comes with changes, uncertainty, and ever-increasing complexity. Leaders may find that turmoil leaves them exhausted.

Solution: Be More Flexible

As a leader, you must develop new capabilities to meet the oversized challenges of leading. Leading requires making judgments and adjusting to further information as it becomes available. As one saying goes, today's solutions are tomorrow's problems.[4] You must develop competencies and implement strategies for flexibility for yourself, your team, and your organization.

Demand 5: Leaders Think They Must Act Alone

Leaders think they need to act alone for two reasons. First, many leaders have learned to trust their judgment. Their early leadership experiences revolved around self-sufficiency and individual efforts, so it is natural to think that leading is an individual activity. Second, leaders may have been lured into the myths associated with heroic leadership—that a single leader is responsible for success or failure. This myth is perpetuated by media and popular culture, which tend to praise or blame individual leaders.

Solution: Build a Coalition of Social Support

Leading is not a solo activity. Successfully leading depends on others across teams and organizations. Although success is often attributed to a single leader, every leader who has accomplished great things has relied on a team of experts who offer support, advice, and implementation. Even though leaders depend on others, successfully leading outside your comfort zone comes with the expectation that you, as a leader, must be prepared to lead.

THE NECESSARY STEPS FOR LEADING OUTSIDE YOUR COMFORT ZONE

Leading outside your comfort zone results in—resilience, growth, and well-being—as shown in figure 0.2. These are developed through four steps:

1. Cultivating novel experiences. Moving outside your comfort zone starts by cultivating new experiences that generate tensions and challenges. Seek out novel experiences as you move from stagnation to growth. Initiate new experiences, face new challenges with an open mind, and discover untried solutions.

2. Accepting unpleasant emotions. A range of pleasant and unpleasant emotions will emerge when leading outside your comfort zone. Learn to become aware of, accept, and act in these situations.

3. Implementing learning strategies. Identify strategies to improve self-awareness, enhance learning, and improve. Each chapter in this book offers evidence-based strategies for learning and helps you identify your strategies.

4. Motivating yourself to learn. Lead by initiating, sustaining, and increasing effort toward learning.

FIGURE 0.2 How to Lead Outside Your Comfort Zone

ORGANIZATION AND CRITICAL INSIGHTS OF THE BOOK

Throughout the book, you will encounter surprising ideas about leadership. These counterintuitive ideas emerge from neuroscience, psychology, and leadership studies research. Some of these insights will challenge your current beliefs about leading. For example, you may believe that only pleasant emotions can motivate learning, but research tells a different story. Unpleasant emotions play a valuable role in learning. Another counterintuitive insight is about resilience. You may think you are born with resilience, but research shows resilience is a competency that can be learned. Further, although following popular goal-setting methods is essential for leading, you will see that many tried-and-true goal-setting techniques fall short in contemporary leadership.

The book is organized into three sections:

Section 1 offers foundational insights into leading beyond your comfort zone. Section 1 maps the challenges of leading in a complex, changing world and explains how these challenges place new demands on leaders.

Chapter 1 shows how leaders at Netflix, a contemporary technology company, must address different and more challenging problems than business leaders in past decades, such as Jack Welch at General Electric. A key difference is that leading in contemporary organizations requires a focus on resilience, growth, and well-being for the leader and their team. The chapter outlines five myths associated with leadership: (1) leadership skills are only needed by those at the top of the organization, (2) only new leaders need to learn, (3) leading relies mainly on leveraging power and resources, (4) leading for resilience is primarily about overcoming traumatic experiences, and (5) leaders are heroes who sacrifice their well-being for the sake of the organization. These myths are embedded in a false dependence on heroic leadership, the belief that a leader is all-powerful and must sacrifice their well-being for the sake of the organization. The chapter discusses four new ways to think about the demands of leadership: dealing with a changing and restless workforce, exercising judgment in the face of shifting and competing demands, building self-awareness and accepting public review, and leading for the well-being of self and others.

Chapter 2 explains how the growing use of the language of resilience informs everyday leadership challenges. Resilience primarily focuses on adapting to significant adversity, such as trauma and hardship. Still, leading with resilience is more than dealing with situations involving trauma and severe hardship. This is called positive resilience, which includes seeing resilience as initiating, sustaining, and increasing effort when faced with the everyday challenges of leadership. Lessons learned from resilience research include strategies to respond to and recover from setbacks, the need to develop a positive outlook on the future, and the value of a mindset that sees opportunity in obstacles. Resilience research also reveals the importance of building a network of economic, social, and psychological support.

Chapter 3 describes a central challenge of leading outside your comfort zone—balancing learning with performing. Learning involves taking chances and gaining new insight and skills. In contrast, performing entails demonstrating existing knowledge and skills while minimizing the chance of failure. Leading outside your comfort zone requires balancing the interplay between learning and performing. The goal lies in reaching optimal improvement. The chapter advocates developing a dual mindset that embraces learning and performing. The chapter offers insights on how to build confidence for learning but also cautions that excessive reliance on confidence can be harmful because it detracts from learning.

Chapter 4 argues that successfully leading outside your comfort zone requires seeing adverse events as opportunities for growth. Leaders can learn how to maintain well-being in adverse events beyond their control. This involves self-awareness of how you, as a leader, respond to certain emotional situations involving triggers, sensitivities, and transitions. Examples from US and European football show how external forces can shape performance and that many factors associated with leading may fall outside the leader's control. Methods to respond to external events are presented.

Section 2 provides a deep dive into the specific process associated with leading outside your comfort zone, as described in figure 0.2.

Chapter 5 describes how leaders can cultivate novel experiences that support learning through: (1) common challenging situations and opportunities for growth, (2) the amount of practice and experience, (3) the underlying feelings of experience, and (4) stories of resilience. Methods to reflect and learn from these experiences are offered.

Chapter 6 advocates for learning to accept unpleasant emotions through enhanced emotional self-awareness. Accepting frustration and other painful emotions can lead to growth. It offers strategies to improve your understanding of emotions and shows why a better understanding of your emotions becomes vital to growing as a leader.

Chapter 7 presents five research-based strategies to support learning: building positive emotional engagement, creative problem-solving, developing a learning identity, enhancing flexibility, and building social support.

Chapter 8 outlines the benefits and mechanisms of learning and how they contribute to resilience, growth, and well-being while leading. Leading outside your comfort zone requires rekindling your natural ability to learn. Learning is an underlying mechanism of resilience, as learning helps leaders adjust, solve problems, and self-regulate in the face of unpleasant emotions.

Section 3 applies the insights from the previous sections to specific situations, including improved focus, leading teams and organizations, and goal-setting.

Chapter 9 describes ways to enhance focus under different conditions, ranging from time management to mindfulness and breathing exercises. The world is filled with distractions. Leading requires overcoming these distractions to meet short- and long-term objectives. The chapter outlines eight distractions or threats to focus: shifting between activities, multitasking, mind-wandering, rumination, timing, cognitive overload, off-loading, and time pressure.

Chapter 10 offers advice on applying ideas from previous chapters to leading a team. Leading teams provides a unique challenge. Teams are full of emotions, and leading a team requires effectively managing the emotions of self and others.

Chapter 11 recaps the lessons of the book for leading an organization. Leading an organization requires a unique set of competencies. Building resilience at the organizational level requires strategic thinking, communication, and other skills that go above and beyond those needed when leading at other organizational levels.

Chapter 12 offers tiered goal-setting as an alternative to traditional goal-setting processes such as SMART and stretch goals. By focusing on growth and well-being, tiered goal-setting involves setting three simultaneous and incrementally challenging goals and adjusting the goal based on self-guided feedback. A template for setting tiered goals is offered, and methods of assessing progress toward goals are suggested.

The conclusion summarizes the insights and tools presented throughout the book into three simple lessons for leading outside your comfort zone: moving, sleeping, and learning. Physical movement, adequate sleep and recovery, and the joys of learning form the basis of resilience, growth, and well-being and provide both a starting and an ending point for leading outside your comfort zone.

Foundations of Leading

ONE

Moving Outside Your Comfort Zone as a Source of Growth and Well-Being

OVERCOMING THE ANXIETY-RIDDEN
DEMANDS OF LEADERSHIP

Today, leaders face unique challenges. They inherit a restless workforce. They respond to the competing demands of stakeholders. They exercise judgment with limited information. They offer their personal lives to public scrutiny. They wrestle with the gaps between organizational and individual values. They become the screen onto which others project their emotions. Leading requires moving outside your comfort zone at every moment.

This chapter compares the challenges leaders faced in two organizations at different times. Leading at Netflix, a contemporary company, requires resilience, learning, and self-awareness. In contrast, leading at General Electric in the 1980s and 1990s focused on power, resources, and authority. Comparing these two companies highlights common leadership myths. Leaders often fail because they continue to hold onto these unproductive myths, which were relevant in the past but no longer provide a true basis for guidance. Holding onto these myths will prevent you as a leader from meeting contemporary leadership's challenges, resulting in learning the wrong lessons.

The chapter outlines four myths: the belief that leadership skills are only needed by those at the top of an organization, that only new leaders need to learn, that leading relies mainly on leveraging power and resources, and that leading for resilience is primarily about overcoming traumatic experiences. Taken together, these reinforce the myth of the heroic leader. The chapter then outlines the real challenges of contemporary leadership: leading a changing and restless workforce, exercising judgment in the face of shifting and competing demands, building self-awareness and accepting public review, and leading toward consensus and the well-being of self and others.

LEADING NETFLIX VERSUS LEADING GENERAL ELECTRIC: THE CHANGING NATURE OF LEADERSHIP

Netflix began as a promising business upstart; it provided a mail-order DVD rental service, a mail-in version of the Blockbuster video rental chain. Then, broadband internet service replaced dial-up. The large amounts of data that could be delivered directly to homes and businesses threatened the very existence of the DVD format. The company's leaders saw the threat. At first, the path to navigate this change was unclear, so the leaders offered Netflix up to its biggest rival, Blockbuster. However, Blockbuster declined to buy the struggling mail-order company.[1]

Blockbuster's decision to ignore Netflix turned into one of the most ironic failures in corporate history. Netflix transitioned from a mail-order DVD rental service to a full-fledged production studio, while Blockbuster, once its potential financial lifeline, filed for bankruptcy. Investors became so optimistic about the transition at Netflix that analysts valued it alongside top technology firms such as Facebook, Apple, Amazon, and Google. Taken together, these companies were known as the FAANG stocks, the most valuable companies in the world.

But things started to change after the COVID-19 pandemic. With viewers no longer stuck at home, the number of subscribers to Netflix's streaming service began to fall. As a result, the high stock price, relied upon by its leadership to fund the production of elaborate films and TV shows, began to wane. While recruiting and retaining new subscribers proved difficult, navigating the social landscape proved just as challenging. Leadership became mired in controversies. Leaders at Netflix were lauded for offering a significant amount of diverse content but found themselves facing a situation that seemed beyond their control. The concern was that some of its content went too far and was offensive. Some employees staged a walkout in protest. One employee was fired for interrupting a meeting and making demands that leaders saw as unreasonable. Many custom-ers threatened to cancel their subscriptions if Netflix did not drop certain con-tent they saw as offensive. Co-CEOs Ted Sarandos and Reed Hastings publicly defended Netflix's content but backtracked after the backlash began. Sarandos admitted to having "screwed up" in his response and reflected on the need for more "humanity" moving forward.[2]

These co-CEOs were lauded as one of the world's most influential corporate leadership teams just weeks before and were now embroiled in a public relations crisis. But in the current environment, even seasoned leaders like Hastings and Sarandos needed to adapt to the quickly changing situation. Sarandos expressed a desire to learn and consider the positions of multiple stakeholders. Even more critical, he publicly recognized the need to validate the emotions of these various stakeholder groups.

These leaders survived because, as co-CEOs, they were committed to learn-ing.[3] This helped them develop the resilience necessary to navigate the unpre-dictable business landscape. The challenges at Netflix illustrate how leaders face new and ever more challenging demands from multiple stakeholders.

Few leaders could have imagined that employees, let alone outside interest groups, would yield such power over a company's future as they did at Netflix. Consider Jack Welch, the former CEO of General Electric, an industrial giant and one of the most influential companies in US history. Welch may be one of the most influential business leaders of all time. His commitment to leadership development within the company produced many of the most significant cor-porate leadership development programs in a generation. He viewed leadership development as important at all levels, but it is unlikely that his approach would be successful today. He once complained about outside interest groups trying to hold GE accountable for billions of dollars of environmental damage. He mini-mized the influence of these "do-gooders" and insulted their approach. He even blamed the environmentalists for the loss of US competitiveness.[4]

Today, Welch's sentiments about being a leader appear old-fashioned and un-likely to be persuasive. Welch personified the ultimate "command and control" leader molded in the Cold War image of a military leader ready for battle. For all his strengths, Welch's approach would yield little success in today's environment. Welch reigned when American manufacturing was waning. The US was losing manufacturing jobs at a historic rate and hundreds of thousands of jobs were moving overseas. During Welch's reign, profit margins in GE's notable industrial businesses, such as lightbulbs, appliances, and jet engines, were shrinking. It is no wonder that by the time Welch stepped down in 2001, a significant portion of GE's revenues came from nonindustrial products. GE Capital, a financing arm of GE, overtook manufacturing as GE's primary income source.

Jack Welch ranks unquestionably as a great manager, increasing GE's value multiple times during his tenure. However, he based his decisions on assumptions about leadership that are no longer relevant. Welch made a name for himself as a leader by squeezing corporate margins but failed to create a resilient business model. Ultimately, he may have developed thousands of good managers capable of allocating resources, but he could not develop leaders who could imagine GE's future. Welch successfully led GE during the significant shift from industrial to knowledge work. Still, even the best leaders, like Welch, struggle to build time-tested and resilient organizations. In the aftermath of Welch's time as a leader, GE experienced a catastrophic fall in stock price, ran through several top leaders, and struggled to identify a successful strategy. The "GE model," an essential case study once taught in business schools, disappeared from classrooms. The company was broken into three parts, and GE's legendary training center in Crotonville, New York, a place that had developed a generation of leaders, was sold.

MYTHS ABOUT LEADING THAT HOLD YOU BACK

The reverence shown for Welch may be deserved, but we should not hold up post–Cold War leaders like Welch as examples of the leaders we want to foster now. The need for an authoritarian leader, who is always in charge, emotionally distant, and even resentful of stakeholders, is one of many leadership myths. These myths present a false sense of what it means to lead. The myths contributing to our oversized expectations about leading and responses to those myths are summarized in table 1.1 and discussed in more detail below.

Myth 1: Leadership Skills Are Only for Those at the Top
First, consider the myth that leadership skills exist primarily for those at the organization's top. Leaders beyond those of the C-suite also require leadership development. As a professor, consultant, and coach, I meet with emerging leaders, mid-level managers, and top leaders at various levels of government, military, academic, business, and nonprofit organizations. These leaders may not face the

TABLE 1.1 Myths and Realities of Leading

MYTH	REALITY
Leadership skills are only for those at the top.	Leaders and managers at all levels of the organization need leadership skills.
Only new leaders need to learn.	All leaders, experienced and new, need to learn to address new challenges.
Leading relies mainly on leveraging power and resources.	Leadership requires influencing others even when you have little power and few resources.
Leading for resilience is primarily about overcoming traumatic experiences.	Resilience is required for everyday situations and especially important for leading outside your comfort zone.
Leaders are heroes who sacrifice their well-being for the sake of the organization.	Leaders are consensus builders who manage competing demands across multiple stakeholders.

same level of scrutiny as CEOs, but they experience leadership challenges with similar intensity. One leader was frustrated by being caught between upper management's demands to meet increasing performance standards and employee demands for greater autonomy. Another leader struggled to bring new, cleaner technology to a small African village. Yet another leader in a university became despondent as she tried to implement new and innovative teaching methods in a system that could not see beyond narrow outcomes.

Workers at all organizational levels can be leaders, and everyone can benefit from leadership development. While stories of top leaders such as Hastings and Sarandos are familiar, stories of leaders across every level who find themselves perplexed by the conflicting demands of leadership are just as important. Many leaders hold no direct reports but benefit from learning to be more resilient in their work, career, and lives. For example, at Netflix, several individuals questioned the company's policies to stand up for an issue they believed in. They took a public stand that risked their careers for a greater purpose. Aren't those who challenged the status quo at Netflix leaders, too?

In short, all leaders, formal and informal, experienced and novice, can benefit from developing the skills associated with leading outside their comfort zone. Learning to be more resilient helps them navigate the daily challenges of leadership. As an organization grows, expands, deals with crises, and transitions to new business areas, employees need to understand the dynamics of these changes and learn to thrive in the changing environment.

Myth 2: Only New Leaders Need to Learn

A second myth is that only new or inexperienced leaders must learn new skills and acquire knowledge. One executive I worked with, Bill, believed that only new managers deserved leadership development. Bill ignored the fact that all the leaders in his organization faced a changing workplace, a constantly evolving set of regulations and customer demands, and emerging technology that could alter the course of the organization. Bill overlooked the problems that arose when employees transitioned from individual contributors to leading others. This critical period often makes or breaks one's professional career, but unpleasant emotions, such as self-doubt, fear of failure, and anxiety, are shared by leaders across the organization. Bill failed to understand that leaders need resilience across the organization and at every level.

Further, the myth persists that learning occurs mostly in the classroom and is a formal process. Learning conjures images of sitting in a lecture hall, late nights studying, and excruciating exams, but learning also occurs as a continual process of accepting and processing new information. Learning involves adapting to new situations, developing new skills, and acquiring and refining habits. Learning and increasing awareness of the learning process become imperative, as learning is required everywhere and every day.

Myth 3: Leading Relies Mainly on Leveraging Power and Resources

The third myth posits that leadership mainly relies on power and resources. However, leadership depends on understanding oneself and using power and access to resources for the common good. The best source of power is the power to act. Consider, once again, the protesting employees at Netflix; despite having no formal authority or resources, these individuals brought their viewpoints to the forefront of discussions about employee involvement. Their resources arise from their conviction and ability to influence those in power, but they do not require formal power.

Resources still matter, but expertise, knowledge, creativity, and personal power are even more critical. The rise of information technology, social media, and the interconnected world allows new voices to rise to power. Once housed in monasteries, libraries were the gatekeepers of knowledge, but information has become more democratic. Aspiring leaders hold access to significant resources requiring little more than a smartphone. Ironically, the retired Carnegie libraries, once hubs of information in cities across the US, have been converted into stores that sell Apple iPhones!

Myth 4: Leading for Resilience Is Primarily About Overcoming Traumatic Experiences

The fourth myth suggests that resilience is about overcoming traumatic events or hardships. Indeed, many such situations require resilience. However, Heidi Brooks, from the Yale School of Management, coined the term *everyday leadership* to emphasize leaders' daily challenges. Leaders address novel and challenging situations regularly. Brooks teaches her students to face the complexity of leadership and helps them gain insights into their leadership style, values, and abilities. These everyday leadership challenges, setbacks, and frustrations prove more common and are just as likely to derail leadership efforts as trauma and crisis. Leading requires constant resilience.[5]

Since resilience no longer applies simply to overcoming trauma and is no longer confined to medicine and psychiatry, its expanded definition is broader and more immediate. Resilience reflects the ability to engage natural learning processes and acceptance that setbacks are inherent to leadership.

Myth 5: Leaders Are Heroes Who Sacrifice Their Well-Being for the Sake of the Organization

The previous four myths can be summarized as the myth of heroic leadership. Too often, leaders ignore the need to improve their self-awareness and instead embrace myths associated with self-control and courageous action. Being the hero requires demonstrating great personal sacrifice for the sake of the larger organization. The myth relies on a mistaken belief that neglecting one's well-being somehow translates into organizational success. Being a hero may make leaders feel good about themselves, but these sacrifices will not likely impact the organization positively. More likely, these heroic actions will have a detrimental effect on leaders and followers.[6]

Heroic leadership can result in many dysfunctions: excessive work hours and demands, a rescuer to save the day, a single person who can solve all your problems, and a dramatic change that puts others at significant risk. One example of the excesses of heroic leadership arose when Elon Musk called for "production hell" as Tesla was ramping up production of its autos. Production hell resulted in long hours of exhausting work. Musk sacrificed sleep and when he did sleep, it was on the production floor. He would later try to instill this same view of self-sacrifice into his employees at Twitter when he purchased the company, proclaiming that only the "hardcore" would be spared layoffs—pictures of Twitter employees folding out makeshift beds under their cubicles circulated on social media. The show of self-sacrifice came in the service of corporate production.

Unfortunately, heroic leadership may boost the leader's self-esteem but does little to build their self-awareness. Many of the employees at Twitter described Twitter's version of "production hell" as unsustainable, and many more were fired. Other leaders left the company out of frustration. In the end, heroic efforts such as these prop up the leader's self-image but come at the expense of the individual and the organization, negatively impacting long-term performance and mental health.[7]

In other cases, leaders might embrace extreme measures to demonstrate their level of self-care. Young leaders find this a potent force as they adopt public personas around self-care as self-deprivation. Tech start-up cultures appear particularly vulnerable to leadership from a self-deprivation angle. Jack Dorsey, the founder of Twitter, publicizes his self-care regime, which includes fasting, cleansing, and self-imposed exiles, where he refrains from speaking for days at a time.[8] These actions go beyond focusing on self-care and often move into public displays of self-sacrifice that reinforce the notion of heroic leadership. But heroic leadership as self-care ignores well-being and lacks staying power. Self-care effectively relieves stress in the short term, but the benefits of these practices are often fleeting without a focus on long-term resilience and learning. Leaders must concede that self-awareness does not equal self-care or self-sacrifice. Instead, leaders should focus on improving self-awareness, which can result in profound insights into how actions impact the organization.

Holding on to these myths gives rise to false confidence about leading. Leading today involves more than being the hero, acquiring power, or holding formal authority. Leading requires resilience, growth, and a focus on well-being. Leading requires adjusting to change, exercising judgment, and acting in the face of competing demands.

CHALLENGES AND OPPORTUNITIES OF LEADING

Leaders face a daunting set of challenges. Russ Vince, professor emeritus at the University of Bath in the UK, suggests that unpleasant emotions like anxiety remain pervasive in leaders.[9] Vince advocates that leaders understand leading in the context of these emotions. Recognizing these emotions allows leaders to thrive, providing challenges and opportunities for leading, which are summarized in figure 1.1

Leading a Changing and Restless Workforce

To begin with, leading requires facing an increasingly restless workforce and changing demographics. Leaders face fundamental challenges in the demographic makeup of the workforce, such as an aging population in developed economies, fewer entrants into the workforce, a backlash against immigration in Western countries, slowing birth rates, and increasing retirement rates among

FIGURE 1.1 Challenges and Opportunities of Leading

older workers. Leaders must find creative ways to address worker shortages that may extend for decades.

It's not just the demographics of the workforce that require attention; it's also how workers value work. The relationship between workers and their work has changed. Work-life balance, work identity, and employee burnout are some factors that require more thoughtful leadership. Leaders must create meaningful work where employees can pursue their own goals and purpose. Employees no longer value longevity and loyalty to their employer like they once did. Employees demand more than just a place to work; they are asking for leaders to make work more fulfilling by creating cultures that support well-being. Employees want a workplace that will improve their daily lives beyond work. At the same time, they demand higher pay and better working conditions.

Leadership in organizations requires understanding well-being in an increasingly complex environment where crises and threats are everyday events.[10] Leading requires identifying ways to support others by becoming purposeful partners and working alongside employees to create an environment of growth and well-being. Leaders are called to develop policies that accommodate workplace well-being trends and assist employees in finding their larger purpose and goals, not just at work but in all facets of their lives. Leaders are asked to build a more equitable and flexible workplace and to find ways to support the entire person, not just work-based identity.

Leaders must accept that employees struggle with well-being, mental health, and burnout. Well-being plays a central role in supporting organizational effectiveness. For example, the World Health Organization recently classified burnout as a global concern, and the U.S. Surgeon General called burnout a moral issue that devastates workers. Leaders must address challenges associated with workers' focus, additional work and home pressures, anxiety, concerns over finances, and mental well-being. In particular, the need for resilience has escalated among college students and the Millennial generation due to the challenges these groups face with mental health such as stress, anxiety, fatigue, and depression.[11]

Exercising Judgment in the Face of Shifting and Competing Demands

Leading outside your comfort zone requires judgment despite competing stakeholder demands. Leaders rarely hold access to complete data, the data they possess often needs to be revised, and deep analysis takes precious time. In situations like these, leaders rely on their accumulated experience. They count on their judgment. Judgment is developed through experience and requires acting in the face of ambiguity, uncertainty, and doubt.

Judgment requires learning how decisions affect the well-being of stakeholders since each will see the choices differently. Leaders need to understand multiple viewpoints, even those appearing in polar opposition. Judgment does not require giving up one's perspective and embracing both views. Instead, judgment requires engaging others in decision-making and understanding the consequences of decisions. Consensus building replaces direct authority as the key factor in judgment. Terry Price, a professor of leadership at the Jepsen School of Leadership at the University of Richmond, described how leaders often fail to consider the opinions of others when making decisions and often miscalculate the implications of their choices. In addition to including multiple stakeholders in crucial decisions, he recommends that leaders be flexible and willing to shift or modify their decisions after they see the results. Flexibility is a hallmark of good leadership. Judgment requires updating perspectives based on new information and always being ready to adapt.[12]

Leaders face new and increasingly complex challenges. We expect leaders to be resilient despite ever-increasing potential failures and setbacks. For example, the newly appointed Disney CEO Bob Chapek found himself the target of negative publicity by both progressives and conservatives for his response to a new Florida law that targeted how gender identity could be taught in schools, only to be relieved of his position after eleven months. Decisions made seemingly in private become public fodder. Consider Vishal Garg, CEO of Better.com, who fired over nine hundred employees on a Skype call, only to see his message posted on online chat boards. Despite the negative publicity, he returned to ask another group to quit weeks later.

Leading requires diving head first into new challenges that hold uncertainty. Successfully navigating these challenges requires taking risks and acceptance of an unclear path. For example, Lisa Su, appointed CEO of chip maker AMD in 2014, spent her first year dodging bankruptcy. Su diligently brought the company back to life and positioned it for a revival as the demand for computer chips soared. However, this revival was not certain when Su took the helm, but leaders must search for opportunities in uncertain circumstances.[13]

The challenges of competing stakeholder demands are evident in the embattled university president. University presidents, a once highly sought-after leadership role, hold one of the most challenging leadership roles in the US as they navigate issues of student mental health and generational change, calls to union-ize various arms of their workforce, external stakeholder demands, and budget woes. University presidents face calls to step down and even receive death threats. Changing societal expectations put university leaders in a bind: they have little power over faculty who often hold lifetime employment through tenure or long-term contracts, but stakeholders, such as politicians, donors, and even faculty, call for change. University leaders show no leader is insulated from the stressors of their job and that resilience is needed more than ever, as leaders experience the same challenges to well-being experienced by others in the workforce.[14]

Building Self-Awareness and Accepting Public Review

Increasingly, leaders serve as the public face of their organizations. Because their actions can reflect on the organization, leading requires greater self-awareness. Leading requires understanding how others will perceive values, strengths, and weaknesses. The link between leading and self-awareness is measurable among business leaders. A survey of nearly a thousand CEOs from nineteen countries found that 80 percent strongly agreed that they, the CEO, needed to change and focus on self-improvement for their organizations to succeed. According to the study, the key to effective self-improvement was greater self-awareness, develop-ing the next generation of leaders in their organizations, and seeking feedback from others.[15]

Individual actions can have significant consequences in a highly connected world. As leaders become public-facing figures, their actions remain under con-stant scrutiny. When Ursula Burns took the CEO role at Xerox, she was the first woman of color to become CEO of a Fortune 500 company. She was also the first woman to succeed another woman in the role! She quickly learned that her actions reflected on Xerox. Every action she took and word she said was seen through the company's lens. As a result, her self-awareness became a key to her success. She noted every action and how it reflected on her leadership and the company.[16]

Leading for the Well-Being of Self and Others

Ursula Burns, Elon Musk, Jack Dorsey, and others reveal a tension between per-sonal values and organizational needs. Leading requires accepting that individ-ual goals may conflict with organizational goals. There often comes a time when leaders must make tough decisions about their values.

Consider Natasha Harrison, the top attorney at a leading New York law firm. Harrison was appointed deputy chair, the second highest position in the firm, in December 2020, the height of the COVID pandemic. She navigated the firm through a difficult time. But leading what many consider one of the world's top trial law firms proved unsatisfying. Harrison wanted to change and reimagine how law firms do business, so she left to start a new firm. She recognized that law firms' traditional model of charging clients by the hour was a significant factor in burnout and dissatisfaction, especially for younger attorneys. In an interview for the *Financial Times*, she noted that the model created a perverse set of incentives, where attorneys wanted to keep a case open to bill more hours while clients were suffering through an issue, hoping to make it as short and painless as possible.[17]

Rather than try to reform an old-school law firm, she took what, for many, would be a counterintuitive action. Starting a new firm allowed her to focus on employee well-being by changing how law firms paid their employees. This meant abandoning the goal for a certain number of billable hours, often exceeding two thousand hours a year. Instead, Harrison was reducing the hours in her new firm so attorneys could work on cases they found energizing and engaging. In many situations, this meant working pro bono. She would have struggled to make this change in her old firm. While reducing the billable hours may impact the bottom line, Harrison believed that reducing the hours would decrease burnout and turnover and make the work more fulfilling, ultimately leading to a more substantial and fulfilling career for attorneys.

Harrison represents the emerging trend of leading with a focus on well-being. A leader in this movement was Helena Morrissey, the mother of nine children and former fund manager at firms like Newton Investments. She was Britain's model working mother through the mid-2000s. But, noting her difficulties in seeking work-life balance, she reevaluated her role-model status and corporate role. She formed the 30% Club, a project to ensure that women represented at least 30 percent of corporate board members. She later questioned her goals and influence, asking whether she perpetuated the myth that leaders can do it all. But trying to do it all reinforced the myth of heroic leadership at the expense of well-being. Harrison and Morrisey represent two leaders refocusing their careers and leadership on well-being.[18]

MOVING OUTSIDE YOUR COMFORT ZONE

As you embark on your leadership development, reaffirm your commitment and capacity to learn. Reaffirming your self-worth, appreciating your current skills, and building on past successes can help support resilience. The changing leadership landscape brings emotions to the forefront of leading. Anxiety and other emotions can derail leadership goals. Leaders who affirm their commitment to growth and well-being are better equipped to address the challenges. Begin the affirmation process by completing Exercise 1: Affirming Your Commitment to Learning as a Leader. Affirmations such as these support successful change across several activities, such as weight loss, academic performance, anxiety reduction, and general well-being.[19]

In addition, identify two or three individuals who can support you through this process. The individuals can come from work, personal life, or other areas, but they must be people whose opinions you trust and whom you believe will work in your best interest. These are your change coaches. Richard Boyatzis has spent decades studying the benefits of formal and informal coaching and the impact of social support on effective change. He confirms that leadership development is most effective when we work with others. Seek feedback, support, and inspiration from others, including family, friends, peers, mentors, and other leaders who have blazed the trail you seek to pursue. Peer coaching groups can also be a form of social support in these change efforts. Ask others for their opinion and input. Undergo a 360-degree feedback process to understand how others view you. Observe others who have already achieved what you aspire to achieve.

Embarking on a leadership development effort means acquiring a beginner's mind. This involves accepting that you don't have all the answers, being open to the opinions of others, and being open to being wrong in your own opinion. Keeping a journal of daily thoughts and actions and paying attention to the physical aspects of health and well-being are good tactics for gaining a beginner's mind. Journaling helps clarify values as well as refine future aspirations as a leader.[20]

Moving outside your comfort zone becomes a common aspect of leading and is accompanied by anxiety and other unpleasant emotions. To accept the challenges of leading, leaders must abandon the old myths about leading or risk failing to develop the skills, insights, and resources necessary for leading in this environment. Successful leaders will embrace the challenges of leading a diverse and ever-changing workforce, learning to adapt and change, and working toward building well-being in themselves and others.

Exercise 1: Affirming Your Commitment to Learning as a Leader

Research shows that affirming your commitment to yourself and your value improves outcomes. In this exercise, you will create affirming statements about your ability to deal with complex and frustrating learning situations. Select a phrase from Section A (1 through 3), then choose one of the phrases in Section B to complete the sentence.

Section A

1. When learning and frustrated, I will . . .

2. When challenged by something, I will . . .

3. When learning something new, I will . . .

Section B

4. . . . think about the things I value about myself.

5. . . . remember things that I have succeeded in.

6. . . . think about people who are important to me.

7. . . . think about things that are important to me.

Write the entire sentence by combining the sentence stem from Sections A and B.[21]

TWO

What Research Says About
the Practice of Personal Resilience

LEADING FOR RESILIENCE, GROWTH, AND WELL-BEING

Leaders rely on the language of resilience more than ever. With the COVID-19 pandemic, global warming, globalization, and other crises, the language of resilience has surged in popularity. For example, during the pandemic, business leaders turned to the language of strength to reassure employees about the future of their organizations. CEOs reminded employees they had the necessary capabilities to lead through the crisis. Leaders drew on the language of resilience to communicate with employees, respond to shareholders, and reassure customers. The language of resilience reached across the organization to show that everyone could handle challenging situations, reassuring that all were competent to work through emotionally charged situations. During these uncertain times, leaders invoke resilience to motivate followers through the day-to-day challenges.[1]

Despite this, many leaders still need to learn the value of resilience. Definitions of resilience vary across industries, professions, and academic studies, making it difficult for leaders to know how resilience can help them lead. This is unfortunate, as resilience is essential for leading outside your comfort zone. Resilient leaders turn the anxieties of leading outside their comfort zone into opportunities for learning. Challenges create growth.

This chapter describes how the research on personal resilience informs leadership. From the start, understand that resilience goes beyond crisis and trauma; resilience is needed to lead every day. This is positive resilience: adapting to everyday adversity and challenges. Resilience implies mental toughness, the ability to continue working toward goals despite adversity associated with unpleasant experiences, and the ability to lead a return to normal and stable states. The critical takeaway from reviewing hundreds of studies on resilience is this: leaders need to adopt resilience strategies to support the well-being, growth, and productivity of themselves and their teams.

LEADING OUTSIDE YOUR COMFORT ZONE: TURNING CHALLENGES INTO OPPORTUNITIES

Psychologists initially used the term *resilience* to describe recovery from hardship, such as potentially traumatic events, chronic stress, or significant loss. The connection to leadership becomes clear: leadership requires responding to crisis-driven problems, potentially traumatic events, or hardship. However, most leadership situations will not rise to the intensity associated with chronic stress, significant loss, or trauma. More common roadblocks to leading arise from daily unpleasant challenges, setbacks, and frustrations. These more common roadblocks are the most likely factors to derail a leader's career. A definition of resilience for these more common situations implies building the capacity to initiate, persist, and direct effort toward learning when experiencing unpleasant situations.

A baseball analogy proposed by two psychologists, David Sherman and Geoffrey Cohen, highlights the need for resilience. In major league baseball, they argue, most attempts to hit the ball result in a strikeout. Imagine how you would feel if you had a setback seven out of ten times. Like major league baseball players, people face constant setbacks when leading. The baseball analogy gives us a good starting point: imagine that you will lead outside your comfort zone at least 70 percent of the time![2]

As someone who wanted to learn about resilience and leadership, Jaye exemplifies how overcoming these challenges can help you lead outside your comfort zone. She had experienced discrimination in many forms but also knew that she had been the beneficiary of a supportive family and other support systems. She graduated at the top of her class and earned her PhD. After teaching in a university setting, she knew she wanted to make an impact beyond the classroom, so she landed a job at a top military university that had only recently started accepting women.

After years of working in higher education, she often shared the challenges of being a woman of color in a white male–dominated institution. Despite her success, she knew that resilience was not something she was born with or took for granted. Instead, she saw resilience as something that she needed to focus on each day and cultivate throughout her life. She strongly advocated building resilience in all students and relied on her experience to support them in developing theirs.

Jaye knew that being a leader required her to understand her emotions and the emotions of others. Leadership required her to learn and grow and support others in their growth. Like many resilient leaders, Jaye had learned to cultivate positive emotions when learning something, but she was aware of the unpleasant emotions that can arise during moments of learning. She saw these emotions as indications of challenges that caused her to test her assumptions. Even more importantly, as an advocate of lifelong learning, she believed that finding ways to learn from all her experiences, both pleasant and unpleasant, was at the heart of her resilience. The increasing demands placed on leaders like Jaye in their personal and professional lives require a new and deeper understanding of developing and sustaining resilience.

Jaye turned challenges into opportunities for learning. Cohen and Sherman offer a list of common opportunities that move leaders out of their comfort zone (table 2.1).

TABLE 2.1 Opportunities for Learning

- Experiencing performance demands on the job or in class
- Becoming frustrated by new goals or aspirations
- Not being able to obtain accurate information
- Being asked to challenge long-held beliefs
- Experiencing illness, fatigue, or burnout
- Encountering the defeat of one's pet project or major initiative
- Finding out that you might be on the wrong track
- Realizing you lack support for a project or initiative
- Receiving negative feedback
- Being rejected for a job offer or promotion
- Receiving actual or perceived social slights
- Leading a team where conflict requires unpleasant discussion
- Providing feedback that is uncomfortable

Adapted from Geoffrey Cohen and David K. Sherman, "The Psychology of Change: Self-Affirmation and Social Psychological Intervention," *Annual Review of Psychology* 65 (2014): 333–71.

POSITIVE RESILIENCE

Jaye demonstrated positive resilience. My research over the past twenty-five years has focused on how leaders learn, how they respond to challenging events, and how they can prevent disasters from happening. I conclude that many leaders fail to move outside their comfort zone because they are plagued by fear, anxiety, and frustration. These unpleasant emotions prevent them from gaining the skills, implementing the strategies, and finding the support they need to learn and grow as leaders. They assume a position of retreat. The language of resilience, well-being, and growth can move leaders out of the position of retreat and toward action.

Resilience involves learning skills and competencies for dealing with these challenges. Ned Powley created the term *positive resilience* to describe proactively responding to challenging situations and taking advantage of personal and organizational resources to support resilience when needed.[3] Positive resilience reflects the confidence to act, even in doubt. Positive resilience offers long-term strategies, support, and skills that move leaders and their teams outside their comfort zones in an exciting way. Resilience reflects the ability to withstand unpleasant events, work through challenges, and remain focused on learning during difficult situations. The result is the enduring capacity to act despite experiencing these unpleasant emotions and the confidence to learn new skills in the face of novel challenges.

WHAT WE KNOW ABOUT RESILIENCE THAT CAN SUPPORT LEADING

To understand positive resilience, it is helpful to see how the research on resilience contributes to navigating everyday leadership situations. Resilience has been offered as an explanation for how people (1) adapt to adversity, (2) acquire and demonstrate mental toughness, and (3) support an organization as it returns to normal after a crisis or trauma.

Adapting to Adversity

Adapting to adversity focuses on how to recover from psychological trauma, traumatic events, acute stress, or posttraumatic stress. It includes recognizing the developmental potential that can emerge after significant life setbacks. George Bonanno of Columbia University has studied resilience for decades. While looking at resilience in a healthcare setting, he identified a resilience paradox: despite having experienced traumatic events, many individuals often lead healthy, productive lives. Yet, hundreds of studies with thousands of individuals failed to reveal why. In short, while resilience is a healthy response to trauma, we know little about the factors that predict posttraumatic resilience.[4]

Bonanno noticed a few recurring patterns. Resilience requires an ongoing adjustment to changing circumstances and the need for self-regulation. Also, he observed that everyone might achieve resilience slightly differently, and recovery from the aftermath of trauma may require different resilience strategies for different people. Bonanno concluded that resilience requires slow steady progress when overcoming trauma. Progress is built upon identifying and redefining solutions as you go along. Self-regulation and adaptability are key to resilience.[5] He speculates that a few things may be essential. First, individuals should focus on cultivating a basic disposition that includes openness to new experiences and improving emotional stability. Second, social and economic stability are key; financial resources, job security, and education are the foundation of resilience. Much of resilience, his work suggests, may flow from our social and economic situation, which points to the importance of work and livelihood underlying resilience. Stable and productive work is vital to building resilience. Other factors include maintaining a positive outlook and finding meaning in daily activities, factors often related to work and economic activity.[6]

In a similar approach, Richard Tedeschi studied how people responded to significant life setbacks and loss. He looked at those who suffered from a severe illness or an accident, the loss of a loved one, or a traumatic experience. To his surprise, not only did many of the people he studied return to normal, but eventually, they saw their loss as a turning point for progress and growth. The bad experience, ultimately, helped these individuals take stock of their situation and served as a launching point to a productive and meaningful life. He came to understand resilience as a form of posttraumatic growth, which he described as the ability to achieve a fulfilling and happy life in the wake of trauma. In one of his studies, Tedeschi and his colleagues observed resilience in a population in China. They found that three factors were vital to posttraumatic growth: deliberate rumination and thoughtfulness about the events, coping based on self-sufficiency, and social support.[7]

Both Bonanno and Tedeschi make us consider that although resilience in the face of hardship is not inevitable, it is possible. The good news is that resilience may be more common than we think, even if the causes of resilience remain a mystery. According to psychiatrist Richard Friedman,[8] citing a comprehensive study, over 90 percent of Americans report having experienced traumatic events, but only about 7 percent report long-term symptoms such as posttraumatic stress disorder because of these events.[9] In other words, most people recover from periods of acute stress brought about by potentially traumatic events, such as 9/11, an earthquake, or a significant life crisis.

The challenges brought about by the acute nature of traumatic experiences may offer clues to how to address the day-to-day challenges that most leaders will encounter. Let me be clear. Overcoming trauma brought about by hardship associated with crisis, significant loss, and disaster is essential for leadership, but these factors account for only a small percentage of leadership situations. Leaders should remember that individuals will respond to challenges differently. Resilience requires thoughtfulness about events, taking small steps to work through the situation, being open to new experiences, and accepting anxiety. Resilience involves becoming self-sufficient and requires remaining optimistic about the future. Even more important may be access to economic and other resources.

Mental Toughness

Mental toughness also plays a complex role in resilience. The toughness perspective entails maintaining positive movement toward goals, even when experiencing emotional hardship.[10] The mental toughness approach has received particular attention in sports and performance-enhancement psychology. Mental toughness involves regulating emotions and focus, which helps us handle pressure, failure, and success. It emphasizes the ability to tough out difficult emotional or physical situations by continuing to pursue the goal despite these emotions. The mental toughness approach emphasizes self-control—the mental strength to overcome negative emotions and continue toward goals.

The mental toughness approach permeates our conception of what a resilient leader should be. Resilience, the conventional wisdom suggests, is about controlling your emotions to achieve a goal with a higher purpose. The mental toughness perspective suggests "toughing it out" no matter the unintended consequences to our physical or psychological well-being. So mental toughness has a downside, and there is a penalty for overriding our negative emotions. Toughing it out for too long inevitably leads to sustained stress. Extended periods of stress result in exhaustion, while self-control, the main ingredient in mental toughness, is quickly depleted. Further, the mental toughness approach may perpetuate negative stereotypes of masculinity and self-sufficiency by emphasizing the short-term benefits of overriding negative emotions. Limitless expression of mental toughness can also lead to negative social consequences. For example, a study on Special Forces training showed that those recruits who expressed high levels of willpower were judged less favorably by those around them. At the same time, the expressed willpower was not related to increased performance.[11]

Psychologist Angela Duckworth describes how passion and perseverance motivate achievement. Those who have the ability to maintain progress toward their goals and endure the hardships that arise are described as having grit. Duckworth's research supports the notion that perseverance and passion work as forms of resilience and are important characteristics, above and beyond general intelligence and other innate talents, that support successful goal achievement. Duckworth distinguishes emotional self-control from determination and explains grit as the unwavering ability to pursue one overarching, dominant goal at the expense of other goals for extended periods, despite what obstacles might be in the way.[12] Grit has gained wide appeal; however, research points to the fact that grit is another form of conscientiousness, a personality factor that has long been associated with success in careers, leadership, and academic achievement.

But grit, too, is only sometimes desirable. When we start pursuing a goal, we need an understanding of the nuances and complications of the situation. Judgment is required to reevaluate our priorities as we pursue the goal and gain more information. Mindlessly following our goals becomes problematic unless we adjust to the emerging circumstances we experience as we pursue goals.[13] The unintended consequences of continuing to pursue a goal can be counterproductive and can result in burnout, stress, depleted energy, and low self-esteem. Further, mental toughness research fails to account for regret. One marathon runner I spoke with relied on her grit to train for and complete marathons. Only later did she realize that the stress of long-distance training had done long-term harm to her body. In reflecting on her experience, she decided her persistence in pursuing the goal was destructive.

Grit, conscientiousness, and other related ideas on mental toughness offer an approach to resilience that requires an uneasy but essential embrace. Leaders must persevere in the face of challenges and hardship and develop strategies to regulate emotions and the learning process. However, mental toughness in leadership involves more than unwavering persistence in pursuing a single, unchanging, and unmodified goal. Leadership requires flexibility and adaptability to change, including changing directions over time. Definitions of mental toughness should be expanded to embrace learning, including paying attention to shifting goals, backtracking, and abandoning destructive or irrelevant goals. Leading requires stamina and dedication.

Returning to Normal

A third approach focuses on resilience as a "return to normal." The focus is on better understanding "how employees respond to severe challenges and adversity" and on resilience as a form of "positive adaptation despite experienced adversity."[14] Diverse fields of study, including military leadership, aviation, sports, and sports management, provide essential insights into why and how resilience matters for leadership. Resilience can be described as a process of bouncing back and returning to a "normal" equilibrium state, which involves recovering from past events and informing future actions.[15]

Organizations have adopted a range of resilience training practices. Resilience training in organizations often supports a range of performance outcomes such as increased achievement of goals and increased efficiency of production; physical and biological effects such as reduction of fatigue or stress; psychological factors like increased positive affect; work factors such as satisfaction, engagement, and decreased burnout; and mental health factors such as well-being and a reduction of stress, anxiety, and depression.[16] Resilience training can help leaders improve organizational and leadership outcomes, such as well-being, increasing self-efficacy, and taking preventative measures against adverse outcomes such as burnout, fatigue, and stress.

BUILDING BLOCKS OF RESILIENCE

Taken together, research on personal resilience offers valuable insights for leading. Resilience is how individuals respond to setbacks, including challenges, hurdles, and unpleasant experiences. These setbacks range from traumatic experiences to minor challenges experienced daily, and resilience is a process that involves taking steps to address these challenges. There is no preset path, and everyone must determine their path forward. Everyone has a unique resilience profile.

Resilience is vital before, during, and after challenging events. It supports purpose, well-being, motivation, and productivity. Leading with resilience engages strategies that provide a sense of direction, offers the tools to manage stress, and can lead to the confidence to meet the challenges of leading. Leading with resilience involves developing a positive outlook that provides hope for an improved future. The result is an optimistic but realistic outlook—no one gains by expressing an overly rosy view of the future. Instead, leaders serve as catalysts for growth and change by setting the tone for a new, different normal.

Resilience is a learned competency, a set of attitudes, skills, and mindsets about one's capabilities. These competencies are not fixed; although there may be elements of personality that support resilience, no one's resilience is set at birth. Self-regulated learning strategies, such as developing emotional stability, self-awareness and management, and openness to experience, are key resilience competencies. Resilience involves the desire and motivation to learn and grow in the face of unpleasant, even traumatic, experiences and the motivation to find a path forward when prospects appear grim.

Resilience entails a mindset, a way of looking at the world that sees obstacles as potential paths to growth and transforms obstacles into opportunities to grow. Unpleasant emotions are not suppressed or ignored but seen as inevitable. Unpleasant emotions are recognized as sources of information, and in some cases, they are the catalysts for change as they generate problem-solving, information-seeking, and learning. Resilience implies a long-term mindset, so unpleasant experiences can be overlooked in the short term while considering possible future learning and improvement.

Resilience is a finite resource that may require shifting attention from accomplishing immediate goals and outcomes to supporting long-term well-being. Because resilience is essential for learning, growth, and leading a fulfilling life, it must be constantly nourished and replenished. In other words, resilience is more than mental toughness; resilience sees unpleasant situations as transient but recognizes that sustained stress, unpleasant emotions, or extended periods of poor well-being are unproductive in the long run. Resilience is also a privilege. It may rest at the mercy of external resources such as emotional support, economic capacity, and social support. With the support of external resources, resilience can be attained.

Resilience does not signify a life free from pain or unpleasantness. The purpose of resilience is not to retreat from unpleasant emotions, even if fleeing from negative emotions may be a viable short-term strategy. Resilience is not simply remaining positive in the face of negative emotions or unpleasant events. Positive resilience involves seeking new challenges despite frustrations and fears and emphasizes learning in the face of unpleasant emotions, challenges, and setbacks.

MAJOR LEAGUE BASEBALL PITCHER R. A. DICKEY LEARNS THE KNUCKLEBALL

The story of major league baseball pitcher R. A. Dickey and how he developed his unconventional pitching style illustrates the importance of resilience as a learned competency. In his early twenties, just out of college, Dickey looked forward to a promising career as a pitcher and signed a six-figure contract with the Texas Rangers. But when a physical exam revealed a mechanical anomaly in his pitching shoulder, Dickey was relegated to the minor leagues before throwing his first professional pitch. The club was unwilling to take the risk as the probability of a debilitating injury proved to be too high. Despite the initial promise of a major league career, Dickey worked as a semi-professional player, which paid so poorly for the first ten years of his career that he struggled to pay his bills. Still, Dickey had faith in his upward trajectory.

Occasionally, he would move up to play a single major league game, but he needed more consistency when given this rare chance to perform. Dickey examined his progress each year, and although he was confident in his ability to improve, he remained disappointed with his performance. He wasn't progressing, and he wasn't consistent; this was a source of frustration year after year.[17]

Dickey started an unconventional program to salvage his career, but it was a long shot. Rather than giving up pitching due to his physical limitations, Dickey focused on developing a new skill and switched from striving to be the best fastball pitcher to becoming the top knuckleballer. The knuckleball is the most challenging pitch in baseball. It was uncertain that anybody could do what he set out to do—throw a competitive and consistent knuckleball to the best hitters in the world. Few major league pitchers throw the knuckleball consistently enough even to consider this strategy. The knuckleball is unreliable, and learning to throw it always proves brutal; pitching a consistent knuckleball would be frustrating. According to sportswriter Jeremy Stahl, learning to throw a knuckleball isn't only about teaching your body to throw it. It's not just about physical capability and motor skills. Success at a knuckleball requires a disciplined mind, especially when performing at the highest levels of baseball.

Dickey understood the physical and mental demands he would face and the complex mental challenges of the knuckleball. His focus on the process rather than a predetermined outcome demonstrated his approach to learning. He estimated he put in thirty thousand hours perfecting his new pitch. It required slow, steady change over more than six years, and doubt set in regularly. Day after day, he went to the gym and struggled, wondering if he would get it right or if he was making progress.[18]

Dickey had several sources of technical and emotional support. He not only had the support of his wife, but he also received help from pitchers such as Orel Hershiser. He even sought the advice of a highly select group of former professional knuckleball pitchers, including Tim Wakefield, who were all too eager to help the next generation of pitchers learn to pitch, thereby keeping the tradition alive.[19]

After six years, he had his shot at the major leagues again, but things didn't go well. To hint at how bad it was, the opening chapter of his autobiography was titled "The Worst Night I Ever Had." He gave up six home runs. It was not just the worst night for Dickey, but it was recorded as the worst pitching night in the history of major league baseball. His major league career seemed doomed.

Nevertheless, Dickey was determined to master the difficult pitch. At the same time, he continued to practice other, more traditional pitching techniques. He considered the knuckleball only one of his strategies. He would need to use the knuckleball discriminately as one of many pitch variations in his arsenal. Over time, he introduced the pitch into his lineup of different angles, speeds, and spins to throw off the batter. It wasn't just about trying to throw the knuckleball. The knuckleball served a strategic purpose in his pitching sequence: to disorient and confuse the batter. The variation in his pitches became his signature.[20]

Dickey worked through years of frustration, challenge, and setbacks, but his resilience paid off. In 2012, eighteen years after being drafted into professional baseball, Dickey was the leading pitcher in the major league with two hundred strikeouts. That year, Dickey was awarded the Cy Young award, the highest honor for a pitcher.

REFLECTING ON YOUR EXPERIENCE

Building resilience starts with reflecting on your experiences as a leader. As a leader and lifelong learner, you have already demonstrated resilience. As a formal or informal leader, you have experienced challenges and setbacks as a foundation to learn and grow. Begin reflecting on your resilience by working through Exercise 2 at the end of this chapter. The exercise will help you recognize challenges that have helped you learn resilience.

A common characteristic of resilience is learning from past experiences and developing a positive outlook on the future. Resilience involves seeing unpleasant events, such as setbacks and hardships, as temporary and moving beyond these momentary experiences to see the future as a time of fulfillment. Consider when you experienced a setback and how you addressed and coped with that situation.

Resilience holds many facets and can mean different things. As you reflect on your past leadership experiences, consider creating a personal definition of resilience. Review the elements of resilience in figure 2.1 as a guide to creating your definition of resilience.

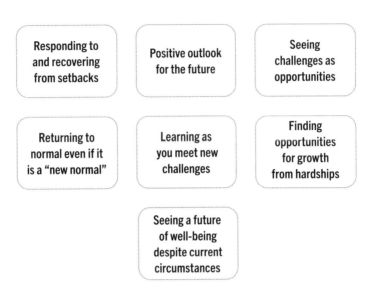

FIGURE 2.1 Building Blocks of Resilience

This chapter reviewed how research on personal resilience serves as the basis for leading outside your comfort zone. Leaders readily adopt the language of resilience, but the implications of resilience as a leadership strategy have yet to be fully realized. Leading with resilience becomes essential for overcoming many unpleasant situations and is critical for meeting the everyday challenges of leading. Leaders face many challenges, and resilience entails seeing these challenges as opportunities to learn and grow.

Exercise 2: Reflecting on Your Resilience as a Leader

1. What challenges have you faced in your life and career, and how have you addressed these challenges? As a guide, turn to the leadership development opportunities offered by Sherman and Cohen in table 2.1.

2. Provide at least one example of how you can use opportunities like those in table 2.1 as opportunities for growth and development. In other words, how can a challenging situation help you improve your resilience?

3. What skills or approaches might help you deal with these challenges as you progress in your leadership development journey?

THREE

Achieving Optimal Improvement
Through Learning and Performing

MOVING BEYOND THE UNREALISTIC
EXPECTATIONS THAT UNDERMINE LEADING

If you have invested in reading this book, you are a leader who wants to perform at your best. You know firsthand that developing yourself as a leader requires a tricky balance of setting and maintaining high-performance expectations while simultaneously taking time for learning. You have achieved a level of success in one or two areas. Yet, you have probably kept reading because you struggle to meet high expectations of yourself as a leader.

The prior chapter offered new ways to look at leading through the lens of resilience. This chapter describes two essential mindsets for building resilience and leading outside your comfort zone. It then describes how leaders balance the dual demands of learning and performing, presents four distinct modes of learning and performing, and explains why each mode is essential for improving as a leader.[1]

THE LEARNING VERSUS PERFORMING DILEMMA

Consider Kari, an executive in our courses who sought to balance learning and performing. Kari's promotion from top sales rep to regional sales manager was bittersweet. Kari excelled at sales, enjoyed meeting with customers, felt challenged by winning over her most demanding clients, and thrived on problem-solving. Her long hours and persistence led to consistent sales successes and confidence that these successes would continue. She learned all the details of her product mix early on so she could spend her time working with her customers and not updating her knowledge of new products. But in her new job as regional manager, she no longer worked directly with the customers. Instead, her days consisted mainly of reading sales reports and generating spreadsheets. The role of the regional manager required her to monitor industry trends and track shifting customer demands. She was in daily contact with her sales force but seldom spoke to customers directly. Despite success in her prior position, she felt ill-prepared for her new job.

Kari illustrates how prior orientation may need to change when a leader takes on a new role or faces a new challenge. Kari was no longer confident that her efforts had a direct impact on sales. As regional manager, the feelings associated with winning new business had disappeared. The new job proved multifaceted, and she now relied on success from a wide range of sales territories, making forecasting unpredictable. Kari struggled to accept that her performance now depended on the success of her sales force rather than her direct effort to sell to customers.

In our research, we saw a frequent challenge experienced by leaders like Kari: having had stunning success in one area, these leaders faced new challenges that led to frustration. Kari needed to shift her expectations about her role. She could no longer rely on her experiences; she needed to focus on learning new techniques and skills. She needed a new mindset.

Top performers like Kari want to be successful and focus on things they do well, but their existing skills may not easily translate into a new role. The stories of successful people failing are familiar—the admired CEO who feels like a failure as a parent, the sports hero who goes bankrupt. A business executive fails to convert a command-and-control leadership style to the consensus-building associated with politics. Even Michael Jordan, one of the greatest basketball players of all time, tried to transfer his skills to baseball and was largely unsuccessful.

Chris Argyris's influential *Harvard Business Review* article, "Teaching Smart People How to Learn," argued that intelligent people with a track record of making good decisions are highly sought after, supported, and promoted in organizations. However, this early success leads to problems as they climb the organizational ladder because they have never learned how to learn. They have only learned how to succeed. Argyris taps into the fact that learning is difficult for everyone. But, more importantly, he emphasized that learning is complex.[2]

Learning is difficult for many reasons. Fear of failure, discomfort with novelty, and concern about appearing incompetent can explain why some leaders fear learning. When they fail to meet high expectations immediately, leaders may return to their comfort zone. However, leaders can overcome these challenges by adopting a dual learning and performing mindset.

LEARNING AND PERFORMING: A DUAL MINDSET

Learning and performance describe two mindsets. Mindset reflects an attitude, and attitudes are often unconscious.[3] These attitudes guide our behaviors. Both learning and performing are essential for improvement. Learning requires taking chances, setting aside old ways of doing things, and not getting too caught up in failure. On the other hand, performing implies putting existing skills to work and demonstrating existing capabilities. Performance reflects staying within your comfort zone and executing well-rehearsed patterns.

Psychologist Anders Ericsson describes how to achieve this dual mindset.[4] For Ericsson, all individuals face a dilemma—whether to focus on learning or performing. Performing results in short-term success but requires that individuals forgo long-term improvement. Some individuals, however, engage in deliberate practice, a type of self-directed learning. Deliberate practice is the ability to pursue high performance through improvement. It involves monitoring that performance, learning from it, and adapting it over time. Some people reach an effortless, "autonomous" performance level, where the interplay between learning and performing becomes natural.

In applying Ericsson's scenario to leaders, you can see that leaders may be forced to forgo their learning in the service of performing. While this strategy may be adaptive in the short term, it may stifle learning. A similar relationship between learning and performing emerges from the research on competency development and adult learning. Boyatzis and Kolb focus on the differences between the here-and-now experience (e.g., performing) and long-term development (e.g., learning). Learning and performing reflect distinct but necessary modes of progress toward achieving our full potential.[5]

Psychologist Carol Dweck distinguishes between fixed and growth mindsets. The phrase "what you got is what you got" captures the performing mindset, while a learning mindset, also called a growth mindset, is reflected in the statement, "I am not limited in what I can learn." Dweck and others have conducted extensive studies on the growth mindset. Those with a strong growth mindset believe they can develop their intelligence and possess the potential to learn, grow, and improve. They assume they can overcome challenges because learning is possible, and this positive expectation is reflected in their attitude toward learning.[6] Those with a fixed mindset believe their intelligence is fixed and cannot improve. They show less perseverance and focus on demonstrating existing skills. Those with fixed mindsets performed worse than those with growth mindsets in some activities. For example, students with a growth mindset perform better on standardized tests than those with a fixed mindset in studies.[7]

Distinguishing between learning and performing is more than just an idea. Evidence shows that learning and performing involve different underlying neurobiological processes, each associated with different emotions. For example, performing at high levels requires extensive focus, suppressing stress and unpleasant emotions. Learning, in contrast, is accompanied by anxiety, frustration, and other unpleasant emotions. While anxiety and stress are necessary for learning, they may interfere with performance.[8] Meanwhile, the kinds of stress that enhance learning can reduce performance.[9]

Successfully leading outside your comfort zone requires a balance of learning and performing. Performance is necessary for successful execution, while learning is essential to improve. Learning focuses on the long-term commitment to improvement while performing concentrates on getting things done here and now. Performing is demonstrating competencies while learning is developing new ones. Table 3.1 summarizes some of the differences between learning and performing.

TABLE 3.1 Learning and Performing

LEARNING	PERFORMING
Develop new strategies for accomplishing tasks	Rely on existing ways of doing things
Focus on the process	Focus on the outcomes
Seek new challenges in activities you have not yet mastered	Demonstrate competency in things you already do well
Seek new experiences	Rely on existing methods for getting things done
Take calculated risks	Concentrate on measuring outcomes
Evaluate as you go along	Focus on the completion and narrow outcomes
Seek opportunities for development	Seek recognition for successes

SERENA WILLIAMS OVERCOMES A SIGNIFICANT CAREER SETBACK

Serena Williams regularly balanced learning and performing throughout her career. Recognized as the best tennis player of her generation, she is one of the highest-performing athletes of all time. She has more top titles than any other female tennis player in history and was the number one tennis player in the world for longer than anyone. She holds twenty-three Grand Slam titles and four Olympic medals.

How has Williams been able to maintain such a high level of success? A clue lies in a less publicized distinction she once held: the most comeback wins. She often fights her way back after being down earlier in a match. In the same year, she won four major Grand Slam tournaments and led the field in returning to win a match while trailing her opponent. As one headline described, Williams has "mastered the art of the comeback."[10] Williams shows this resilience both in particular matches and across her career.

Williams initially ascended to the top ranks of female tennis in 2002 and subsequently fell out of the top fifty-three times in the next fifteen years. In two of those periods, she returned to the top ranks again. In one period, she held the top spot for nearly four years. In a third effort, she reached as high as the top ten. One thing is clear: Williams spends as much time improving, fighting her way back to number one, as she does performing at the top of her game. It may seem surprising that even the world's most outstanding player spends so much time trying to improve—striving to play at her full potential.

One situation illustrates Williams's resilience. In 2012, Williams was thought to be at the top of her game. She was the favorite to win the French Open held in Paris. Despite the high expectations, or maybe because of them, Williams lost to an unranked player in the tournament's first round. This was a devastating loss for her. One headline claimed that she was no longer queen of the court and that her crown had been taken away.

At thirty-one, most players would have retired after such a defeat, but Williams took another route. She found a new coach and began practicing for her next tournament, even before leaving Paris. Williams chose an unlikely new coach, Patrick Mouratoglou. A mid-level tennis player, Mouratoglou had forgone the opportunity to work in his father's business to follow his passion for tennis. Over the years, Mouratoglou developed a reputation for his unique training style, yet he had not coached any top players. Working with him, Williams improved in specific areas of her game and identified new winning strategies.[11]

According to Mouratoglou, he helped Williams update her game, and she developed a more complete and better game than she had as a twenty-year-old. She reworked her schedule to address the demands of playing tennis in her thirties. In 2013, Williams came back to win the French Open. In the following years, Williams accumulated more top titles than any other player in the modern era of tennis, even winning four of the five top tournaments in a single year.[12]

Williams's thoughts and feelings after her defeat at the 2012 French Open will remain a mystery, but what she demonstrated was seen in many individuals we studied. They had once been at the top of their game but felt they no longer had the competitive edge they once held. In other cases, they had achieved stunning success in one area but saw themselves as unaccomplished or struggling in another. They needed to learn and adapt.

Rather than puffing up self-esteem and ego, leaders like Williams focus on enhancing the quality of their experience, leading to sustained learning. Confidence comes not from building self-esteem but from building skills and improving awareness of one's motivation. Rather than emphasize the outward fruits of success, they turn inward to reflect on their capabilities. By combining a mindset of learning and performing, leaders can overcome the negative factors that hinder improvement. They learn to accept and assess what actions they can take to face the next challenge. These leaders view frustration as an opportunity to learn and consider setbacks as a normal part of the development process.

THE IMPROVEMENT MATRIX

Improvement results from the interaction between learning and performing. Both can operate simultaneously and coexist at various intensities. Four modes of improvement arise from the interaction of learning and performing (see figure 3.1):

- *Stagnation.* The stagnation mode arises from the intersection of low performing and low learning. Stagnation is defined by slow improvement. It often occurs when beginning a new activity but can appear anytime during an improvement process. Stagnation likely results in frustration with improvement efforts.

- *Deliberate learning.* The deliberate learning mode arises from the intersection of low performing and high learning. Deliberate learning describes a situation where you are learning but not putting your learning into practice. You may be improving, but you still need to put that improvement to the test in a performance situation. When you are engaged in learning, you can improve by applying your learning to practical problems and routines.[13]

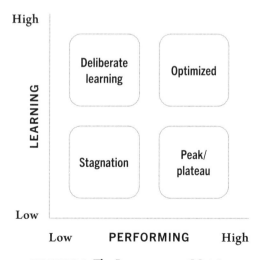

FIGURE 3.1 The Improvement Matrix

- *Peak/plateau.* The peak/plateau mode arises from the intersection of high performing and low learning. This mode occurs when performing well, but there is a need to grow, get better, improve, or find more enjoyment from an activity. A peak or plateau typically occurs when you are already good at doing something but want to achieve more. You are getting results, but you need to get better. Many reach a point where they stagnate. Improvement is either slow or nonexistent. For Ericsson, experts could rise above stagnation and continue to improve, whereas novices reached a peak and could not rise above their current level of performance. The result is a plateau, where the novices no longer improve but have reached the top of their performance abilities unless they can learn new approaches or strategies to improve.

- *Optimized improvement.* The optimized mode arises from the intersection of high learning and high performing. This situation occurs when you have achieved a balance between learning and performing. Optimized improvement results in getting better by applying your knowledge to solve problems or do well in performance situations, achieving incremental gains, and seeing improved performance results.

PATTERNS OF IMPROVEMENT

The improvement matrix provides a visual space to explore relationships between learning and performing. Leaders can identify their current location on the grid and make plans for the next steps. For example, you can move toward learning if you are in the peak/plateau mode, characterized by high performance, but frustrated with a lack of progress and growth. If you are in the engaged deliberate learning quadrant, move toward performing and look for opportunities to demonstrate your newly developed skills. If you are in the stagnant quadrant, move toward deliberate learning or the peak/plateau quadrant. Finally, you can move to the optimal quadrant from any location on the grid as you seek to balance the immediate demands of performance with longer-term learning needs.

A typical improvement pattern follows the matrix's U shape. With this pattern, leaders move from learning to stagnation. With more practice, leaders become more proficient and performance increases, reaching optimal improvement. The U pattern emerged from the idea of a learning curve, which represents a normal process of improvement where errors decrease at a steady, predictable pace.[14]

However, not all improvement efforts follow a perfect U pattern. The original learning curve came not from observing human improvement but from monitoring manufacturing process improvement. The original learning curve was called the Curtis-Wright curve, named after a company that built aircraft in 1936. The Curtis-Wright curve showed that aircraft manufacturing errors decreased steadily over time as companies learned from their mistakes. New technology helped contribute to streamlining processes and operations.

Human improvement follows a different set of laws and does not provide as clear a picture of improvement as manufacturing. Recent research sheds new light on how leaders develop and shows that modern statistical methods often smooth out complex changes in how leaders learn. Development does not follow predictable patterns, nor does it follow a U shape. Leadership is characterized by many ups and downs. Stops and starts are common. Progress can be slow or fast.[15]

Leaders should look for additional patterns in their improvement and not become discouraged by periods of slow progress or setbacks in their improvement, where their skills and abilities appear to regress. Consider other patterns, such as a Z pattern across the improvement matrix. With this pattern, leaders begin something new by learning and quickly optimize performance, then experience periods of slow progress. As a leader, identify your pattern of improvement.

MAINTAINING SELF-CONFIDENCE FOR IMPROVEMENT

Both learning and performing require self-confidence. You must believe in yourself and that you can learn and perform. Self-confidence involves feeling that we deserve and are capable of growth and well-being. Studies support this well-established fact: when we are confident about our abilities to be successful, we can improve. Confidence in our abilities reinforces our willingness to put in effort, push ourselves to succeed, and overcome obstacles.

However, confidence works in subtle ways. It is the product of faith built up across many situations, both successes and failures. With each successive goal sought, with each new challenge, confidence grows a little at a time. Confidence can create a mindset for new challenges requiring new skills, perspectives, and resources. Unfortunately, leaders often overestimate their ability to respond effectively to new challenges and easily confuse confidence with actual competence. Confidence rests in the belief that you will succeed; competency involves holding the skills to succeed.

Confidence involves a tricky balance. Too much confidence can be distracting because confidence does not directly lead to solving problems. Focusing too much on boosting self-confidence can lead to complacency, where leaders reassure themselves that they are capable and worthy of their leadership role but don't seek out the necessary learning and resources to address the current challenges. We can become so confident in ourselves that we overlook the need to learn.[16]

Too often, leaders attempt to thwart threats to their confidence by reassuring themselves that they are valuable leaders. The focus on building confidence creates significant problems for leaders and those they lead because they expend effort to reassure themselves in their leadership role rather than explore new learning methods. This can make leaders less likely to accept setbacks, become less likely to recognize that they need to update their skills, and more likely to blame others or outside factors when encountering failure. The balance requires having just enough confidence to take bold action but not too much confidence that you fail to learn.

Building self-confidence without simultaneously considering self-improvement can be a trap. Self-confidence should not serve as a substitute for improvement. This is especially true when it comes to dealing with negative feedback. Stanford psychologist Carol Dweck and her colleagues noticed that when subjects in their studies received negative feedback, the result was overwhelmingly the need to boost confidence. It was as if reaffirming one's talents served as a psychological buffer to negative feedback. However, the negative feedback led to different outcomes based on the actions that the individual took after boosting their confidence. For some, the boost in confidence resulted in self-improvement. When this group of participants received negative feedback about their performance, they turned their attention to their talents to boost confidence. Such self-assurance helped them identify what they needed to do to improve. For these individuals, reaffirming their talents was essential for maintaining personal growth and improving performance. By reaffirming their talents, they regained their confidence and sought further improvements. However, in other individuals, their process of growth stopped short. They reaffirmed their talents but never sought further improvements. For this group, what seemed most important was to reinforce their self-esteem. Maintaining positive self-esteem was the end of the story. For these individuals, boosting their self-esteem was both the starting and the stopping point for their improvement efforts, as the need to consider the feedback never seemed to enter their minds.[17]

One of my colleagues, Travis, helped me think of a metaphor for the role of confidence and self-concept. Travis began his career as a helicopter pilot for the US Army. He has taken the lessons he learned as a pilot and applied them as a successful business consultant. He described that when flying a helicopter, he was always aware of a potential landing spot in case he needed to make a quick and unexpected landing. A good helicopter pilot displays vigilance in looking for a safe landing spot, even if it is rarely used.

Self-confidence works similarly. We always need to be on the lookout for a place to land to refuel our confidence, as it provides us with a time to reflect on our strengths. Improvement efforts can be emotionally complex. This safe landing spot allows us to move forward again and again. The lesson is that self-confidence is a vital launching point for improvement but doesn't necessarily mean a lack of frustration. Self-confidence may give us hope, but it doesn't provide improvement strategies. Finding a safe landing spot after a threat to our confidence is essential for improvement.[18]

Several years ago, I studied a group of mountain guides who became confident in their abilities to lead climbers to the top of Mount Everest. They believed they could escort even novice climbers with little experience to the summit. John Krakauer's bestselling book, *Into Thin Air*, chronicled these events. The guides believed they could get everyone on their team to the top but failed to publicly acknowledge that many success factors were out of their control. Harsh weather, poorly conditioned and exhausted climbers, interteam rivalry, and a crowded mountain created unanticipated challenges for the climbing teams. Yet, the guides pushed to the summit and constantly reassured themselves and their followers of their abilities. This resulted in a tragedy as several climbers from multiple teams died, including the two primary leaders.[19] Overconfidence led to a deadly disaster.

BUILDING A DUAL MINDSET

Moving outside your comfort zone requires building a mindset that allows you to learn and perform. Begin by completing Exercise 3, Assessing Your Learning and Performing Mindset. This will help you become more aware of your orientation relative to learning and performing a particular activity. You can complete this exercise several times, using different activities to see how you learn and perform and how these change across different situations. You can also complete this exercise during an improvement effort. Improving as a leader is a process with varying patterns of improvement. Assess your current situation to determine if you need to focus on learning or performing.[20]

Consider how you can support learning and performing in others. Return to table 3.1, which highlights the difference between a learning and a performing orientation. Present this table at a team meeting or an informal session. Ask the session attendees to take mental notes of which items in the table most represent their viewpoint. Are the individual's problems more likely to be solved through a learning or performing orientation? How can the team develop the attitudes that support learning and performing?

Research on resilience can also help address the challenges posed by self-esteem. When experiencing negative emotions about yourself, consider setbacks, loss, and challenges temporary. Consider that these states can be overcome. Reframe unpleasant situations as unfortunate episodes rather than reflections of who you are. Studies on teen depression show that when teens develop an optimistic outlook in the aftermath of setbacks, they are more likely to stave off depression. Further studies show that shifting to a positive outlook can improve brain functioning. This is likely because an optimistic outlook and confidence encourage learning and growth and limit the negative impact of stress.[21]

The chapter described how improvement requires balancing learning and performing. Learning and performing require different mindsets, which are essential for leading outside your comfort zone. Learning and performing require a positive sense of self-esteem, which provides the launching point for successful improvement efforts.

Exercise 3: Assessing Your Learning and Performing Mindset

This exercise will help you understand your attitude toward two critical leadership mindsets: learning and performing. It will also help you identify the types of activities needed to improve as a leader or in other areas. Follow the four steps below.

Step 1

Think of an activity you are currently doing. The activity can be associated with work, hobbies, or other areas of interest. Write the activity here:

Step 2

Consider how you are progressing on the activity you just wrote down. Below is a list of statements about the activity. Rank each statement on a scale of 0 through 7 based on how the statement is like you or not like you while working on the activity.

   0 = least like me while working on that activity

   7 = most like me while working on that activity

SET A

1. I select a challenging way to approach the activity.

2. I look for opportunities to develop new skills and knowledge in the activity.

3. I read materials to improve my knowledge of the topic.

4. I focus on challenging areas of the activity where I'll learn new things.

5. I take risks to get better at what I am doing.

6. I try new strategies to improve, even if it means not doing a great job at first.

7. I prefer to work on areas that require me to develop a new higher level of ability and talent.

8. I try to find new ways to improve on what I am already doing.

SET B

1. I prove that I have abilities in the activity to do well on it.

2. I work on parts of the activity where I can already perform well.

3. I avoid asking what might appear to others to be "dumb" questions because I should already know the answer.

4. I focus mostly on my strengths.

5. I take action to make others aware of how well I am doing.

6. I believe I should already be capable of success before doing anything too difficult.

7. I focus on doing it right every time.

8. I like to prove that I can do it well.

Step 3

Add your scores for all questions in Set A. This is your learning score: _____.
Add your scores for all questions in Set B. This is your performing score: _____.

Step 4

1. Based on your survey scores on learning and performing, what is your highest score, and what does it say about how you are approaching the specific topic you wrote about in Step 1?

2. Which of the four improvement quadrants—deliberate learning, optimized, stagnation, or peak/plateau—best describes your situation? Why? For example, what are you doing that reflects that quadrant, and how do your scores reflect that?

3. What kinds of activities do you do that are associated with learning and performing in your improvement efforts? What activities can you engage in to optimize your improvement?

FOUR

Turning Adverse Events into Opportunities for Growth

ACCEPTING ADVERSE FACTORS BEYOND YOUR CONTROL

Your success at leading outside your comfort zone rests on turning adverse situations into opportunities for learning. Accepting that opportunities arise from challenges marks a crucial turning point in your leadership growth. As a leader, you will encounter an array of constraints and barriers. Many of these factors are beyond your control, but what is in your control is how you respond to these challenges. This is the basis of resilience, growth, and well-being: continuing to learn despite setbacks and barriers.

This chapter explores three factors influencing how you respond to external events: triggers, sensitivities, and transitions. More importantly, the chapter identifies techniques and considerations for addressing these factors. The chapter offers an assessment tool to turn adverse events into opportunities for learning.

FORCES BEYOND YOUR CONTROL: LESSONS FROM US AND EUROPEAN FOOTBALL

As a leader, you must accept that certain factors are beyond your control. For example, success as a leader in a sales organization could be negatively impacted by a competitor that could undermine your sales based on price and quality. Lack of cooperation among team members results in difficulty building consensus. Even hiring practices within an organization can constrain your performance. For example, opportunities for promotion may be limited if only a few associates can be promoted to partner. Another constraint comes from power struggles, as others may seek to challenge your leadership. Economic and social challenges beyond your control can derail a once-successful strategy. In short, leading requires responding to many factors beyond your direct control. As a leader, you can turn these seeming challenges into opportunities to learn and grow.

An example of how external forces shape leaders occurred during the 9/11 attacks on the World Trade Center. At the time, early in his presidency, President George W. Bush was among the least popular US presidents in history. But just after the tragic events of 9/11, his approval rating rebounded over thirty points. An external event—in this case, an international crisis and terrorist attack—generated the country's strong sense of identity. Bush captured the attention of the country. Throughout his presidency, Bush's approval rating did not remain as high as during the terrorist attacks. Still, he rode his popularity for the next few years to winning his reelection bid by a wide margin.[1]

Two examples illustrate how external factors can influence resilience in unexpected events. One example is from American-style football, and one is from European-style football. Researchers reviewed data that came from three positions on US football teams. The first position was the quarterback, who oversees each play, is the first player to handle the ball, and is responsible for executing the first part of any play. An effective quarterback must develop an ability to control the ball, dodge tacklers, pass the football while off balance, and sometimes run with the ball. A quarterback needs to make quick decisions, as he needs to size up the opposing defense and decide how to execute a play within a fraction of a second. The second position the researchers reviewed was the running back. Running backs are fast and flexible, able to run with the ball and evade tackles. The third position was the wide receiver. Wide receivers are speedy, have good hand-eye coordination, and can move smoothly to their position to catch a pass. The researchers could account for most or all ball handling in any game by looking at these three positions.

Using a strategy to measure performance they borrowed from fantasy football, the researchers developed a performance indicator for each player. They then recorded external forces that might impact the player's performance, such as the opposing team's strength. They also tracked the performance of other teammates to see how their performance might impact the performance of the three primary positions.[2]

The results showed that players differed in how they dealt with external constraints. Sometimes, players adjust to the opposing team's strategies and abilities. In other cases, players experienced a significant decrease in performance based on the opposing team. Playing skills mattered, but an even more powerful influence on performance were circumstances mostly outside the player's control: the opposing team. The most significant impact on performance was not how the players performed but the competing team's performance.

The example from American-style football shows that external forces can shape our resilience, but more importantly, it shows that leaders can influence situations that seem beyond their control. The way they influence these situations may be subtle and small, but they can greatly impact outcomes over time. For example, leaders may find ways to relate to those around them. Leaders often pick up on the emotions of others, and these emotions impact their success.

The sport of soccer (or football as some call it) demonstrates the subtle and unexpected ways leaders can influence their environment. Geir Jordet, a Norwegian School of Sports Science researcher, studies sports performance. In one study, he reviewed every single penalty kick and every shootout conducted in international football that had taken place over a decade. He even went as far as to contact individuals who had recorded older competitions on VHS tapes, often rummaging through dusty garages to uncover older tapes of kickers.

Jordet watched the recordings for nuances in the behavior of the kickers and their teammates. He even observed the crowd. He sought to decipher what might influence the kicker in these high-pressure situations. Shootouts and penalty kicks often decide the outcome of a game. They place immense pressure on the kicker because all the attention is on the kicker and goalie. A single kick can be the difference between a win and a loss, particularly in a shootout at the end of a matchup when two teams are tied. In this scenario, five players from each team have a chance to score a goal, and the team with the most goals at the end of the game wins. Jordet was especially interested in how an athlete could gain a slight edge when faced with an evenly matched opponent.

Jordet and his team watched the behavior of athletes after a successful kick. They paid particular attention to how athletes express emotions and how those emotions might influence (or be influenced by) those around them. The player's behaviors included a small smile or a short fist-pump. Jordet's team coded their observations using detailed methods and subjected them to rigorous statistical analysis. They learned that a single player's expression of emotion could significantly affect the team and had a contagious effect.

When players showed post-goal celebrations, like pumping their arms in the air, the kicker's team was likelier to win the overall shootout. Further, when a player celebrated a successful kick with other team members, the team was more likely to win the game. Celebrating with a fist pump and arms in the air seemed contagious; the feeling of confidence expressed after a successful shot was transferred from one teammate to another. Jordet's lesson: even though leaders do not control all the variables, they can gain a slight edge by working within a set of constraints over which we have limited or no control.[3]

TRIGGERS, SENSITIVITIES, AND TRANSITIONS

The football and soccer analogies, as well as the presidential approval rating, illustrate how external constraints serve as opportunities for learning. Opportunities to learn from experience arise from three primary sources:

- *Trigger:* An external event that creates a strong emotional response

- *Sensitivity:* An external event that makes a weak but uncomfortable emotional response

- *Transition:* A change in life, situation, or series of events that generates unpleasant emotions

Triggers are events, situations, or experiences that provoke strong emotional reactions. Triggers might include anger in response to change or encountering a situation that brings up past experiences. Mood and emotions are often associated with challenges in self-monitoring and self-control. Consider Charlie as an example. One thing Charlie knew about himself was that he didn't like to be challenged in public. So, when a young, talented, but socially unaware associate asked about the recent changes at the company, Charlie felt his emotions bubble up. When challenged in public, his first instinct was to put the associate in his place, but was that the tactic for an aspiring vice president? Charlie was aware of this trigger but needed to offer a different response. Putting people in their place, as he called it, was not a part of his company's culture.

Sensitivities are another external factor that can generate unpleasant emotions, but the onset of the internal response is more gradual. Sensitivities emerge throughout one's life or career. Deirdre, a professor at a prestigious university, frequently taught classes to companies and universities around the globe. After three trips in one year, she thought she had learned to deal with jet lag. She had been sleeping just a few hours the night before each presentation. Tired, dehydrated, and under the weather, she wasn't sure she could bring her usual enthusiasm and wit to the class. To deal with this sensitivity, Deirdre took a stand on her well-being. After returning to the United States, Deirdre decided to limit overseas travel to twice a year and conduct more web-based talks so she could still reach her audience but stay closer to home. By doing this, she would avoid her sensitivities to jet lag and lack of sleep.

Transitions are sustained events, situations, or changes. They can take many forms. Common transitions include life and career changes, new opportunities to learn and grow, pandemics, and cultural shifts. Unlike triggers and sensitivities, transitions unfold over time and are often difficult to identify when they first occur. People organize transitions in their minds in a variety of ways. These transitions provide milestones for reflection and can catalyze your development as a leader. A common way to view a transition is based on career changes, such as moving from new employee to management to leadership through retirement. Another way to organize transitions is based on your physical moves, which help you to organize your mental life in concrete ways. Transitions can follow job changes, from one employer to another, or be based on changes in your life circumstances, such as transitioning from child to teenager, to young adult, to working adult.[4]

Angela, a twenty-one-year-old college student, always enjoyed working with people. She led a student organization and was very social. Unlike some of her peers in the business school where I taught, she had little to no enthusiasm for numbers. It took her only two classes (one in accounting and one in finance) to realize she should only take jobs requiring little time working on spreadsheets. At the same time, she didn't know precisely where her talents and interests would lead her. At least she had a starting point: any job that required her to spend more than two hours a day on a spreadsheet was a nonstarter! Angela interviewed and landed her dream job, working at a tech firm in human resources. The job wasn't all Angela expected. She quickly learned that she would need to manage a budget and conduct detailed performance analyses in her unit. She would need to focus on analysis to be effective in her job. It turned out that Angela had to spend at least some time working on spreadsheets. But when she faced this new situation that required developing new skills and enhancing existing ones, she continued to believe in her ability to grow and develop. She learned how to do the spreadsheets as necessary for her job.

LEADERSHIP TRANSITIONS

A model developed by learning theorist David Kolb to understand common career transitions can also help clarify leadership development transitions.[5] Leadership transitions consist of three primary phases: novice, expert, and resilient leader. In the novice stage, the leader acquires new knowledge. This is also known as the beginner or the knowledge acquisition phase. When acquiring knowledge, a leader gains knowledge and abilities in different areas. The acquisition phase is the first phase of learning, in that leaders are introduced to new concepts but are not yet proficient in applying them. Here, a leader is introduced to new approaches—for example, by taking a seminar, reading an article, watching a short instructional video, or working through a do-it-yourself project from observing others or through trial and error—but is not yet proficient or able to replicate the skill.

In becoming an expert, a leader applies the knowledge they acquired. This is the application phase of leader development. Learning involves using newly acquired knowledge, skills, and abilities (KSAs). In this phase, an individual learns a skill but one that is not generally transferable to other activities. For example, learning to play the piano, solve math formulas, or learn a new accounting system all involve general learning. Notice that this step requires learning specific KSAs. However, a particular KSA set may or may not help one perform other activities.

The final stage is the resilience stage, which involves building knowledge that is durable and transferable. Resilience is associated with more general, long-term capabilities that help individuals improve their learning. Resilient leadership rests on building abilities to cope, deal with change, respond to setbacks, and meet new and more complex challenges. Often, this step leads to a general improvement mindset because of the broad set of abilities that are transferable to all aspects of life, not just a single task. To paraphrase David Kolb, leaders free themselves from the confines of specialization in the expert stage, characterized by the narrow rules and procedures associated with the field. This freedom results in seeing the world holistically, where old assumptions are challenged, and the boundaries of culture and profession are seen as one piece of a giant puzzle.[6]

ACTOR TOM HANKS'S CAREER TRANSITION

Transitions don't always come about naturally; some transitions must be cultivated. For actor Tom Hanks, a career transition was an opportunity to learn and grow. Hanks spent his early acting career playing a distinct role: young, likable, and naive. As radio host Terry Gross has said, he played "one-dimensional characters." In one movie, *Big*, Hanks played a child trapped in an adult's body. In *Splash*, he played a man in love with a mermaid. The roles were easy, and Hanks quickly became typecast as the playful and nonthreatening but uninspiring best friend. Producers and the viewing public loved Hanks in this role, and he became one of the most popular and successful actors around.

Hanks wanted the opportunity to play more challenging roles, which required more of him professionally and emotionally. While he enjoyed making the audience feel good and laugh, he also wanted them to think and learn. Hanks began to evaluate his future as an actor and deliberately decided to take a role beyond a one-dimensional character. Most actors would have gobbled up the high-paying jobs that came their way. But Hanks, with the support of his wife, went nearly a year rejecting tens of millions of dollars in acting jobs that looked the same.

At one point, he had waited so long that he thought the proper role might never come, and he would have to resort to the same tired characters he had played before. Then came an opportunity. Ron Howard was directing a feature film, *Apollo 13*. Hanks would play the role of Jim Lovell, the hero astronaut who helped his team return to Earth after a fire forced them to abort their mission to the moon. Looking for the right opportunity became a wise career move for Hanks. His success in *Apollo 13* led to a series of complex, challenging, and exciting roles, eventually leading to two Academy Awards for his roles in the movies *Forest Gump* and *Philadelphia*.[7]

This story illustrates one reason Hanks has been such an enduring actor: he has shown resilience in his career. He sought out the right opportunity to learn and grow. Even before that opportunity arose, he spent time developing characters and learning the craft of acting. Although he eventually became bored with these characters, he understood that this boredom would not define the future of his career. The boredom with the roles he was offered and his willingness to reject them meant he was striving for something more. Ultimately, Hanks rewrote the narrative of his career so that it was no longer a story told by others where he was the "funny guy."

RESPONDING TO TRIGGERS

Leadership requires special attention to emotional triggers. Emotional triggers arise and disappear quickly and seldom last for more than a minute. This is due to the biopsychology of triggers which emerge from the part of our brain responsible for responding to threats— the flight, fight, or freeze response. We sense the threat, and the body responds. Eyes dilate to take in more immediate information. Stress hormones fill the body. When we feel a threat, our body automatically enlists all our physical and mental resources to respond. All nonessential processes in our body and mind are put to rest. For a short time, our digestion stops, as does the energy processing in many parts of our body. The brain enlists every single cell in response to the threat.

This mechanism may have been quite helpful for early humans. For modern-day leaders, these triggered responses are the source of problems. Few situations faced by contemporary leaders require a fight-or-flight response. Yet, the mechanisms have survived for millennia and still arise on occasion.

As a leader, recognize the events or situations that trigger this response. When these triggered emotions become sustained over time, they lead to unproductive stress. The sustained and heightened level of emotions results in several problems, such as anxiety, chronic stress, and even physical illness. The heightened emotional state can hurt decision-making and block important learning mechanisms even in the short term. Over time, elevated stress levels can damage key brain parts essential for long-term memory, such as the hippocampus.

Once a trigger has become established, it can lead to renewed negative experiences that interfere with leading and developing as a leader. When we encounter the same trigger in the future, our body will likely respond with the same heightened level of emotion, even though there is no threat. This is because our brain stores the emotions in a different location than our rational thought, which results in an emotional response that lacks a clear explanation. We experience the emotion, but the brain cannot track the emotion to the precipitating event, since the rational part of the brain runs behind the emotional part. Even as the emotions proceed the rational brain by a fraction of a second, the result may be an action we regret.

Psychologists believe that the proper way to respond to triggers is to allow the rational response of the brain to catch up with the emotional response. This requires not letting the emotions drive action but instead allowing ourselves time to accept that the emotion may be counterproductive and beyond our control. However, we can wrestle control back by allowing the emotions to emerge and dissolve, creating room for our thoughts to drive our actions.

One effective way to deal with the immediate onset of emotions is through the STOP technique. STOP is an acronym for stop, take a breath, observe your feelings, and proceed. The STOP technique was developed from dialectical therapy based on mindfulness practices. Mindfulness encourages increasing awareness of our inner experiences, such as emotions, body functions, and other sensations.[8] The STOP technique buys you time by letting the rational brain catch up with its emotional reaction. By stopping or slowing down our response to external events, we develop the capacity to respond more constructively. The technique provides a path to more productive responses to triggers.

Leaders need to develop the ability to handle unpleasant and intense feelings. Professional athletes have perfected this skill. Unpleasant and intense emotions can mean the difference between winning and losing. Millions of dollars, public scrutiny, and reputations are on the line. Novak Djokovic, a leading tennis professional, says he can turn his emotions around in five seconds. Early in his career, he was the underdog. Famous players like Rafa Nadal and Roger Federer were fan favorites, and when Djokovic played against them, the crowds often taunted him. He learned how to turn the negative energy into a positive. If the crowd chanted his opponent's name, he imagined it was his name they were chanting. Through years of mental training and practice, he developed a technique that has helped him turn negative emotions into positive ones in seconds.[9]

Exercise 4 offers an opportunity to review the eight most essential leadership experiences that can catalyze learning. These represent the types of adverse events that can support learning and development as a leader.

This chapter has outlined triggers, sensitivities, and transitions—three external factors impacting resilience. Leading requires learning to recognize these factors, assessing how they impact learning and performance, and determining the appropriate action. In some performance situations, leading requires overriding unpleasant emotions, but that does not mean all unpleasant emotions should be ignored.

Exercise 4: Turning Adverse Events into Learning Opportunities[10]

Learning from your experience is essential for your development as a leader. This exercise will help you learn about eight situations that are the foundation of leadership development. When completing this inventory, you will think about your involvement in these situations, how you reacted during these experiences, and how to cultivate these situations in the future.

The types of experiences that support learning include:

- Interactions with others

- Responsibilities for leading

- Overcoming challenges

The inventory has two sections. Complete both Section 1 and Section 2.

Section 1

In Section 1, you will take an inventory of eight types of situations that you may have experienced. These include conditions arising from work, in clubs or other organizations, and your personal life. If you have never experienced some of these situations, that is okay; go on to the next question.

1. Describe a time when you faced unfamiliar or new responsibilities.

2. Describe a time you had to create a change, introduce new procedures, or put into place new processes to get things done in new ways.

3. Describe a time you had to take on higher levels of responsibility in an organization.

4. Describe a time when you had to work across boundaries, for example, working with people from other departments, with different responsibilities, or on a different project to accomplish a goal.

5. Describe a time when you had to manage a diverse team or workforce.

6. Describe a time when you had to make a job transition where you took on new responsibilities.

7. Describe a time when you had to work with peers where you did not have direct authority over them but still had to motivate them to get things done.

8. Describe a time when you faced obstacles you needed to overcome to accomplish individual or organizational goals.

Section 2: Review Your Responses

Below is a summary of the eight leadership situations you just reviewed. Learning to deal with these situations is critical for leadership development. Circle those experiences where you had a response and leave it blank if you have not faced these situations.

1. Faced unfamiliar responsibilities or new responsibilities

2. Created change or introduced new procedures or processes to get things done

3. Took on higher levels of responsibility

4. Worked across boundaries

5. Managed diverse teams or workforce

6. Experienced a job transition where you took on new responsibilities

7. Worked with peers where you did not have direct authority over them

8. Faced obstacles that you needed to overcome

Questions for Reflection

1. Which situations were left blank?

2. Looking at the situations you circled, what essential experiences have shaped you as a leader?

3. Considering your responses, how prepared are you as a leader?

4. What have you learned from these experiences, and how have they shaped you as a leader?

5. How might you find opportunities in areas you left blank or areas that need further development?

Fundamental Processes

FIVE

Cultivating Novel Experiences

_____

THE EXPERIENCES THAT COUNT FOR
DEVELOPING AS A LEADER

This chapter begins a four-chapter sequence associated with the four processes of leading outside your comfort zone. Chapter 5 outlines the experiences related to growth as a leader. Chapter 6 introduces the second process, which involves accepting unpleasant emotions and outlines the various emotions associated with resilience, growth, and well-being. Chapter 7 introduces five learning strategies. Chapter 8 provides an in-depth look at resilience as a process of initiating, sustaining, and increasing effort toward learning.

Leading outside your comfort zone requires making the most out of your experience. This includes cultivating learning opportunities across career, work, personal life, and formal education. This chapter explores four characteristics of experience that support learning: (1) the challenges and opportunities for learning, (2) the duration or amount of time spent practicing, (3) underlying feelings and emotions when learning, and (4) stories about prior learning and resilience.

CULTIVATING NOVEL EXPERIENCES

Jim is frustrated. He has yet to be promoted to a full-time team lead. He met with his supervisor to discuss opportunities to take on additional responsibilities, and he took professional development classes through his employer's human resource development program. His boss offered assignments as a team lead, but these were only short-term. He wonders if his employer only sees him as someone to fill in until a real manager can be hired. After each assignment, he returns to his regular job and waits for the next opportunity.

Consider another side of Jim. Jim is a devoted father and husband, and he volunteers in his community. He spends his summer vacations working at a local camp for underprivileged children. He rose to a high-level position in his church, an organization he is passionate about, which chose him to represent the congregation at the next national church meeting.

Jim struggles in one area of his life but excels in another. He displays considerable leadership skills at his church yet remains frustrated when he demonstrates these qualities at work. Jim decided to dive deeply into his leadership development and explore what he needed to learn to get that promotion. Jim knew he already had meaningful leadership experiences in his community and religious activities but needed help to translate those leadership experiences into his work. Jim was like many seeking to develop as leaders, taking stock of their leadership experience and transferring their positive leadership experiences to other situations

We have all heard that experience matters for leading, but what kinds of experiences matter, and how can experiences lead to building more resilient leaders? Leaders need to understand that experience alone is not enough. For experience to be valuable, it must provide learning opportunities and last long enough to support learning. Learning requires addressing the internal emotions and thoughts generated from these experiences and communicating this to others in an inspiring and convincing way.

EXPERIENCES THAT PROVOKE MOMENTUM TOWARD LEARNING

The influential philosopher John Dewey asked, "What is the character of experience that leads to learning?"[1] Dewey's question implies that it is not just the experience itself but the character of the experience that matters for learning. Since

Dewey's time, significant resources have been directed toward understanding experiences that support learning, but one characteristic stands out. Experience must provoke momentum within the leader: the desire to learn. Four kinds of experiences provoke momentum to learn: (1) experiences that generate challenging opportunities, (2) experiences with a duration sufficient to provoke learning, (3) experiences that provoke an emotional connection in the leader, and (4) a meaningful narrative that arises from experience (table 5.1). We can respond to Dewey by digging deeper into these four characteristics of learning experiences.

Challenging Situations and Opportunities

All experiences hold learning opportunities. These opportunities can challenge the leaders' current competencies and push them to develop new insights about themselves and others.[2] Research provides a short list of these opportunities, including taking on unfamiliar responsibilities, creating change, gaining high levels of responsibility, working across boundaries, and managing diverse teams and workforces.[3] The exercise in chapter 4 provided a preview of these types of opportunities. They involved interactions with others, taking on responsibilities for leading, and overcoming challenges.[4]

Amount of Practice and Experience

The second characteristic of experience that supports learning is the duration, amount of practice, or time spent working to develop a skill. Duration is accumulated experience. Accumulated experience is like a résumé; it is collected, measured, and lived over time. Some common forms of learning include tenure in a job or career, age, or time spent learning and developing a skill.[5] Leaders often learn from experiences that require repetition, exposure, and ongoing adaptation. The research consistently links time spent in a particular role and leadership success. One study in a healthcare setting showed that individuals and teams become more proficient as they spend more time learning new procedures. Similarly, studies show that time spent in a leadership role can translate into leadership skills.[6]

Spending the appropriate time developing leadership skills is essential, but how much time is needed remains in question. Some rules of thumb provide insight into how long these developmental opportunities must last. For example, in the US Army, officers are rotated to new leadership roles every three years. It's not uncommon for business leaders to rotate responsibilities at a similar

TABLE 5.1 Experiences That Support Leader Development

CHARACTERISTIC	HOW EXPERIENCE SHAPES RESILIENCE	QUESTIONS TO SUPPORT LEARNING
Challenging situations and opportunities	Demonstrate resilience in the face of challenge and opportunity. Show how you seek out and take advantage of opportunities to learn.	Do I seek out new opportunities and challenges and learn from them to become a stronger leader? What do I learn from these experiences? What do I want to contribute as a leader?
Amount of practice and experience	Show continuity, long-term commitment, and accumulation of lessons learned.	What would I like to do in the future? What experience, skills, or knowledge do I need to progress as a leader? How long should I stay in this position?
Feelings and emotions when learning	Demonstrate resilience in the face of unpleasant emotions, conflict, and different opinions. Identify situations that generate emotions. Describe how you respond to setbacks. Develop an understanding of what motivates you and how you respond to emotions.	What motivates me to be a better leader? What fears, frustrations, or other unpleasant emotions keep me from improving? Why is becoming a better leader important to me, and how can I support others as a leader?
Stories about prior learning and resilience	Communicate and demonstrate resilience through stories about how you navigated challenges and how you made the most out of your experiences. Describe how you overcame challenges, hardship, or disadvantage.	How do I communicate and present my values as a leader? What stories can I tell that demonstrate who I am and what has shaped me as a leader?

pace. Yet, the systematic study of learning durations doesn't provide a definitive answer. Evidence also shows that too much experience and time in a single role can lead to complacency and rigidity. Experts, for example, believe they have seen it all and have nothing left to learn. This is called the curse of expertise—where experts may become wiser but more rigid in problem-solving with time.[7]

One debate about the time it takes to learn something well centers around the 10,000-hour rule. The idea was initially proposed by psychologist Anders Ericsson and popularized by Malcolm Gladwell in his book *Outliers*.[8] It was hypothesized that the development of expertise in any area is associated with at least 10,000 hours of deliberate practice. The 10,000-hour rule emerged from Ericsson's research of highly accomplished and specialized performers—violinists, chess players, athletes, and others—as they developed specific skills. It revealed that 10,000 hours of concentrated practice with feedback and a deliberate focus on learning was required to become a top performer in these areas.

Researchers applied the 10,000-hour rule to study tasks more relevant to leadership development. By viewing time spent learning activities across many different skills and careers, researchers found that learning time impacted improvement but depended on the type of performance gains sought. For example, learning time matters for improvement in well-structured activities with clear rules, such as games, music, and sports. Ericsson studied these activities—learning time accounted for between 18 percent and 26 percent of performance outcomes. In other words, there was a strong relationship between the amount of time spent in deliberate practice and the final level of performance on well-structured activities. More time learning led to better performance. However, the connection between time spent learning more complex and unstructured tasks remained unclear. For example, for leadership development activities, time had a negligible impact. Time spent learning accounted for less than 5 percent of outcomes in leadership development activities.[9] The takeaways: learning to be a leader is more complex than most tasks, and just spending time learning may not be enough in and of itself when it comes to developing as a leader.

Feelings and Emotions When Learning

A third characteristic of experience also supports leadership development. This involves the leader's inner world and the emotions experienced while learning—the quality of the experience matters. Pleasant experiences may not be the most relevant set of experiences for learning, which surprises many leaders. After all, many psychologists advocate for enjoyable experiences such as happiness, positive thinking, affirmations, and happiness. Advocates for these positive experiences fill our newsfeeds, the popular press, and self-help books for good reason. Pleasant experiences can motivate and help us celebrate successes. A previous chapter discussed the role of confidence, a positive experience, and its role in supporting actions that support learning and performing. Positive inner states play an essential role in learning but do not tell the whole story about the nature of experiences that support learning. Positive experiences play a specific role, not a universal role.

Flow, also called optimal experience, is one way to understand the role of positive internal experience. Psychologist Mihaly Csikszentmihalyi describes flow as the effortless action people feel when doing something they enjoy. These experiences stand out as the best in their lives. With flow experience, individuals are so engaged in the activity that they lose track of time; they don't realize what is happening around them because they are so focused on what they are doing. Flow occurs when people (1) hold a clear set of goals to work for, (2) receive immediate feedback from the task on activities directly linked to meeting those goals, and (3) are working on something challenging enough but not too challenging based on their current level of skill.[10] Alex Honnold is the first and only person yet to climb the monstrous El Capitan rock cliff with no supporting ropes. He describes the process as being completely immersed in the climb, focused on each specific foot and hand placement, knowing exactly if each placement is correct immediately. The process is not easy, but he doesn't consider it risky because he knows exactly what he needs to accomplish at each step and has completed the climb numerous times with safety ropes.[11]

Flow is linked to happiness and is essential to feeling good and motivating us to work toward a goal, but flow doesn't happen often. Even Csikszentmihalyi lamented that most days are dull, boring, and filled with anxiety. These are not flow states.[12] If flow is about a flash in time, what are we to do with the other twenty-three and a half hours in a day, many of which may be filled with anxiety and boredom?

The question is this: Flow may be an optimal state of happiness, but is flow an optimal learning state? Characteristics of flow—a clear goal, immediate feedback, and a challenging task that we are adequately prepared to perform—set the stage for optimal experience, but are these characteristics associated with the optimal development as a leader? Flow is more likely to occur during well-structured chess or mountain-climbing activities. Does flow also support leadership development, characterized by complexity, uncertainty, and social change?

Flow offered a hot topic in a conversation with current and former Olympic athletes, some of whom had been competing for a decade or more. This conversation made me wary of the value of flow as an optimal improvement or learning state. I asked this group of top-performing athletes how often they had experienced flow in either competition or practice. The answer: not much. The flow experience happened sporadically, and they explained that it was more luck than planned. The limited time spent experiencing flow made it almost inconsequential to their training and performance. Some athletes said pain management, dealing productively with disappointment, and motivating themselves through bouts of depression were much more valuable than flow. The experiences of these top athletes were supported by studies that show that people spend less than five minutes per day in a flow state. I concluded that resilience and overcoming anxiety, boredom, and discomfort were more critical for becoming top performers than flow.[13] These athletes suggested that learning and improving generated the most positive emotions. They experienced improvement as enjoyable and motivating, but they also needed to motivate themselves through periods of stagnation and physical pain. The insight I gained was that peak performance experiences such as flow play a different role in performance than they do in learning.

The question remains: Is there an optimal experience that supports learning when leading outside your comfort zone? Psychological research suggests that some unpleasant experiences, especially slightly unpleasant experiences, serve as catalysts for learning.

Consider frustration. Video game designer Shigeru Miyamoto has reached celebrity status among video game players as the creator of popular games like Super Mario Bros., Donkey Kong, and Legend of Zelda. He explained the guiding philosophy behind the design of his games: build in frustration, just enough so the player can overcome the frustration to move forward and worry less about the ending and resolution of the game.[14]

Frustration catalyzes learning by setting a leader on the path to problem-solving. Frustration, which can be thought of as a low-level unpleasant experience, activates leaders to seek answers to resolve it. The experience is unpleasant enough to motivate effort but not so unpleasant that it inhibits action. Like anxiety, frustration is an aroused state of being, but it is far less unpleasant than full-blown anxiety. While anxiety has a decidedly negative connotation, frustration implies a challenge that can be overcome.

Consider how frustration emerges. Experiencing frustration signals a particular state of experience that facilitates learning. Leaders often experience low frustration levels across activities. For example, leaders may experience frustration when preparing for a public speaking engagement, when a project doesn't go as planned, or when they cannot motivate a struggling employee. Frustration accompanies many transition phases and commonly occurs with leadership experiences like taking on a new job, meeting a new challenge, or shifting to a new line of work. From an experiential standpoint, frustration often signals that more negative emotions, such as anxiety, may follow if the frustration is not addressed.[15] By addressing frustration, leaders can potentially avoid more complex anxiety-related feelings. Because of this, frustration motivates us to act and resolve tensions.

According to neuroscience, frustration may activate learning. Because frustration starts as a slightly unpleasant internal experience, it motivates knowledge-searching behaviors associated with learning. The search for knowledge decreases the unpleasant feelings that accompany frustration. Frustration activates the motivation and reward system, and dopamine is activated, even though the external reward is never realized. Neuroscientists call this "reward prediction error."[16] The dopamine release sends the leader searching for an answer because the desired outcome is not achieved (resulting in frustration) and generates physiological arousal. The neurobiological processes associated with activated frustration are displaced rewards, an expected reward that never comes.[17] These neurobiological processes may also explain how experiences of frustration are related to building resilience. By learning how to respond to unexpected failures, leaders learn mechanisms to respond productively when they fail to achieve expected rewards. Resilient leaders can better overcome setbacks and continue forward, seeking new knowledge and setting new goals, even in the face of failure.[18]

The experience of frustration activates other brain systems linked to learning.[19] A study in an exercise context found that frustration was associated with unpleasant emotions, fatigue, and psychological distress when doing challenging exercises and progressing toward exercise goals.[20] However, self-motivation played a buffering role, cushioning the individual from these unpleasant emotions, and those who showed self-motivation were more easily able to overcome the other adverse effects of frustration. This reveals that positive experiences play a buffering role in frustration. For example, someone might experience unpleasant feelings toward exercise, like guilt or feelings of low self-worth due to not exercising. Increasing the amount and intensity of exercise lowers the unpleasant feelings associated with not exercising.

Frustration may activate what Kate Whalen refers to as "positive challenges,"[21] which involve being able to withstand the uncomfortable emotions associated with moving outside your comfort zone. Frustration may lead to positive action, such as taking more chances or increasing effort. Unlike flow states, which offer clear goals, specific actions, outcomes, and pleasantness, frustration introduces a level of uncertainty; frustration is accompanied by unpleasant feelings and the search for information.[22] As leaders embark outside their comfort zone, they are more likely to feel frustration than they are to feel flow due to uncertainty over goal achievement and related rewards. Thus, flow as a pleasant experience and frustration as an unpleasant experience serve two purposes. Frustration serves to motivate, and flow serves as a reward.

Russ Vince, professor emeritus at the University of Bath in the UK, has suggested that learning emerges with the anxiety that arises during leadership. Similarly, Edgar Schein, one of the early proponents of learning and leadership, said that anxiety is the underlying motivator of learning. While this idea is exciting, I think the term *anxiety* may be overstating the primary experiences that motivate learning. Anxiety is only one experience characteristic that supports learning and may not be the most important.[23] In summary, both pleasant and unpleasant experiences provide the basis for learning and provide a catalyst to learning when leaders approach these situations with a learning orientation.

Stories of Resilience

The fourth characteristic of experience that supports learning emerges from how we retrospectively conceive the experience. This involves narrative or storytelling, the process by which leaders put meaning and continuity into experiences. Learning arises from experience over hours, days, weeks, months, or years. Experience may be discontinuous, but we recollect experiences with a strong sense of continuity. In our research, we often ask participants to recall learning experiences. We may ask them to remember a time when they were learning and making progress or to recall a time when they were frustrated with their learning. When we analyze the results and feed the information back to the participants, they are often surprised that the experiences were not continuous. The participants experienced these learning activities as connected in time and space, but upon reflection, they noted that the experiences were not connected.

One example stands out. Angel recalled a home improvement project, redoing his bathroom, as a source of frustration while learning. In his reflection, he recalled many learning experiences, such as watching YouTube videos on replacing tile and demolishing his bathroom. He recalled the trial-and-error learning of performing tasks like laying tile, putting in drywall, and caulking his bathtub. When Angel reflected on his story, he realized these project tasks occurred over many months and sometimes over a year. Yet, in his recollection, it was one continuous project, even though the actual events were spread across a year, and his activity remodeling his bathroom was separated by weeks at a time. When Angel shared this story with his partner, he, too, recalled the experience with a sense of continuity. To be philosophical, the space-time continuum only sometimes matches how we recollect our experiences.

Angel's experience highlights how we view our learning experiences with a sense of continuity, even though they may not be continuous in time or location. This sense of continuity exists because we organize our experiences into episodes. We organize our experiences by themes and mark them by events. We find activities that form a coherent pattern and link them to the goals we are trying to achieve. Therefore, when thinking about our learning experiences, we can think of these experiences as "episodes" with a theme of continuity. Episodes provide a template for leaders to develop narratives of their experiences.[24]

If the work of a leader is to create meaning and purpose out of uncertainty, then turning experiences into narratives may be the central work of a leader. Narratives are stories that put the unstructured experiences into a sequence that makes sense and allows the leader to communicate a message. For learning to occur, experiences must be turned into narratives which then, in turn, become part of the sensemaking process and allow experiences to be preserved and transmitted to others. In our research, we found three basic categories of learning and leading:

- *Work/professional learning spaces* involved job, career, or experience learning episodes. This might include developing work-related knowledge. Examples include leading a team, learning leadership skills, learning a new software package, and learning a language to improve at work.

- *School/formal educational learning episodes* focus on institutional learning. They involve specific classes and academic achievement experiences, including developing critical thinking or higher-order thinking skills and other cognitive development skills associated with higher education. Other examples are improving in an accounting class, improving study skills, learning Python, and learning a language in class.

- *Personal development episodes* focus on activities outside formal work and education, including health and wellness activities, hobbies, pets, and childcare. Examples include training a puppy, baking bread, developing a healthy lifestyle, and learning to drive. Other examples are working on a language for travel, self-improvement, or undefined organized sports.

Karl Weick is an influential social psychologist who studies sensemaking—a process of retroactively describing one's experiences. Sensemaking entails organizing our prior experiences into coherent and meaningful stories we tell ourselves or display publicly. Leaders constantly make sense of their experiences and use storytelling techniques to learn and communicate with others. Many leadership stories explain how past unpleasant experiences shaped a leader's values. For example, politicians may discuss how they overcame poor economic circumstances or social inequality and how these struggles built their resilience as leaders. Business leaders may discuss how their childhood experiences running a small business, such as a paper route or selling items door-to-door, demonstrate their fortitude to succeed in business. Nonprofit leaders may explain how losing a loved one or a medical emergency inspired their push to support a related cause. These are stories of resilience, overcoming challenges, and how these challenges led to growth.[25]

LAMONT HAWKINS OF WU-TANG CLAN RESHAPES HIS IDENTITY

Lamont Hawkins (aka U-God of the rap group Wu-Tang Clan) realized that he needed to change how he viewed himself and his life and update his narrative as he became famous. He chronicled his transition from drug dealer to "mainstream rapper," which required that he change his view of his world and himself. Having spent months in prison, he realized that his old life as a drug dealer came with drawbacks and that the entire world around him was changing as he reached a new level of economic security brought about by increasing fame.

At the same time, he reconfigured his identity; he brought with him tools that had made him successful. His ability to work with others stayed with him through the transition from dealer to becoming a more mainstream business-man; he talks about how he used his skills to convince cops not to arrest him, how these skills were later used to resolve conflicts within his musical teams, and how he used these skills to work with managers and agents. He relates his resil-ience, for example, when he was booed off stage in his first appearance with the Wu-Tang Clan but used the defeat to become more disciplined with his music. Despite his years of success, he continued to manage stage fright. This is a fasci-nating story of how skills obtained in one area can be transferred across different career stages.[26]

Even more interesting, Hawkins described how his view of himself changed. He drew on the skills he already had but needed to change how he viewed him-self as he reached higher fame and fortune. He was no longer the kid who was always in trouble but a person who could help others and solve problems. The changes also resulted in feelings of alienation and contradiction. He valued his past experiences but wanted to move beyond them and create a life free from the troubles he had as a youth. Hawkins learned to tell a different story about his life and rewrite his leadership narrative from a tale of hardship to success.

YOUR DEVELOPMENT AS A LEADER

Experience provides the raw material for the lessons you learn as a leader. Begin by taking stock of your experiences and understanding which experiences have led to your learning as a leader. Exercise 5 provides an opportunity to reflect on the experiences that have shaped you as a leader. The exercise offers a structured storytelling method to help you shape the reflection in a way that can be commu-nicated to others. The technique can reveal to others how you overcame adverse events and how these events have shaped your values as a leader. Another tool is a 360-degree feedback process. Organizations provide commercially available 360-degree feedback processes through human resource development and train-ing programs, professional coaches, or leadership development consulting firms. These are excellent places to start your leadership development.

After-action reviews provide another way to review the experience and ef-fectively improve individual and team learning. These reviews engage active learning, where individuals review past events using multiple forms of information. Learning how to debrief after-action reviews is a powerful leadership skill. Debriefing an after-action review involves a team reviewing previous projects, actions, or events. It emphasizes identifying areas for improvement and developing questions that focus on learning, such as what went well and what you should continue to do. Also, ask yourself what you want to change or improve upon in your next try.

This chapter outlined four characteristics of experience that support learning and leadership development and identified how each characteristic could support learning to be more resilient. Moving outside your comfort zone may be uncomfortable, but it provides learning opportunities. It results in developing competencies, a better understanding of the underlying feelings associated with experience, and putting those experiences into a narrative. The chapter responds to John Dewey's question about the nature of experience introduced at the chapter's opening. Learning experiences involve multiple facets, including opportunities for new experiences to emerge, a measure of time, an internal experience, and a retrospective element of sensemaking. The next chapter examines pleasant and unpleasant experiences and their role in developing as a resilient leader.

Exercise 5: Turning Your Experience into Stories About Overcoming Adversity[27]
In this exercise, you will develop a story illustrating how overcoming adversity shaped your leadership values. Keep in mind the key elements of a successful story:

1. Is graphic and easily visualized.

2. Has a beginning, a middle, and an end.

3. Has a moral that is easy to understand.

4. Is short, taking less than three minutes to tell.

5. Grips people emotionally.

Consider an experience in which you faced adversity and how this experience shaped you as a leader and put it into a story. The story should illustrate a value you hold or demonstrate as a leader and how you learned from adversity. The adversity does not have to be traumatic but can be an obstacle or setback that taught you a lesson. Use the template below to help you think through the story. The story should illustrate the value you are demonstrating, show action and transformation, but not explicitly state its value. Here are a few prompts to consider:

- A time I learned something about myself and my values

- A time I stood up for something I believed in

- A time I took a risk

- A time I learned a lesson

- A time I made an escape

- A time I broke a rule, but it made things better

- A time I faced a challenge

Describe the experience that has shaped you as a leader.

Once you have identified an experience, put this into the form of a story or narrative including the three stages described below. Use the story template below to organize the elements of your story.

- Stage 1: Beginning (where I was, what my state of mind was, what I was like, or what I believed)

- Stage 2: Middle, part 1: Inciting incident (what happened, what I accomplished, what events took place, how I reacted to the events)

- Stage 3: Middle, part 2: Challenge to overcome (the challenge I faced, what I tried, whether it worked the first time)

- Stage 4: End state (where I was at the end, how I was transformed or changed, what the ah-ha moment was, how this shaped me as a leader)

Template to Organize Your Story

Value that the story conveys: _____

- Beginning (what did I believe or what was I like before?)

- Middle (what was the event?)

- Middle (what was the challenge?)

- Middle (how did I overcome the challenge?)

- End (how I am different now?)

Evaluating the Effectiveness of Your Story

Now, answer the following questions about the story. You can continue to refine the story as needed to answer the question. Seek feedback from others on your story.

1. Was the story graphic and easily visualized?

2. Is there a clear beginning, middle, and end?

3. What is the story's moral, and is it easy to understand?

4. Is the story short, taking less than three minutes to tell?

5. Does the story grip people emotionally?

6. What value does the story illustrate about your leadership?

SIX

Accepting Unpleasant Emotions

GROWTH FROM FRUSTRATION AND
OTHER PAINFUL EMOTIONS

Leading outside your comfort zone requires taking on new leadership challenges despite experiencing unpleasant emotions. As leaders push outside their comfort zone and into new leadership territory, they experience confusing and complicated emotions. Ignoring emotions often derails leadership efforts, and leading requires productively acknowledging and dealing with emotions. The key is to notice which emotions enhance or inhibit learning. This chapter presents ways to increase emotional awareness, accept unpleasant emotions, and channel these unpleasant emotions toward growth.

Unpleasant emotions might derail your leadership efforts in a variety of situations.

- One executive missed the opportunity for a promotion—not because the company overlooked his talents but because he was afraid the new position was beyond his capabilities. Rather than find out, he delayed applying for the job. He let the fear of anticipated unpleasant emotions limit his career trajectory.

- Another emerging leader continued to put off studying for the CPA exam, even though he knew he needed to pass it to keep his job. He realized that going to work and solving problems was far more interesting than studying for the exam, and his procrastination resulted from boredom with studying.

- Another leader became uncomfortable when she needed to sell her ideas to upper management. She felt this was not genuine and that selling her ideas made her appear incompetent. Shouldn't the benefits of her proposal be obvious? She tamped down her enthusiasm for the project and almost threatened it.

- One leader quickly became uncomfortable with her newfound responsibilities. Her thoughts were consumed with negative questions such as, "Why was I chosen for the job when others had more experience?" These thoughts distracted her from working on her new role.

- Another leader was a perfectionist, and she feared that her contribution needed to be better. Despite her prior successes, she was afraid to try new things and take risks out of fear of failure.

Read just about any book on leadership. You will quickly see that emotions are characterized as something like dragons lurking in a cave. The message is clear: emotions are animal spirits that must be avoided, tamed, managed, controlled, reevaluated, overridden, or buffered. However, these characterizations of emotions fail to capture the value of emotions in leading. Emotions can serve as important signals. Rather than be seen as dragons, emotions are to be cultivated. These inner experiences that we call emotions serve as the raw material of growth and well-being. Failing to address unpleasant emotions can limit your leadership growth and development. Excessive rumination, procrastination, and avoidance become coping mechanisms for these unpleasant emotions. Leadership suffers. Leading outside your comfort zone requires increasing self-awareness and developing proactive mechanisms to support your emotions.[1]

RECOGNIZE AND ENGAGE WITH EMOTIONS

Scholars have differing views on a standard definition of emotions or the role that emotions play in leadership.[2] *Emotion* is often used interchangeably with other words, such as *mood, affect,* or *feeling.* The word often becomes confused with affect, the feelings we directly experience. Affect reflects the inner experience, while emotion is how we express the inner experience through visible means such as facial expressions, body language, or words. In other words, emotions represent how we communicate our internal experiences, while affect describes the inner feeling, sensation, and meaning placed on an experience.

Psychologist Lisa Feldman Barrett and her colleagues suggest that affect serves as an "inner barometer" of our internal sensations at any time.[3] These sensations arise in response to perceived threats and opportunities outside of ourselves or an internal state. Sensations are not always easy to label, which explains why we might say, "I can't express how I feel right now."[4] We say this because we struggle to find words that reflect the range and complexity of our experience. The language of emotion is vast. One approach to emotions tracks over 620 positive and 744 negative emotions, so there are many ways to express emotions.[5] Still, we struggle to express ourselves in language. Even with the vast vocabulary associated with emotions, our language is not granular or precise enough to convey the experience.[6]

Emotions are a complex mix of biological, psychological, and social factors. Awareness of emotions becomes invaluable to resilience, growth, and well-being. As you become more aware of your emotions and the sources of these emotions, you can learn how these experiences shape your actions. You can learn how pleasant and unpleasant emotions motivate you differently. The first step is to name these experiences—that means putting emotional labels on inner experiences. Psychologists call recognizing, categorizing, and documenting these experiences interoception—or body and mind awareness. When you become aware of your body and mind, you can draw on these signals to understand the force of emotions, how they motivate you, and how they may hold you back.

One study examined how adults on the autism spectrum could learn to recognize their inner experiences. Individuals on the autism spectrum tend to have higher anxiety levels than the general population and tend to be less skilled at understanding the source of their anxiety. In other words, they have low interoception skills. Interoception training helps these individuals reduce their general anxiety by improving their perceptions of their inner states. The study focused on a central internal bodily cue for emotions: heart rate. Researchers asked if these individuals could learn the causes of their anxiety by becoming more aware of their heart rates. The researchers divided the participants into two groups. One group received training on how to improve how well they sensed their heart rate. The group was trained to monitor their heart rate and, in turn, became more aware of their inner states. A second group received no training at all. They found that after three months of training, the group that had received training on monitoring their heart rate had significantly lower anxiety levels than those who did not.[7]

The study reveals important insights for leaders. Improving awareness of inner experiences, such as heart rate, can increase understanding of emotions such as anxiety, leading to more beneficial actions. Leaders can learn to track their heart rate like the participants in the study by using the heart rate monitor feature available on most smartwatches. Try it yourself. Put on the watch and hit the button, and your heartbeat appears on the screen. But before monitoring your heart rate, first take off your watch. Now, listen to your heartbeat without the aid of the smartwatch and its sensor. For most people, the heartbeat is challenging to detect. This is where the intervention comes into play. Assuming you are in good health, do an activity that will increase your heart rate by just a little. For example, climb several stairs, run for a hundred yards, do burpees, or take a brisk walk. Now sit still and feel your heartbeat, but don't rely on your smartwatch or take your pulse; see if you can become more aware of your heartbeat. With physical activity, your heartbeat increases in time and intensity, so you should be able to feel your heart rate now. Count the beats and measure the heartbeats you hear for one minute. With training, you might improve both the accuracy of your counting and the ability to sense your standing heartbeat without physical activity. Monitoring heartbeat is one of the ways leaders can improve their awareness of emotions. Developing an ability to monitor the origins of your emotions can increase awareness and help address situations such as stress and burnout.[8]

LEADING THROUGH EMOTIONS

Leadership and emotions are connected through emotional intelligence.[9] Emotional intelligence describes the ability to understand and manage your emotions and influence the emotions of others. Emotional intelligence involves four dimensions: (1) understanding emotions of oneself and others; (2) using knowledge of your feelings to support and direct thinking; (3) understanding how your feelings interact with various outcomes and with other emotions, including knowledge of what might be motivating your feelings; and (4) regulating your feelings so you can act even in the face of certain emotions.

Learning about emotional intelligence results in a clearer understanding of how emotions motivate leaders and their teams. Leading requires identifying, assessing, experiencing, and responding to various emotions. As the examples from the opening of this chapter illustrate, the inability to address unpleasant emotions can prevent growth and learning as a leader. How people learn from unpleasant emotions has been studied extensively in business failures associated with entrepreneurship. My colleagues George Solomon and Vivianna Fang He led a study that found that entrepreneurs varied in their ability to deal with the emotional demands that accompany failure.[10] The ability to deal with unpleasant emotions was vital to successfully respond to failure, such as assessing why the failure occurred, identifying ways to decrease the chances the failure would happen again, and productively moving on to the next project.

A key mechanism for dealing with emotions involves self-regulation. The self-regulation of emotions can be described as a four-step process.

1. *Identification.* In the identification phase, leaders determine if current emotions must be addressed. Whether to address the situation involves being aware of the emotion and then deciding how the emotion will motivate. Are the felt emotions helpful in increasing motivation and engagement in learning activities? Or does the emotion serve as a barrier to action? For example, suppose you experience anxiety, and this motivates problem-solving. In that case, there may be no need to address the unpleasant experience if you still feel in control. However, if the anxiety prevents you from taking a new job that you want, you may need to evaluate this emotion and its role in your life.

2. *Selecting regulation strategies.* The second step involves seeking out strategies to address unpleasant emotions. Throughout this book, you will learn about evidence-based strategies to support self-regulation of emotions. Chapter 7 presents specific strategies for self-regulation.

3. *Implementation.* In this step, leaders identify tactics to manage the emotional state. Implementation is tricky because it requires determining if the leader has the resources to address the problems caused by the emotions.

4. *Monitoring.* Once a regulation tactic is chosen, leaders monitor the experience and ask whether the regulation should continue and whether it is working.[11]

Following these steps increases emotional resilience by accepting, labeling, and identifying strategies for emotional self-management. Track these steps over time to identify patterns. Identify specific times or situations where the emotions are most prominent. Identify triggers or sensitivities from external events that may initiate unpleasant emotions. Finally, understand which activities support positive emotions in these situations. Reframe the emotion by looking at its positive or generative side: emotions such as anxiety and fear can motivate discovery. Realize that some unpleasant emotions can be productive too. Often, unpleasant emotions can motivate learning. For example, anticipation of an event may appear as anxiety. Fear can reflect the fact that you care about an outcome. Emotions are also short-lived. Those feelings of anger and fear will only last a few minutes. Accept unpleasant emotions as a natural part of life. Embrace the realization that unpleasant emotions are required for any fulfilling life.

Here is an extended list of ways to address unpleasant emotions offered by psychologists Vivian Kraaij and Nadia Garnefski.

- Blaming yourself for actions you took

- Blaming others

- Ruminating, especially with negative thoughts

- Thinking of the worst possible outcomes

- Finding perspective, considering possible positive outcomes, and accepting that things will get better

- Refocusing, generating pleasant thoughts

- Rethinking, finding the good in events, even adverse events

- Accepting the situation

- Taking action, developing strategies to take the following steps[12]

LEARNING AND EMOTIONS, BOTH PLEASANT AND UNPLEASANT

Many leaders become overly tied to the idea that pleasant emotions are a powerful source of resilience. Pleasant emotions are related to well-being, happiness, flow or optimal experiences, and positive attitudes. For example, the broaden-and-build theory of resilience suggests that positive emotions promote activities associated with learning.[13] Pleasant emotions link to joy, excitement, and support actively working toward goals. Positive emotions may increase focus, which is an essential ability for leading.

Unfortunately, leaders tend to overemphasize the value of positive emotions.

Leaders often believe they must be cheerful when confronted with a challenge, even when it is accompanied by unpleasant emotions. Because of the emphasis on positive emotions, leaders become tempted to hide or suppress unpleasant emotions. Unpleasant emotions arise as a part of leading, too. How leaders address these undesirable emotions will be a key to successful leadership. Ignoring these unpleasant emotions is ill-advised, as all experiences, not just pleasant experiences, serve as raw material for learning. Masking, ignoring, or trying to suppress unwelcome emotions may hurt leadership outcomes. For example, one study showed that hiding negative emotions harmed how healthy companies integrated after an acquisition suggesting that leaders need to prepare for a range of pleasant and unpleasant experiences.[14]

We developed a research program to learn more about the relationship between learning, emotions, and motivation. We asked participants to describe what kinds of emotions they were experiencing while learning. We first asked participants to recall when they felt frustrated while learning. This prompted them to think about a slightly unpleasant learning experience but one that may have continued to be motivating. We then asked the participants to remember when they were making progress while learning. This second question was designed to evoke a pleasant experience while learning. Participants recorded their thoughts and feelings during the two situations.

We expected unpleasant emotions such as anger, fear, or anxiety to be associated with frustration. After all, frustration would be linked to more unpleasant emotions, and progress would be linked to more pleasant emotions. However, we learned a far more complicated relationship between emotions and learning existed. We learned that:

- When learning, leaders have a combination of pleasant and unpleasant experiences.

- When making progress while learning, leaders tend to experience pleasant or neutral emotions, but in many cases, progress is also associated with unpleasant emotions such as frustration, concerns, or anger.

- When frustrated while learning, leaders experience more unpleasant experiences, but the unpleasant emotions do not necessarily mean less learning; frustration and other unpleasant experiences can also support learning.

An insight into the nature of resilience and emotions emerged. We estimated that 25 percent of those we studied learned under both conditions, when frustrated and making progress. In other words, a subset of leaders is highly resilient because they don't let emotions—either pleasant or unpleasant—get in the way of their progress when learning.[15]

The relationships between learning and emotions are more complicated than we initially thought. Learning entails a complex mix of pleasant and unpleasant emotions (see table 6.1). Returning to the body of research on emotions and learning, we noticed patterns largely consistent with our findings. We could break down which emotions were associated with learning based on whether these emotions were pleasant or unpleasant and if they enhanced or inhibited learning. Despite the variety of ways unpleasant emotions can lead to adverse outcomes, our research shows that unpleasant emotions can support positive outcomes in many situations. Unpleasant emotions have been associated with increased motivation for exploration, curiosity, the ability to anticipate problems, motivation to overcome stumbling blocks and challenges, the ability to identify discrepancies in information, and improved judgment.[16] Anger, a robust unpleasant emotion, can inspire solution-seeking and curiosity and spur goal pursuit.

TABLE 6.1 Relationship Between Emotions and Learning

	PLEASANT EMOTIONS	UNPLEASANT EMOTIONS
ENHANCE LEARNING	Curiosity	Frustration
	Positive engagement	Anger
	Happiness	Low levels of anxiety
	Positive expectations	Low levels of stress
DIMINISH LEARNING	Complacency	Boredom
	Satisfaction	Disinterest/avoidance
	Lack of challenge and stress	Procrastination
	Overconfidence	

THE SURPRISING UPSIDE OF FEELING DOWN

Paul Bloom, a professor of psychology at Yale, took the value of unpleasant emotions a step further. He argued that unpleasant emotions are essential for growth and learning. In contrast to common mantras that point to happiness and joy, Bloom explained how unpleasant experiences open us up to new possibilities. Having unpleasant experiences supports a more productive and fulfilled life than seeking only pleasant experiences. We continually pursue goals that put us in unpleasant situations, but we become fulfilled by pursuing these goals.

At other times, supporting our values surpasses our need for pleasant experiences. Bloom concluded that meaning and purpose often result from suffering and then offered several examples of unpleasant and potentially traumatic experiences. For example, having children often leads to unpleasant experiences, including sleepless nights, sacrifices, and a life of worry. Indeed, happiness may result from having children, and despite the unpleasantness associated with much of parenting, most parents' lives would be unfulfilled without children. For Bloom, leading a purposeful life is more important than avoiding unpleasant emotions. He argues that a purposeful life is almost impossible without unpleasant feelings.[17]

Bloom's recognition of the value of unpleasant experiences will resonate with many leaders. Unfortunately, many would-be leaders have removed themselves from potential leadership roles due to the fears and anxieties over the responsibilities associated with organizational leadership. This is why human resource management professionals struggle to identify, cultivate, and develop new leaders. They are challenged to help would-be leaders understand that the unpleasant experiences of leadership are often outweighed by the contributions that a leader can make. Organizations can support leaders by helping them understand the importance of these emotional barriers and how to use unpleasant experiences to support positive changes and contribute to their overall success. These positive outcomes often serve as a counterbalance to the unpleasant emotions experienced during leadership.

Leaders must accept unpleasant emotions as necessary for learning in facing life's challenges. A study on getting over heartbreak from a romantic relationship showed that allowing unpleasant thoughts about the former partner was the most effective way to overcome the broken relationship. Participants in the study were put into three groups. One group was asked to think about something else.

This was the avoidance group; they avoided thinking and feeling about the situation altogether. The second group was asked to think about the good times in the relationship. This was the positive feelings group, focusing only on the positives of the relationship. The final group was asked to recall those unpleasant experiences with their romantic partner, including things that were annoying about their partner or that caused conflict. Not surprisingly, those who thought about unpleasant aspects of the relations expressed the highest level of unpleasant feelings. Still, they were the ones who were most likely to get over the relationship. None of the groups, however, wanted to think about the past relationships at all. The outcome suggests that reflecting on the most negative attributes offers a valuable regulation strategy for dealing with unpleasant emotions. At the same time, all three strategies worked to some degree, suggesting leaders can adopt several strategies for dealing with unpleasant emotions.[18]

CHANGING YOUR EMOTIONAL MINDSET: NAVY SEALS SHOW MOTIVATION THROUGH UNPLEASANT EXPERIENCES

Leading outside your comfort zone requires accepting unpleasant times when you feel stress, anxiety, or frustration. Resilience is formed when you learn from these situations and turn these unpleasant experiences into opportunities for learning and growth. Turning unpleasant experiences into opportunities for growth is essential for resilience and is often referred to as the "emotional mindset" approach. This mindset says that how we approach our experiences impacts the potential outcome. When we view unpleasant experiences as necessary, even essential, to learning, then we become more resilient. The mindset approach says that rather than seeing unpleasant emotions as debilitating, we can take full advantage of the positive aspects of unpleasant emotions, enhancing our learning.

A study of Navy SEALs demonstrates how the mindset approach works.[19] Navy SEAL training is among the most demanding physical and mental leadership training programs. The team is called SEALs because they can perform successfully on sea, air, and land. Less than 20 percent of those who begin training complete the entire four-week program. Even the 20 percent statistic fails to capture the full extent of the challenges because those who start the training program are among the most elite in the US Armed Services.

One hundred seventy-four recruits started the program. Week four of the training is characterized as hell week, where candidates have drills and tasks nearly nonstop while receiving only forty-five minutes of sleep a night. Forty-four recruits began hell week, but only twenty-five remained at the end.

The study sought to determine what emotional factors contribute to persistence and performance. It focused on how the various mindsets of the recruits played out as they worked through the final phase of their training. Researchers used the concept of mindset as the basis for their study. Mindset can be understood as a group of attitudes, emotions, and deeply held beliefs of a person or group. These beliefs are so strong that they guide the individual or group's actions. In the case of the Navy SEALs, the mindset entailed the value of persistence and performance in completing the grueling training.

Researchers wanted to understand how three mindsets might contribute to resilience. The first category was stress mindsets: Did the leader-in-training believe that stress was debilitating and decreased performance, or that stress enhanced, contributed to, and boosted performance? Second, they were interested in a failure mindset: Did the leader believe that overcoming failure leads to improved performance or see failure as debilitating? Finally, the researchers examined the willpower mindset, whether willpower is viewed as unlimited or limited. These three mindsets have apparent connections to underlying pleasant and unpleasant emotions. Stress and failure are typically associated with unpleasant emotions. Still, those with an enhancing mindset might feel a positive or neutral effect, thus avoiding the negative connotations associated with these unpleasant emotions.

The findings provide clues on how to accept the content of our emotions and even turn unpleasant emotions into opportunities to learn. Those recruits with a robust stress-as-enhancing mindset were more persistent and performed better in objective measures such as time on an obstacle course. These same recruits were also ranked more highly by peers and supervisors. In sharp contrast, those with a solid failure-as-enhancing-performance mindset were slightly less persistent; that is to say, when trainees saw failure as enhancing, they were likely to have lower persistence, but only slightly. Those who felt they had unlimited willpower received more negative comments from fellow recruits, but there was no relation to actual outcomes.

Few leaders will experience the intense stress and hardship of becoming a Navy SEAL. Still, all leaders can learn from these experiences and adopt a mindset that says unpleasant and pleasant emotions can support our learning and perseverance. Leaders can learn from the extreme environment of the SEAL study.

When you see an unpleasant emotion, such as stress, as something that enhances your performance, you can translate unpleasant emotions into higher levels of learning and performance success.

We can also turn unpleasant experiences into motivating experiences that build our confidence. Dr. Nate Zinsser is a military psychologist who has worked with top performers in various fields, including military leaders, corporate executives, and professional athletes. His approach to mindset is to see setbacks, unpleasant emotions, and other potentially debilitating events as temporary. That way, we see that the situation is only a setback, not a permanent state.[20]

ENHANCING YOUR EMOTIONAL AWARENESS

As organizational psychologist Matthew Eriksen pointed out, emotions and experience are not just factors within the person. Emotions are relational. Emotions emerge from various social processes, including our past and future expectations about situations and our existing and anticipated relations with others. Leadership requires awareness of these inner experiences, but leadership also requires understanding the relational aspects of experience. While resilience may involve increased self-awareness and self-regulation, we must also understand how these factors arise in social situations.[21]

In some studies, emotional self-awareness accounts for only a tiny percentage of emerging leaders' ability to attenuate unpleasant experiences. The ability of employees to deal with unpleasant experiences associated with failure can be traced to the larger organizational culture, not just the individual leader.[22] Leaders hold an opportunity to shape cultures that support emotional self-awareness and emotional resilience in the face of setbacks and failures. Leading for improved growth and well-being means leaders are crucial in managing anxiety. Leaders support others who are experiencing stressful situations by helping others manage shifting ideas and change, especially during changing times.

Leaders can help create groups that serve as means to buffer stress and help build what Jarrett and Vince call "emotional coalitions," groups of individuals who understand each other's emotional reactions to events.[23] Leaders in these situations serve as sources of containment for these emotions. Leaders play a dynamic role as others depend on the leader to relieve their anxiety. Vince explains that unpleasant emotions, such as anxiety, can support or inhibit learning. Emotions help us learn when we accept anxiety. But if we develop defenses—attempts to explain away, ignore, or blame our emotions on events or others—we lose the opportunity to learn from our emotions. This means that not all attempts to understand our emotions are productive for learning. Some strategies can inhibit learning. A helpful exercise is to think of an unpleasant emotion you experienced last week and then describe how you addressed that unpleasant emotion. The goal is to offer insight into how individuals deal with unpleasant emotions such as anxiety. Leading outside your comfort zone is more than just generating pleasant emotions; leaders must strive to create cultures that support, recognize, and share unpleasant emotions.

In some situations, leaders must balance confidence with feeling powerless.[24] When you identify the source of unpleasant emotions, you can reverse their adverse effects and build awareness of your emotions. Learning to address emotions through self-regulation techniques will improve your influence and stamina.[25] Although significant differences exist among people in how they deal with unpleasant emotions, leaders have tools to help maintain learning in the face of unpleasant experiences. Labeling unpleasant experiences can help us turn unproductive emotions into productive ones, and by putting words to our feelings, we can make negative emotions a less potent force.[26]

Author and psychologist Guy Winch summarized what to do when we want to move on from past unpleasant emotions: don't overidealize the situation. He argued that we tend to focus on the positives of the past when we face a change, and in doing so, we overidealize the past, making it difficult to move forward and accept change.[27] One strategy to overcome this tendency includes cognitive reappraisal. Consider how unpleasant emotions can serve as motivators for learning.[28]

Emotions are also related to stress. The researchers who looked at Navy SEALs found that how people view stress can impact their effectiveness at dealing with stress. They found that when people view stress as something that enhances their performance, it is likely to have that effect. Still, when we view stress as a negative, we experience it as such, and it hurts performance. Unpleasant emotions are also associated with boredom. Van Tilburg has studied boredom for years and found that boredom is related to negative emotions such as frustration and anger toward others. But boredom could turn positive over time as people seek new and exciting ways to make activities more enjoyable. Boredom is often a turning point to innovation and creativity.[29]

The emphasis on pleasant and positive emotions may cause leaders to ignore or suppress unpleasant emotions, but suppressing unpleasant emotions can lead to problems down the road. Pleasant and unpleasant emotions play different roles essential for resilience, growth, and well-being. While there is no one profile for addressing emotions, leaders can learn to generate pleasant emotions, take stock of unpleasant emotions, and be prepared to make changes so that the emotions they experience support their leadership efforts.

This chapter shows that acknowledging emotions is essential for resilience, growth, and well-being. Leading requires reading and naming emotions—a process associated with emotional intelligence and self-awareness. Leaders should develop strategies to address, overcome, or change their mindset regarding unpleasant emotions, as unpleasant emotions can support learning. In the next chapter, I outline five of the most common strategies to address unpleasant emotions experienced when learning.

Exercise 6: Thinking Deeply About Emotions While Learning

Awareness of your emotions and what you think and feel will increase your ability to monitor and productively respond to your emotions. This exercise contains two parts. In part 1, you will consider how you are feeling at this moment. In part 2, you will consider how emotions may have impacted your learning in an experience.[30]

Part 1: Improving Emotional Self-Awareness

Look at the lists marked for unpleasant and pleasant feelings below. Rate how you feel right now on the following scale, then answer the questions below.

- 0 = not at all

- 4 = extremely so

UNPLEASANT FEELINGS

- Angry

- Nervous

- Tired

- Unhappy

- Depressed

- Frustrated

PLEASANT FEELINGS

- Happy

- Excited

- Enthusiastic

- Calm

- Relaxed

- Satisfied

How would you describe how you are feeling when learning?

- What impact do these feelings have on you?

- How do these feelings impact your team?

- Are the feelings motivating you or holding you back from taking action?

Part 2: Emotion's Impact on Learning
Think about a time when you were learning but frustrated. This could be an experience at work, in a professional development context, in a personal development context, or a formal education setting.

- Describe the experience.

- What were you doing?

- What were you learning?

- What were you feeling and thinking while learning?

Now consider these questions:

1. How did what you were thinking and feeling impact your learning? For example, did it make you want to learn more or less? Did it motivate you or demotivate you to learn?

2. What were the triggers, sensitivities, or transitions that preceded the thoughts and feelings?

- *Trigger:* An external event that creates a strong emotional response.

- *Sensitivity:* An external event that creates a weak but uncomfortable emotional response.

- *Transition:* Change in life, situation, or event that generates unpleasant emotions.

SEVEN

Implementing Learning Strategies

FIVE STRATEGIES FOR RESILIENCE AND GROWTH

Leading beyond your comfort zone requires developing strategies that maintain learning, even in the face of unpleasant emotions. The last chapter described the need for leaders to accept and identify strategies for addressing unpleasant emotions that arise when leading. This chapter introduces five key strategies leaders can use to support resilience and growth: positive emotional engagement, creative problem-solving, learning identity, flexibility, and social support.[1]

The strategies reveal the hidden motivating potential of learning and methods that motivate learning. The strategies do not involve putting a positive spin on or masking negative emotions. These strategies generate pleasant emotions by uncovering curiosity, interest, and openness to new experiences. They are not about willpower or grit or toughing it out while experiencing unpleasant emotions. The strategies presented here focus on improving the quality of the experience; the approach is to make the developmental activity more engaging.

Psychologist Ayelet Fishbach completed a series of studies that have caused many to question the long-term value of willpower and grit in overcoming obstacles. Her research points to overcoming unpleasant experiences by improving the genuine quality of experience. She studied individuals in various settings and found that most of those in the study could only sustain their developmental efforts if the activity were enjoyable. Goals and willpower only went so far.

Improvement could not be sustained if the participants were experiencing long bouts of unpleasant emotions. Fishbach followed people trying to pursue goals that involved activities that people might need help to keep up with over time, such as working out, doing yoga, and flossing their teeth. Her research found that no matter how committed the individuals were to the goal if they did not enjoy the activity, they were not likely to continue to work toward achieving the goal. Goals and willpower cannot overcome unpleasant emotions over the long haul, and study participants began to shy away from the activity.[2]

The factor that led to maintaining these typically unpleasant activities was how much participants enjoyed the activity. If the activity was intrinsically motivating, they persevered. If participants could find some way to make the activity enjoyable, become curious about the outcome, or generate positive emotions associated with the activity, they were more likely to continue to pursue the goal. Perseverance requires moving beyond outward signs of progress and rewards to a focus on one's growth and well-being. A more internally motivating, engaging, and challenging task overshadowed material outcomes or the self-esteem accompanying accomplishing goals. The five strategies that follow are ways to make any seemingly unpleasant situation more engaging.

FIVE LEARNING STRATEGIES

Learning strategies are actions we can take— behaviors, attitudes, mindsets, and emotional states—which can become routines that support resilience. The right learning strategies help resilient leadership, and the wrong strategies make leadership more susceptible to the vicissitudes of our emotions. Leadership requires focusing on the core learning strategies that matter most.

My colleagues and I were interested in learning strategies that support initiating, sustaining, and increasing effort toward learning. These strategies generate experiences and foster attitudes that support learning by directing our attention to motivating and engaging aspects of learning. We extensively reviewed individual factors that motivated learning. The study included research in psychology, sports psychology, management, neuroscience, organizations, and education. We reviewed evidence and ideas across multiple leadership approaches. Topics included how leaders learn to support change, how they motivate followers, how they persist in facing challenges, and how they handle stress. Additional topics included the role of personality and the processes by which leaders support goals. The review identified five primary factors that consistently help us learn: positive emotional engagement, creative problem-solving, learning identity, flexibility, and social support.

Positive Emotional Engagement

Positive emotional engagement describes generating interest and excitement about learning. When you have positive emotional engagement, you enjoy the action, even if it does not have clear rewards or outcomes; find working toward improvement interesting, exciting, and engaging; and are more open to new experiences. Positive engagement elements, such as curiosity, have been linked to enhanced memory and greater pleasure.[3] In addition, psychologists found that positive engagement with an action resulted in greater concentration, positive feelings about an activity, and lower feelings of being tired and stressed.[4]

Sharon's story offers insights into how positive emotional engagement can support leader development. Sharon had decided to leave her job and pursue an MBA in human resources management. After three years as a marketing rep for a digital marketing firm, she decided that she was interested in helping foster diversity and inclusion in organizations. Her interest in neurodiversity and neurodivergence, how individuals with different brain abilities, such as attention deficient/hyperactivity disorder or autism, could contribute meaningfully to an organization. As someone with different abilities, she had become interested in hiring for and creating an environment where others with different skills could thrive. However, transitioning from a full-time job with a regular salary to a student with significant debt was unnerving.

While she did not realize it then, Sharon sought ways to increase positive engagement in her new academic program. She was excited about studying human resources, management, and related topics. However, how would she stay interested in the other vital courses in her MBA program, such as accounting and finance? She found ways to engage positively with these courses. To her surprise, her finance class proved essential for her further work in HR and in understanding how to manage money in her personal life. She learned that she wasn't getting the best possible rate on her loan and that her retirement savings could be improved. Because she entered these courses with an openness to experience, Sharon could see the connections between these courses and her life and career ambitions. The classes became interesting and engaging.

Positive engagement becomes crucial to learning for leaders like Sharon.

Crystal Tsay, a professor at the University of Greenwich, was the lead researcher on a study with full-time and part-time MBA students. She wanted to identify the most critical factors associated with a significant life transition, like getting a graduate degree. Life transitions such as these can be stressful, and the successful transition to graduate school from the workplace is essential to the careers of many leaders. MBA students are representative, as most are either employed full-time and returning to school part-time or are leaving successful jobs to study full-time in hopes of finding something new upon graduation. Other students in the study were opening a new chapter in their lives by returning to school after many years in the workforce. Still others were moving across the world or the country to study, causing major upheaval in their lives.

All the students held something in common. They were seeking to improve their lives or make a significant change. They had already achieved some success in their lives, but they sought something more. Tsay studied a range of psychological concepts, including social support, efficacy, and stress, and the impact of these concepts on learning during this transition. Her study found that the most significant predictor of student learning was the degree to which students were open to new experiences. A host of studies have supported a similar finding. When people are open to experience, they are more likely to learn. In addition, being open to new experiences motivates learning by creating emotional and cognitive engagement with the task, independent of external goals or incentives.

Engagement and openness to experience are aspects of positive engagement; another element is excitement about the topic. For example, Charlie Reeve and Milton Hakel, showed a positive relationship between interest and knowledge acquisition (an aspect of learning).[5] In addition to openness to experience and interest, curiosity has been shown to have a positive relationship with learning behaviors such as information-seeking and positive framing.[6]

One leader we worked with was able to look back on both successes and failures and said things like, "I just wanted to see if it would work." He reminds me of many leaders in the tech world who believe that the road to success is paved with failure. But for him, that is not a hollow phrase. He always loved taking on new projects where learning and problem-solving drove the process. Learning to take a new tech product and turn it into a business, pushing the technology to new levels, and identifying new customers remained interesting.

Positive engagement describes how a leader builds interest and excitement about learning. For leaders, making work intrinsically valuable and engaging is essential for motivation. Positive emotional engagement can be improved by finding ways to keep the activity interesting, even when you become bored or uninterested.[7]

Creative Problem-Solving

A second strategy, creative problem-solving, describes ways to be creative and establish challenging and innovative ways to approach learning. Creative problem-solving relies on finding multiple paths to improvement. The game plan for creative problem-solving is rooted in taking calculated chances, trying new and various approaches, and challenging old ways of doing things. Like positive emotional engagement, creative problem-solving generates interest. cultivates positive experiences, and enhances the quality of leaders' developmental experience.

Mark Fitzloff is a creative advertising executive known for reinvigorating brands like Old Spice and creating engaging ads for Nike. Mark admitted, however, that some of his clients have not been as open to creative ideas as those two companies. Like most of us, Mark must do his job, even when the work isn't inspiring. He often faces developing campaigns to which he has no emotional attachment. To continue to perform at his best, Mark has developed a formula— something he refers to as the "being selfish in your work" formula. This involves finding ways to make the work of personal interest. For example, if a client offers a project that doesn't seem attractive, he tests his creativity. He described the process this way: "I'm really into science fiction and fantasy. If that's what you would rather be thinking about, how do I find a way to make the brand [that I'm working with] exist in sci-fi fantasy?" The process involves identifying ways to engage in the project that make it enjoyable.

Film director Francis Ford Coppola became famous for directing films like *The Godfather* series and *Apocalypse Now*. He was also known for going over budget in many of his movies. Because his films run over budget, he gained a reputation as a business risk. He became so legendary for going over budget that an entire documentary was devoted to his excessive style. Many larger studios became wary of signing him up for work for fear of busting the budget. A big-budget blockbuster became out of reach: no one would fund him. He went ten years between 1997 and 2007, without making a film. He reevaluated what was required to create an excellent movie during this period and focused on smaller films. His big takeaway was that external constraints, such as a small budget, enhanced his creativity.[8] The lesson for leaders is that external constraints, including limited resources, can make you more creative and generate new ideas that enhance learning.

Tammy Sihna and Manu Kapur showed the value of creative problem-solving—what they called productive failure—in school-aged children. When students can solve a problem themselves, they are more likely to learn the material than if presented with the solution. In other words, being challenged to find answers alone or in learning groups leads the students to more durable learning.[9] In addition, developing various strategies to solve problems leads to progress. When we learn through multiple strategies, we learn faster, and improvement flourishes.[10] Studies of learning and creativity have supported the connection between creative problem-solving and learning.[11]

Learning Identity

A third strategy focuses on learning identity, which is the belief that you can learn and develop. The game plan for improving learning identity is to seek opportunities to learn something new, test new ways of performing something you have already done, and not worry about failure.

Aurora Trinh, a professor of leadership at Arizona State University, has shown that leaders are more likely to succeed when they believe they can learn new things, grow, and improve. As discussed earlier, confidence should come from past successes and be applied cautiously to future situations. Each case is different, and leadership becomes more complex with more significant leadership challenges. Learning identity motivates learning by creating confidence that the task can be learned. Trinh described four aspects of learning identity: a learning stance toward life experience, a more confident learning orientation, a perception of how one learns specific to the context, and a learning self-identity that deeply permeates all aspects of life.[12]

Learning identity encourages leaders to avoid the temptation of puffing up their ego and massaging their self-esteem—attitudes often acquired from prior success. Instead, learning identity describes how leaders focus their attention on a form of self-confidence that enhances learning. Dweck's growth mindset is consistent with learning identity. A growth mindset is defined by people's willingness or propensity to take chances, risk failure, and focus on acquiring new skills. A growth mindset contrasts with a performance mindset, described as individuals' willingness or propensity to seek tasks they have mastered because they are focused on demonstrating competence and avoiding mistakes. Dweck's ideas highlight the difference between resilience and performance. Learning results in doing better; performance demonstrates doing the same thing well. Like a growth mindset, a learning identity is tied to the expectancy of positive outcomes associated with one's abilities.[13]

Flexibility

A fourth strategy involves flexibility. Flexibility describes adaptability in how you learn, your strategies to accomplish your goals, and your strengths in trying new approaches. Flexibility allows you to change direction and constantly update your assessment of situations and challenges. The game plan for improvement requires taking stock of current progress and actions to improve, changing direction, developing new strategies, and evaluating goals and progress regularly.

Penny liked to consider herself a jack of all trades. Not only did she produce multiple reports each year for her company, but she also managed individual projects for clients. She led a team and served as an expert at the same time. She was rare among her colleagues, who appeared to be either experts in their topic area or great at managing projects, but not both. Early in her career, this was the case for Penny, too. She was an expert at transfer payment taxation, a highly specialized and emerging area of the tax code associated with international tax law. It wasn't until she was transferred to the Berlin office that Penny seemed to learn that her clients were real people!

Once Penny started working with clients directly, she realized she could no longer rely on her expertise on transfer payments alone. Once she settled into the new office, she saw that she also needed to improve her communication skills. In her words, "It was a real disaster at first." One client even spoke with the team lead about Penny's poor communication skills.

Instead of obsessing over these setbacks and the possible poor performance review that would result, Penny saw this challenge as an inevitable part of the learning process. She learned how to better engage with her clients, read their concerns and nonverbal cues, and be flexible.

My colleague Babis Mainemelis studied flexibility in learning from experience. He noted that when people embrace different approaches to learning, they are both more fulfilled and know more.[14] Improvement happens when we develop multiple strategies, realize that many changes and adjustments must be made, remain flexible, and understand the importance of failure. Flexibility, like agility, describes how people adapt to different learning situations by using different approaches to learning.[15] Flexibility has also been linked to resilience in potentially traumatic events; for example, Bonanno explained that resilience requires flexibility and adaptability.[16]

Social Support

The fifth strategy involves social support. Social support consists of two elements. The first is seeking out experienced and capable others as mentors and role models, especially those who have already achieved what you are trying to achieve. This includes watching, listening, and working with others who have already been successful so that you can learn from their mistakes and benefit from their expertise. The improvement plan is to identify several potential mentors who have already achieved what you are trying to achieve and ask them for feedback on your progress. Social support motivates learning through challenges by offering direction, advice, and expert feedback. Ask them what you are currently doing well and what areas need improvement.[17]

The second element involves finding emotional support. Emotional support helps individuals deal with stress, self-doubt, and the unpleasant emotions of new leadership challenges. Social support is essential to emotion and self-regulation since negative emotions can be addressed by deep interaction with supervisors and managers. Social support has also been linked to various forms of resilience.[18]

Recall Tsay's study of MBA students that identified essential types of social support needed for transitions through major life changes. The types of support include technical support for specific areas of knowledge associated with business, such as calculating financial measures, applying cost-accounting rules, or knowing what types of negotiation might be necessary to solve conflict among employees.

Social support in navigating a new culture and set of expectations might include understanding how to interact with other students, successfully engage with teammates, or work through a new job's requirements. Finally, emotional support helps with understanding, accepting, and dealing with the complex emotions associated with taking on a significant new life challenge.

Shrinivas, a consultant, looked for ways to improve his teamwork and leadership of the team. He contacted his organization's organizational development specialists and connected with a senior partner whom he trusted. When Shrinivas was doing this, he adopted the learning strategy associated with social support. He identified individuals who could give him direct feedback on his progress. The late psychologist Anders Ericsson studied social support in his work on expertise development. Ericsson showed how experts learn from observing others before making outstanding contributions. Whether chess champions, leaders in organizations, or top athletes, leaders in most fields found support through expert feedback from others.

IMPLEMENTING LEARNING STRATEGIES

Exercise 7 provides a quick way to assess your readiness for and application of the learning strategies in a specific activity.

There are other ways to support the development of learning strategies. Researchers working in habit formation, such as Wendy Wood, Katy Milkman, and Ayelet Fishbach, have shown that when a job is unpleasant, we are less likely to complete it, even if we have set goals. Ways to improve your learning habits include bundling or mixing a pleasant activity with a less enjoyable activity—for example, listening to music while working out or enjoying a cup of coffee while working on tedious tasks. Sequencing involves rotating or organizing tasks from pleasant to unpleasant—for example, doing a task such as online shopping to initiate work on a spreadsheet. This gets you in the mode of working on a computer. Alternatively, you can work on an unpleasant task first, then reward yourself with something more pleasant. Another approach to increasing positive engagement is seen in tangential immersion, which suggests that people combine less demanding tasks with more challenging ones.[19]

To improve creative problem-solving, consider Aviva Romm's advice to shift away from thinking about a situation from a judgment standpoint or making a quick decision. Instead, engage in creative problem-solving. Rather than taking a position, ask these questions: What is my immediate reaction? Why do I feel this way? What could be going on that might be more interesting than I initially thought? How can I learn more about this situation and take in more information? Harvard social psychologist Ellen Langer often relates mindfulness to learning and creative problem-solving. This involves four steps: (1) view a situation from several perspectives, (2) see information presented in the situation as novel, (3) attend to the context in which we perceive the information, and eventually (4) create new categories through which this information may be under-

IMPLEMENTING LEARNING STRATEGIES 111

stood. Another approach to creative problem-solving involves varying the way you go about learning, training, working, or playing. For example, changing how practice sessions are conducted can make learning faster and more enjoyable.[20]

To develop your learning identity, consider embracing challenges and seeing them as fun and exciting; identify the benefits of engaging in an activity other than the outcome. Focus on understanding your learning skills and recognizing your past successes in learning. Self-esteem is necessary, especially when you first experience a setback. However, focusing too much on propping up your self-esteem can prevent you from taking full stock of necessary changes.[21]

To increase your flexibility, consider multiple ways of accomplishing something and think about different sources of information you can use to succeed. For example, David Kolb has suggested understanding your learning style—your preferred learning mode—to increase flexibility. Kolb's learning model, as a four-phase process of experience, reflection, thinking, and acting, provides a model for understanding the different ways you can learn. Kolb's Learning Style Profile is a commercially available tool to support understanding your preferred learning style and offers insights into improving flexibility in other modes.

To take advantage of measures of social support, take note of the concept of deliberate practice and learning. If you will become a leader in your organization, seek out existing leaders as mentors. If you are learning new skills, find a coach or advocate whom you can learn from. Find ways to receive feedback from those individuals and ensure that feedback is specific so you know where to concentrate your future practice.[22]

This chapter described five strategies to support learning in the face of challenges. Leaders who adopt these strategies can turn challenging situations into opportunities to support themselves and lead others. Learning strategies help leaders overcome the often adverse outcomes of working while frustrated and help to turn unpleasant emotional situations into situations that enhance learning.

Exercise 7: Readiness to Apply Learning Strategies

Learning strategies describe actions you can take to motivate and improve how you learn. In this exercise, you will consider readiness to apply learning strategies in a particular activity.[23] Follow the three steps below.

Step 1: Thinking of a Time When You Were Learning Something
Consider an activity you are working on. The activity can come from any life, social, personal, or work area. Write a short description of the activity.

Step 2: Ranking Your Use of Learning Strategies
Rank how much you agree or disagree on a scale of 1 to 7 (with 1 = strongly disagree and 7 = strongly agree) with the following statements as they apply to the activity you just described.

When learning, I am:

1. curious   _____

2. excited   _____

3. interested in the activity   _____

4. engaged   _____

5. enthusiastic   _____

6. challenged   _____

7. problem-solving   _____

8. creative   _____

9. innovative   _____

10. resourceful   _____

When learning I:

11. believe in myself   _____

12. learn something new   _____

13. am confident I could learn   _____

14. believe in my ability to learn   _____

15. feel confident   _____

16. use different methods to learn   _____

17. am flexible   _____

18. try different approaches   _____

19. consider different methods   _____

20. learn in different ways   _____

21. work with others   _____

22. seek feedback   _____

23. trust in others   _____

24. look to experts   _____

25. build relationships   _____

Step 3: Calculating Your Scores

Add 1–5 _____

> *This is your positive emotional engagement score. This strategy is about being excited, engaged, enthusiastic, curious, and open.*

Add 6–10 _____

> *This is your creative problem-solving score. This strategy involves facing new challenges with innovation, creativity, and challenge.*

Add 11–15 _____

> *This is your learning identity score. This strategy reflects your ability to learn, feel confident, and trust in your ability to learn.*

Add 16-20 _____

> *This is your flexibility score. This strategy reflects your ability to use different modes of learning and to shift among different strategies.*

Add 21–25 _____

> *This is your social support score. This strategy reflects your ability to seek social and other types of support from others.*

Add the five scores and see where you are on the readiness scale to apply learning strategies:

Score of 175–158: Extremely high readiness
Score of 148–139: High readiness
Score of 139–105: Some readiness
Score of below 105: Low readiness

(These scores are based on quartiles of a sample of 400 undergraduate and graduate business students and executive education participants.)

Step 4: Questions for Reflection
Each statement in step 2 is associated with one of the learning strategies. Which strategies are your most vital, and which are your weakest?

Review your score for each question and develop a game plan for improvement by identifying actions to increase your use of the strategies. What other actions can you take to enhance your readiness in each strategy?

Review your scores and answer the following questions.

- Which strategies do you use the most?

- Which strategies will improve how you learn?

- Which additional strategies have you tried to improve your learning?

EIGHT

Motivating Yourself to Learn

THE PSYCHOLOGY OF LEARNING, MOTIVATION, AND RESILIENCE

Leading beyond your comfort zone requires progressing and learning despite setbacks, challenges, and other barriers. Learning becomes a form of resilience essential to leading. The previous three chapters described three related processes associated with leading and learning: (1) generating novel experiences, (2) accepting unpleasant emotions, and (3) implementing learning strategies. This chapter describes how these three processes result in learning, resilience, growth, and well-being.

Learning motivates purpose and the pursuit of growth. Kay Peterson, founder and CEO of the Institute for Experiential Learning, describes how leaders can draw on their experience as the basis for learning. Learning sits at the core of leadership development.[1] It provides a lifelong platform to push for greater responsibility, navigate ambiguity, and strategize in the face of competing demands. Without learning, resilience, growth, and well-being become distant aspirations.

THE PSYCHOLOGY OF LEARNING, MOTIVATION, AND RESILIENCE

A natural relationship between learning and resilience exists. Both learning and resilience involve reflection on past experiences, updating perspectives based on that reflection, and implementing action plans to promote future growth and well-being. Learning and resilience emerge from resolving tensions as we experience new challenges, generate new emotions, and cover new territory. Tension is natural in learning and resilience, and resilience results from continuing to learn in the face of this tension. As leaders increase effort toward learning, they take account of the emotions they experience and evaluate their benefits and drawbacks.

Emerging research and time-tested theories support the resilience and learning relationship. Abraham Maslow offered a well-known theory of human motivation. Despite questions about its foundation, Maslow remains relevant. For Maslow, learning and growth provide the source of motivation. Pursuing opportunities to learn and pursuing goals with self-determination are the highest forms of achievement. More recently, popular authors such as Daniel Pink have drawn on self-determination theory (SDT), which shows that intrinsic motivation emerges from autonomy, competency, and connectedness.[2]

Neuroscience offers a complementary description of learning and resilience. Learning may be a natural process, but it is also a complicated one. Jim Zull, the former head of the Case Western Reserve University Center for Instruction and Teaching, studied the neurobiology of learning and growth. As a biologist, Zull saw a connection between biological processes and learning. His extensive review of the brain and the body revealed learning involves billions of possible neuron connections and pathways. Zull identified over 100 different body functions involved in learning.[3]

Moreover, Zull knew that learning went beyond brain activity. Learning invokes biology, psychology, and social processes. It involves highly interdependent processes that recruit brain architecture, electro-brain processes, biological functions, and behavioral factors such as self-awareness and social context. Learning engages a complex mix of neurobiological processes and generates many "good" chemicals such as oxytocin, dopamine, and serotonin. For example, research in laboratory settings shows that learning is associated with dopamine release in mice. Dopamine is a neurotransmitter associated with pleasure, satisfaction, and motivation. For example, when mice were specially bred so they did not produce dopamine, they were no longer motivated to eat. Even when food was within easy reach, the mice lacked all motivation to seek out the food when deprived of dopamine. They were no longer motivated to learn or solve problems to obtain even life-giving food. If this research is transferable to humans, it suggests that learning is intrinsically tied to motivation.[4]

Neuroscience describes resilience as the result of learning to adjust our expectations. Resilience is closely associated with rediscovering purpose in the face of loss and hardship. Neuropsychologist Mary-Frances O'Connor argues that learning is how we deal with changes, especially loss. Recovering from loss involves reconfiguring our brains, and resilience emerges as we shed old assumptions about the world and gain new ones. For example, when recovering from grief, the brain of the survivor adapts to the changed situation where there is no longer the physical presence of another person. Learning is the driving force for overcoming loss and challenge. The brain constantly predicts future events, and when we plan for one event, but another occurs, we need to adjust our expectations. For example, with the death of loved ones, we expect them to be there because they have been present in the past. Neuroscientists call this prediction error and describe the neurological process of how the brain learns.[5] Learning emerges when we predict future events, acknowledge disconfirming evidence, and adjust our expectations about what will happen next.[6] Learning occurs as we resolve gaps between our expectations of a situation and reality. We continually refine our strategies to fill this gap.

Neurobiologist Robert Sapolsky believes that learning plays a role in resilience because it supports survival and allows us to deal with stress in productive ways. Stress is essential for learning because it helps us encode information and learn from our experiences. These experiences will enable us to adapt and change our behaviors to meet current challenges. Therefore, some stress is not only good; stress is necessary to motivate us to grow and stretch outside our comfort zone. When we are stressed, we learn, improve, and grow. This is called challenge stress, but challenge stress must occur in small amounts and be contained in short periods. One region of the brain called the hippocampus is essential for learning. It moves the information we gather and hold in our short-term memory to long-term memory. It is crucial to learning but particularly susceptible to stress. Too little stress and the hippocampus doesn't respond; too much stress and the hippocampus can become desensitized to new information. If we experience too much stress, we cannot create long-term memories and become unable to learn.[7]

Further, learning provides the fuel for improved well-being. As we progress toward personal goals, this progress results in feelings of well-being. Teresa Amabile and colleagues studied how progress toward personal goals tied to purpose was vital to igniting joy and engagement at work. Amabile also found that well-being involves a social element and that seeking out social support was critical to learning.[8] Studies support this and have shown that participation in learning circles enhances well-being by creating social connections and belonging.[9] Research has shown that activities, such as learning new skills or hobbies and being a member of an arts or music organization, increase well-being across the lifespan.[10] Relationships become essential support for leading outside your comfort zone, and seeking out social support is critical to learning. Expert coaches can provide insight into how to learn, identify what skills need to be developed, suggest areas for improvement, and support the technical aspects of learning. Learning requires feedback as we try new things and learn new skills; who better to provide feedback than someone who has already been successful in these activities? In every area, from absorbing the necessary strategies to play chess to practicing emotional control to be a successful organizational leader, working with knowledgeable and experienced people supports learning. A second area of social support focuses on the emotional side. Learning can involve failure, and reflecting on that failure can be emotionally taxing. Social support can help us through these difficult times as well.[11]

Behavioral economists, too, believe learning results from a tension between what we currently know and what we seek to know. George Lowenstein describes one characteristic of learning: curiosity as the realization of deprivation, a need that requires action, and a tension that requires resolution. We satisfy our curiosity by seeking to fill this knowledge gap. Said another way, curiosity motivates us to resolve a felt tension, an unpleasant experience that fuels action to fill the gap in our knowledge.[12]

FALLING BACK INTO YOUR COMFORT ZONE: THE PROBLEM OF ADAPTIVE ADEQUACY

As a leader, you push new boundaries and discover new routes to success; you always learn. Unfortunately, many factors can undermine your ability to learn. Complacency may set in. A leader's focus can drift in unintended directions, and oversized expectations regarding performance can leave leaders feeling dejected. Leaders, like everyone, can become creatures of habit. The elements of motivation discussed by Maslow and put forward by self-determination theory begin to wane. We may become overburdened in work situations (e.g., lack of autonomy), experience feelings of alienation (e.g., lack of connection), and feel as though we cannot accept change (e.g., lack of competency).[13]

Contemporary organizations focusing on performance and efficiency can contribute to this fatigue. Leaders can quickly become indifferent to what they learn about themselves and others. Sheila, the leader of the tech company, grew frustrated as her team became more complacent. Her team was adapting positively to the situation in the organization, but their adaptability led to adequacy—just doing enough. They were no longer thriving. Their well-being was threatened because the team members were not learning and growing. They became disengaged from their work. Just as important, the team's inability to learn was hurting the organization.

To rekindle her desire to learn, Sheila sought to create an environment where the organization and its members could learn and grow, a workplace that thrived on new challenges and opportunities to solve problems creatively. To rekindle learning, leaders like Sheila must overcome what psychologists call "adaptive adequacy." Adaptive adequacy describes how the natural desire to learn wanes, and employees move from being active learners to creatures of habit.[14] Adaptive adequacy results in adequate but uninspired leadership. The result is boredom, discontent, and fatigue. Well-being suffers when leaders are not learning. When leaders are doing just enough to get by and not pushing themselves to learn and develop, they become disengaged from their role as leaders.

A study offers insight into how adaptive adequacy takes over learning. A research team used a computer simulation to observe children, adolescents, and adults playing a strategy game. The experiment involved generating and implementing new strategies to guide a mouse through a maze. The experiment involved two primary phases. Phase I was a learning phase where the participants could independently learn the best strategy for working through the maze. The participants in the study were all given immediate feedback on which strategies worked the best. In phase I, the three groups, children, adolescents, and adults, all performed well in determining the best strategies to feed the mouse, but the adults performed slightly better overall. This made sense; adults had been learning from experiences their entire lives. Before the second phase, the researchers introduced something new. They explained which strategies would most effectively guide the mice through the maze. Explicit instructions were given, but the instructions involved a trick—they were designed to create failures by making it more challenging for participants to guide the mouse through the maze. In other words, the instructions were intended to decrease performance. The study participants had no clue that the information they were given was false.

In the second testing phase, the individuals were tested on what they learned but received no direct feedback on whether their strategy was successful. In this phase, something interesting happened: the children outperformed the adults! The adults seemed to no longer rely on their own learning experiences but instead turned to the instructors' strategies. The children were affected less by the wrong advice than the adults and were less biased toward the new strategies' rules, norms, and authority. The children relied on their direct learning from experience, the trial-and-error learning that led the mouse to food, just as they had in the study's first phase. The adult performance decreased because the adults unknowingly followed false instructions, replacing their trial-and-error learning.

The research team believed that the children outperformed the adults because the children continued to learn from experience while the adults turned to the more accessible approach. The shift occurs due to the overreliance on a brain region called the prefrontal cortex. The prefrontal cortex is associated with rational thinking—the brain functions that monitor, control, and advise the other parts of the brain. A well-developed prefrontal cortex should result in better and longer focus, the ability to override immediate distractions, and the ability to hold emotions in check. However, in the experiment, the adults' prefrontal cortex overrode the processes associated with learning from experience. Because learning from experience is difficult and time-consuming, the adults in the experiment turned to the shortcuts they had acquired rather than learning for themselves. That meant adopting the advice of others through the instructions rather than plotting their own course through the maze and learning from trial and error. On the other hand, the children outlearned the adults because they experimented more and learned more, even though they didn't have a fully developed prefrontal cortex editing their thoughts. The fully developed prefrontal cortex improved efficiency but also interfered with learning.[15]

OVERCOMING ADAPTIVE ADEQUACY

The previous study reveals how leaders can develop a bias toward taking the easiest path. Overworked and busy leaders seek shortcuts to learning, but resilient leaders overcome this temptation by seeking learning opportunities. Leaders must engage in the learning process to overcome adaptive adequacy in themselves and their followers. Learning from experience is critical to leading: reflecting on successes and failures, updating perspectives based on new information, and testing new ideas. In short, learning is a process of changing our minds based on reflecting on our experiences. It involves gathering and processing information to solve problems and engaging in the continual learning cycle.

To overcome adaptive adequacy, leaders need constant growth and development. This requires seeking new and novel experiences, accepting unpleasant emotions, and identifying learning strategies. David Kolb, professor emeritus at Case Western Reserve University, offers a way to overcome the problem of adaptive adequacy. He developed a model of learning that describes how leaders resolve tensions as they gather and process knowledge.

Learning requires the resolution of two primary tensions. First, you must resolve the tension between thinking and feeling. When experiencing this tension, you must decide if you should dive deeper into an experience, drawing on your intuition to help you, or if you should choose first to gather more information before deciding. For example, if working through a group conflict, should the conflict be addressed directly to help the group resolve the tension? This would put you in the middle of the action, and more interesting experiences will likely emerge. You will directly experience what being part of the team is like. Alternatively, you could consider multiple approaches, talk to human resources, or talk to team members individually before deciding if you should act. By thinking before feeling, you are considering alternatives, which requires gathering more information rather than directly getting involved in the conflict.

The second tension you must resolve is between reflection and action. When experiencing tension that emerges from reflection-action, you must decide whether to act or reflect. For example, if you are considering a new approach to serving customers, do you consider what to do and develop a plan, or jump right in and do it? If you jump right in, you resolve the tension by acting. If you decide to reflect and see what other companies are doing first, you are driven to resolve the tension by reflecting.

Over time, we develop preferences for resolving these tensions. You might become a leader who draws more directly on their intuition—learned from engaging in direct experience, or you may be more adept at using analysis and planning. Perhaps you are a leader who chooses to rely more on gathering more information before deciding, or perhaps others prize your talents for jumping right in and seeing how things turn out, with little concern for taking risks. These are preferences that you develop for resolving these tensions in different ways. Your preferences can reflect strengths in decision-making.

Yet, to fully develop ourselves as leaders, we need to move out of our comfort zone to optimize our learning. Optimization of our learning occurs when we try to take advantage of different ways of resolving these tensions. Kolb talks about learning to resolve these tensions as a cycle. The learning cycle means we should address learning tensions in multiple ways. When we rely on specific learning methods, we may be learning but not optimizing.

To optimize learning, Kolb recommends working around the learning cycle and engaging in four modes of resolving the learning tensions. Learning involves examining our direct experience (our emotions and other factors that occur when we are directly engaged in the world), reflecting on the experience (by looking at the experience from different viewpoints), thinking about the experience (by gathering and considering different options and planning for further actions to take), and then acting (by experimenting, taking some risks, and testing our plans).

The experiential learning cycle supports a leader's capacity to solve problems, think strategically, manage others, make better decisions, and tackle various other leadership processes. When people engage in experiential learning, they improve their judgment and learning capacity. The learning cycle is an indispensable diagnostic tool that helps leaders understand their learning and the learning of others. Leaders can point to the learning cycle to identify ways to motivate unit managers to engage in learning, as depicted in figure 8.1.[16]

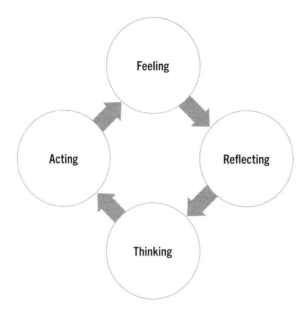

FIGURE 8.1 Kolb's Cycle of Learning

LEARNING IN ACTION

As a leader, you can ask four questions to help others improve learning. Each question is tied to the Kolb learning cycle. (1) Do you have the right experience? The first question focuses on generating new experiences: it asks whether leaders have the right background and experience to be effective learners. The question implies that leaders can improve when exposed to specific learning opportunities. (2) Can you access information and resources? This question corresponds to the reflection step of the learning cycle because it focuses on taking stock of necessary resources for learning. The question focuses on whether you have the information required to learn. (3) Do you know what is happening and why this is relevant to the organization, your team, and your leadership development? This addresses the third stage of understanding and knowledge of the learning cycle. It focuses on whether managers have the right mindset, thinking, and perspective. (4) What action should I take, and what are the potential consequences? This corresponds to the action phase of the learning cycle. This question addresses the range of appropriate actions and considers their broader impact. Leaders can spark the learning process by engaging their managers with these four questions and help them escape the adaptive adequacy mode.

Leaders can improve their learning by introducing additional learning strategies. First, leaders can emphasize self-awareness and understanding strengths, weaknesses, and styles. Increased self-awareness supports overcoming frustrations associated with leadership. When frustrated, individuals are often tempted to focus on self-esteem and generate positive feelings about themselves. While self-esteem is essential, especially after a perceived failure or loss, long-term efforts to support self-esteem can inhibit learning. When leaders focus on self-improvement instead of self-esteem, they build resilience. The approach involves emotional intelligence, learning leadership, leadership without easy answers, and leadership through self-discovery and learning.

Second, leaders can draw on a natural capacity to learn. While the ability to learn and the strengths associated with learning vary across individual leaders, humans hold a boundless power to learn. Learning from experience is a natural process but may ebb and flow over time. Research on learning offers a path forward in understanding how to make the most of this natural learning ability.

Third, leaders can invoke multiple paths to learning. In invoking notions like curiosity, self-discovery, interest, and growth, learning provides a way to build strength. Resilience is defined by stability. Stability is the necessary outcome of resilience, but the path to achieving resilience still needs to be discovered. Consider Bonanno's insight on resilience in the face of potentially traumatic events. Bonanno's recommended path on how to develop resilience tracks the four steps of the learning process. Therefore, the learning process provides methods and descriptions of how leaders can build resilience in themselves and others.[17]

Fourth, leaders can support resilience by recognizing the successes they have already experienced. Regardless of their background, leaders have had successes, failures they have recovered from, and obstacles they have overcome. In this way, they have already shown resilience in different forums. Reflecting on these experiences will enhance the resilience capabilities they have already acquired.

APPLE'S TIM COOK SAVES . . . ELON MUSK'S TWITTER

Consider how Apple CEO Tim Cook responded to Elon Musk's criticism of Apple's in-app purchase policy. No one could say that Musk lacked resources as one of the wealthiest people to have walked this earth, but all these resources could not match Tim Cook's, one of the longest-standing CEOs in Silicon Valley.

Musk had just bought the social media giant Twitter for $44 billion. His decision seemed hasty. By most accounts, he had overpaid by $20 billion or more. At the time of his purchase, Twitter was generating only about $5 billion a year and was losing money. Musk would need to pay over $1 billion in annual interest to cover his accumulated debt to buy Twitter. This may have seemed like a small price for a man who was once worth over $130 billion. The reality was that Twitter was bleeding advertisers, a source of income that accounted for nearly 85 percent of its revenue. Considering these challenges, it is no wonder Musk was frustrated and tweeted that the company might go bankrupt. He stood to see billions of dollars of wealth disappear and would be held responsible.

Despite these frustrations, Musk was about to make the situation even worse by criticizing his largest advertiser: "Apple has mostly stopped advertising on Twitter. Do they hate free speech in America," he tweeted. He even called out Apple CEO Tim Cook by name: "What's going on here @tim_cook?" Apple spent an estimated $48 million a year advertising on Twitter. Why was Musk putting Twitter's most significant source of revenue at risk?

Musk reignited an old argument that Apple was a monopoly. The target was Apple's App Store, where millions of apps were downloaded daily, and Apple took a percentage of every financial transaction in each app. For Musk, that meant that for every potential subscriber to Twitter, Apple would enjoy as much as 30 percent of Twitter's subscription revenue. Apple's practices in its App Store could deprive Twitter of valuable subscription revenue that it needed to make up for its dropping advertising revenue. Musk suggested that the Twitter app might be removed from the Apple App Store altogether.

Despite the constant negative publicity directed toward it by Musk, Apple remained silent. Then, one day, about a week after the negative tweets toward Apple began, Musk tweeted a single sentence: "We resolved the misunderstanding about Twitter potentially being removed from the App Store." The tweet accompanied a photo of a reflecting pond at Apple's headquarters. It appeared that

Musk had been invited to the Apple headquarters to meet with Cook and resolve the dispute. Musk's frustration, at least about the issue with the Apple App Store, appeared resolved.

Reports suggest that Musk overcame his frustration by following the lead of Apple CEO Tim Cook. Cook applied a mix of old and new leadership strategies. Cook moved the negotiation out of the public eye and defused a stressful situation. In contrast, Musk craves public attention, while Cook's public appearances are strategic, and his response to controversies is well-scripted. Even though Cook did not respond publicly to the spat, reports inside Apple, as well as journalists' observations, suggest that Cook orchestrated Apple's response. Tim Cook's leadership, not Elon Musk's, solved Musk's problem.

By drawing Musk out of the public eye, Cook resolved the spat and avoided negative publicity for Apple, which may have saved Twitter, too. Cook, working behind the scenes, silenced a frustrated and vocal Musk. Ultimately, Cook's efforts likely preserved the advertising dollars Apple spent on Twitter, restoring to Twitter a financial lifeline. The move could have accelerated Twitter's downward revenue spiral even further if Apple chose to reply by pulling its ads. Similarly, a drawn-out fight between two of the most public companies in the world would have highlighted the monopolistic potential for both companies. After all, Twitter, too, reaches billions of people and has few, if any, real competitors.

Cook showed the power of focusing on the long term and overcoming the moment's stress. He took the confrontation to a healthy place and focused on making a productive response to this potentially volatile situation. His response took confidence, resilience, and a focus on reducing tension. Leaders like Cook avoid drama. Instead, they focus on building productive well-being. With this emphasis on reducing drama, it is no surprise that Cook has remained the CEO of Apple for more than a decade, twice the time of the average Fortune 500 CEO. That places him among the top 19 percent of CEOs for longevity.[18]

Learning from experience is at the core of leading. Learning supports resilience, growth, and well-being and is intrinsically motivating. However, learning can become stifled, and problem-solving can suffer. Overtime, leaders may fall into adaptive adequacy and fail to optimize their learning. Leaders can overcome adaptive adequacy by adopting the four-phase learning cycle to resolve the tensions and conflicts inherent in learning.

Exercise 8: Learning from Experience

This exercise will help you think about strategies you use to learn and how these strategies support resilience. This involves three steps.

Step 1

Briefly describe a time when you were learning and making progress.

- What were you learning?

- What were you thinking and feeling while learning?

Step 2

Briefly describe a time when you were learning but frustrated with your progress. The situation can be the same or different from what you described in step 1.

- What were you learning?

- What were you thinking and feeling while learning?

Step 3

Compare your responses between step 1 and step 2

- Compare your responses to learning while making progress and learning while frustrated.

- Did you recall the differences and similarities in your thoughts and feelings across these two situations?

- What do the differences or similarities tell you about how you learn in different situations?

Further Reflection

The exercise is designed to help you think about how emotions impact your learning. Both pleasant and unpleasant emotions are required for learning, but often, we equate pleasant emotions with making progress and unpleasant emotions with frustration toward progress. Resilience emerges when we can maintain our learning even when feeling unpleasant emotions like frustration. Consider these questions.

- How do emotions impact your learning?

- What is the nature of experiences that prevent you from learning at your best? For example, are there certain conditions, places, or times where you find it difficult to learn? Similarly, are there conditions, places, or times where you learn well?

- What strategies do you use to overcome unpleasant emotions when learning, and what strategies do you use to enhance pleasant emotions when learning?

- Return to the list of learning strategies outlined in chapter 7. Which strategies can you build into your learning routines to support continued learning, even in the face of setbacks, challenges, and unpleasant emotions?

Applications

NINE

Keeping Focused

Wanted: A leader who can focus for long periods, work in a constant state of alertness, and thrive in an "unfatigued state." These requirements were posted for an actual job ad for the manager of a popular restaurant chain.[1] Not all job announcements require this level of focus, but it points to a new reality—focus has become a primary job requirement for leaders.

The chapter discusses factors that threaten focus and introduces tools to overcome these threats. Lack of focus is among the biggest threats to effective leadership. By cultivating focus, leaders can learn and grow. Daniel Goldman, who popularized emotional intelligence, has called focus an overlooked success factor for leading. In short, focus is essential for leading outside your comfort zone.[2]

Edna could find patterns in any spreadsheet. She always had a talent for numbers. As an analyst for a federal agency, she always took her time, but in the end, she could see patterns in the numbers that her colleagues missed. Now, as a federal agency's division director, she no longer had the luxury of time and was required to think on her feet. The upcoming testimony to an Oversight Committee created significant fears because Edna knew the committee would ask her tough questions. What if she froze and couldn't answer a routine question? What if she said something that grabbed national attention because it was poorly phrased or even wrong?

Edna prepared for months. She worked with other federal leaders who had already given testimony, took a course, and practiced mock hearings with her staff to create the high-pressure conditions she would face in the hearing. She wrote down a timeline of the events of interest to the committee. Next, she anticipated the questions she might be asked during the testimony. Then, in preparation for periods requiring more profound thought, she developed phrases or talking points that she would repeat several times throughout the hearing to emphasize her point.

For Edna, all the preparation in the world would not have made a difference if she hadn't taken stock of her fears. She had to prepare for this challenge because sitting for testimony is essential in her job but does not come naturally to anyone. She went through several strategies to improve her focus.

First, Edna accepted the unpleasant emotions associated with giving testimony. She used her unpleasant feelings as insight, a source of information that something important lay ahead. Even though she initially experienced fear, the fear told her she needed to prepare for the next step. She would not let unpleasant emotions keep her away from the challenge. This awareness put her on a learning path and ultimately set her up for a solid performance. Once Edna took stock of her fears, she thrived and learned how to move forward despite her fears. In addition to learning how to give testimony, the situation taught Edna how to become more aware of her emotions. She knew these emotions did not define her but were the source of insight into her current experience. Her fear of being caught without an answer or staring at the committee with a blank look on her face faded away. She did not need to fear a "brain freeze," where she knew the answer but could not reasonably retrieve the words to express it aloud. This relieved her of the need to think on the spot at every moment.

Second, Edna relied on key phrases that helped her create time to think. Phrases like "I'll get that information for you," "We are still working on those numbers," and "I will refer you back to the official report" were now intuitive to her. This freed up her ability to focus on the here and now of the hearing and relieved her of the demands of recalling specific details, allowing her to stay on message.

These phrases helped her offload the burden of remembering strings of complex numbers. This gave her control over the situation and built her confidence that she held the power to take responsibility for her testimony. In her previous job, she had days or weeks to consider questions and formulate precise and well-considered responses, but now she needed to respond quickly. These techniques helped her buy some time and even helped her communicate the complexity and detail of the situation to her audience.

Finally, Edna developed strategies that helped her focus. Edna could continue to focus on what she knew best, the goals and purpose of her agency; these routines allowed her to display her strengths. She learned to exercise her skills in different situations and could perform confidently, even if the problems were new or different or caused unpleasant emotions. Edna focused on those factors within her control. She also embraced the fact that she had a story to tell. Importantly, Edna did not try to control her fears; she temporarily redirected them to more productive and positive activities.

Notice what Edna did *not* do to enhance her performance. She did not dwell on the potential hazards and adverse outcomes that might happen during the testimony. Nor did she say, "I need to focus harder." Instead, she used routines to organize her thoughts and block distractions.

STAY FOCUSED AND ELIMINATE DISTRACTIONS

At first, Edna's process may seem counterintuitive. Many leaders have heard the advice to stay focused, but that is often impossible. Psychologists led by Daniel Wegner wanted to know how much control people have over their focus. Wegner found that the more people try to suppress thought, the more they focus on their thought processes, the more likely undesirable thoughts will intrude into consciousness. It isn't easy to focus on command, even for those adept at concentrating. Wegner told a group of subjects in his study, "Don't think about white bears," but the more they tried to repress the thought of white bears, the more the thought of white bears came to the forefront of their consciousness. He concluded that one part of our mind is suppressing the thought, while another continues to check in to see if we are suppressing it. We try to repress the thought of white bears, but as other parts of the mind constantly check in,-we are reminded of the thought we are trying to suppress. The white bears experiment represents why the advice to stay focused is not useful. It might even be a recipe for disaster as different systems of the mind compete for our attention. The more we try to stay focused, the more distracted we become.[3]

Wegner's study tells us something surprising. Focus is the ability to manage how we direct attention; in other words, focus requires concentration, but focus also requires understanding our inner dialogue.

INDY CAR DRIVER ARIE LUYENDYK LOSES FOCUS FOR A FRACTION OF A SECOND

For leaders, distraction and the intrusion of thoughts and feelings can be disastrous. Professional auto racing provides an extreme example of the focus demanded of leaders. For a race car driver running at speeds upwards of 200 miles an hour losing focus for even a fraction of a second can result in disaster. Consider the final Indianapolis 500 race of Arie Luyendyk Sr., a two-time winner of the Indianapolis 500. The story of why he failed at his third title rests on the importance of focus. In the Indianapolis 500, like any endurance activity, getting to the green flag (starting the race) requires learning, and getting to the checkered flag (finishing) requires focus. Stress is both physiological and psychological. Environmental demands expose drivers to prolonged noise, intense vibrations, chemical fumes, and heat. Professional race car drivers experience extended periods of stress hormones, extreme fatigue, and dehydration.[4]

It was 1999, and I was at the Indianapolis 500, cheering on Arie Luyendyk, the "Flying Dutchman." Luyendyk had announced that this would be his final year at Indianapolis. He had an excellent chance to claim his third victory as he held the pole, or first position, starting the race. I listened to Luyendyk and his team on a public channel that broadcasts radio communication between the driver and his pit crew. Luyendyk was about 25 percent through the five-hundred-lap race and had taken an early lead. He told the crew, "All I need to do is stay in the lead." Then, something unexpected happened. Coming out of turn four, Luyendyk lost control of his car. It appeared he hadn't even touched another vehicle, although he was cut off and came close to another driver. He had lost focus for a brief fraction of a second.

The setback would be costly, as his car spun out of control, swept across the track, and hit the wall on the other side. His dream of winning a third 500 was gone. In an interview after the crash, Luyendyk lamented his mistake. "I became too complacent and relaxed," he said. He reflected on his state of mind during the race: "I was driving so confidently. Maybe my confidence bit me at the end. I got too greedy."[5]

Few leaders will face the extreme focus demands experienced by professional race car drivers like Luyendyk, but all leaders need focus. Focus is essential for learning. In the next section, I review key threats to focus and attention faced by leaders and, in the final section, outline some of the routines that help overcome these threats.

THREATS TO FOCUS

Leading requires short- and long-term focus. Short-term focus involves attention to the most important things that lead to doing well, keeping distractions away, and knowing when to shift attention to another activity. Long-term focus involves overcoming boredom, remaining focused over time, and staying the course when new and more exciting activities distract us from long-term engagement with the activity.

Maintaining focus requires coordinating across our psychological, social, and physical being—the ability to focus shifts across days, weeks, and years. Focus is essential, but it is a finite resource, and individuals differ in their natural ability to focus. The amount of time the average person can concentrate ranges from as little as eight seconds up to ninety minutes. Focus time varies depending on different factors, including the task and our training. Physical and psychological factors such as diet, blood sugar, heart rate, and hormone levels also play a role. Sleep is another critical factor that impacts focus. Information overload—too much information at once—can also threaten focus. Finally, technology, often designed to enhance focus, can unknowingly deplete focus.[6]

Shifting Between Activities and Multitasking

Shifting between activities and multitasking describe similar activities but have different time frames. Shifting between activities is a deliberate decision to move from one task to another, say, working on an email and then switching to working on a report. On the other hand, multitasking involves doing two activities seemingly at once. You multitask when you simultaneously talk on a remote call and check your email, or when working on a report—shifting between writing a sentence and checking email almost instantaneously.

Some leaders might attempt to improve productivity by shifting and multitasking. Yet, these activities lower our productivity because they drain our focus more quickly. We lose some of our precious focus whenever we change from one task to another. Both shifting and multitasking require anticipation of moving to another activity and planning for the shift. Shifting requires establishing a sequence of mental steps; even if we are unaware of these steps, our mind goes through this process. We *organize*—put the tasks in an order that makes sense for maximum productivity; *initiate*—start the activity and maintain order following the predefined order that you put into place; and *self-monitor*—keep focused on the task and attend to behavior, revising as needed. Shifting and multitasking both rob us of this valuable commodity of focus. Each time we move from activities, we interrupt our focus and expend energy to end one task and begin the next. These activities can trick us into thinking we are more productive, but ultimately, they weigh heavily on focus.[7] Leaders can increase productivity and their capacity to focus by working on one task at a time and creating an environment that eliminates distractions.

To address these focus challenges, refrain from shifting between activities by building transition times between activities and plan time for enjoyable activities like reading, working on crafts, being outdoors, and engaging in social interaction. Set specific times to work on an activity before leaving that task and shifting to another. When engaging in activities that require high concentration, work in fifteen to twenty-five-minute time blocks with breaks in between. Limit the time spent on technology overall and set aside specific times of the day to read emails, social media, and texts. Schedule these activities during times of low productivity, like after lunch. Alternatively, consider checking email and other media once every hour and resist the pull to check every five minutes. You can start by staying off media for a few minutes and gradually increasing your time away. And once again, work on one activity at a time.

Mind-Wandering and Rumination

Another set of challenges are mind-wandering and rumination. Rumination and mind-wandering seem distracting initially, but they are essential for resilience, growth, and well-being. Consider mind-wandering. Mind-wandering was once believed to be harmful. For example, we often use the term *daydreaming* negatively. When we say someone is daydreaming, it implies they need to be more focused and more productive. However, learning requires some degree of mind-wandering, as it helps move what we know from short-term to long-term memory.[8]

A similar process, rumination, is related to resilience.[9] Developing resilience requires simultaneously juggling multiple thoughts. Like the participants who were trying to block out the thought of white bears to focus on more relevant ideas, when we focus, we are not just concentrating on the activity; we are also blocking out distractions and ruminations.[10] When done within limits, rumination provides time to organize complex emotions and develop strategies for action. Taken to an extreme, rumination leads to overemphasizing worst-case or catastrophic events, replaying what-if scenarios, and reinforcing negative thoughts about the past and future.

To take advantage of the mental processes associated with mind-wandering and rumination, schedule these activities, which recognizes their value but also places limits. Ensure your rumination and mind-wandering time do not interfere with your ability to complete specific activities. This helps focus on the here and now but also allows you to consider the broader goals and possibilities. Set daily routines and remove yourself from situations that fuel unwanted rumination. Stop reading social media or news feeds that conjure up unpleasant emotions about unrealistic expectations we hold about ourselves, which can further fuel worst-case scenarios. To further enhance your mind-wandering, set aside time for creative thinking, and set a time limit for rumination, and move on to other activities. Seek out enjoyable activities that serve as a distraction; this will help engage in rumination that generates positive emotions. Finally, avoid rumination at night; focus on breathing or progressive muscle relation exercises instead.

Chronotype: The Best Time to Focus

Like many leaders, Jesse had challenges staying focused. She could only concentrate for a few minutes, and then her mind wandered. As a result, she could not meet critical deadlines and became increasingly detached from her work. While she found relief in gardening, her dog, and meeting up with friends, she dreaded the work she faced. Because she worked as a financial analyst, her job required focusing for long hours on detailed financial statements.

She thought that if only she could focus a little longer each day, she could return to her productive self. She read blogs and short articles on tips to improve focus that dotted the internet and bought popular books on improving her focus. The prospect of improving her focus to work on highly detailed spreadsheets for extended periods was promising. Still, even these techniques proved difficult. While she may have marginally decreased distractions, there was no vast improvement in her focus. However, Jesse improved her focus by better understanding her sleep patterns, also called her chronotype.

Chronotype, our sleep and rest personality, can shape how and when we improve focus. Chronotype proscribes the best time of day to focus. Most people share common chronotypes, which point to two times of day—the morning and later in the evening—when you are likely most productive. However, there are other chronotypes; some people focus best late in the evening or early in the morning. When someone says they are a morning person, they are likely aware of their underlying chronotype, which is associated with high levels of focus in the morning. Someone might describe themselves as a night owl, which means they are most likely to have high levels of focus at night.

Resilience and well-being arise from making the most of your chronotype by identifying times of peak focus and scheduling the most demanding activities for those times. Even though you don't always control your schedule, recognizing your peak times can support learning. Take advantage of these times.

Focus is linked to cortisol, an essential hormone that the body produces naturally as a source of energy. Both our physical and mental strength are dependent on high cortisol levels. The brain draws on cortisol to focus, and the heart uses cortisol for energy. For most people, cortisol is produced in natural and regular patterns. Levels are lower in the morning, just after we awaken. Are you feeling tired in the morning? This may be explained by your body working to generate your daily cortisol. Your body will continue to develop cortisol throughout the morning; by mid-afternoon, it has burned a large amount of your cortisol for the day and is no longer producing it at the same rate it was earlier.[11]

Many people experience an afternoon lapse in their productivity. However, that afternoon feeling of fatigue isn't just caused by the burger you ate for lunch. It also concerns the drop in cortisol. Scientists call this the cortisol slope, which describes how your productivity relates to the levels of cortisol your body creates throughout the day. As your body produces more cortisol, you increase productivity, but when cortisol levels dive, you become less productive and less focused. Researchers have tracked productivity to cortisol levels, as depicted in figure 9.1

Tracking your burger intake may be helpful, but there is a more precise way to estimate your optimal focus time. Using a heart rate tracker found on a smartwatch or other device, track your heart rate while you sleep to determine the time of your slowest heart rate. A slow heart rate is associated with low body temperature. As your body reaches its lowest temperature of the day, it is gearing up to start reproducing cortisol for the next day. Most people will find their heart rate is lowest around 3 to 4 a.m. Then, count four to six hours after that time. That

Morning   **Afternoon**   **Evening**

FIGURE 9.1 The Cortisol Slope of Productivity

would lead to your most productive time between 7 and 11 a.m. Track this over a week and identify an average. You can also increase awareness by tracking your focus throughout the day. What times of the day do you feel most productive? Learning complex material requires deep focus, so work on the most demanding tasks for only about forty-five minutes to an hour during your peak focus time. What times do you feel least productive? Reserve these low productivity times for less strenuous work like responding to emails or for unproductive but required meetings.

In addition to identifying your optimal focus time, take a twenty-minute break every three to four hours; about every twenty to thirty minutes, you should take a five-minute break. During that break, you should focus on something in the distance, such as looking out a window if you have been working on a screen. Use the 20-20-20 method, which supports the release of stress, improving focus, and limiting eye strain. The method encourages taking a break every 20 minutes for 20 seconds and looking in the distance at least 20 feet away.[12] We learn during sleep, too, as our new knowledge moves from short-term to long-term memory, so don't be afraid to nap when necessary. For best results, nap for about twenty minutes and no later than 3 p.m.

Cognitive Overloading and Off-Loading

Leaders are swamped with more and more information. Our brains can only learn and hold so much information at a time. When we confront more information than we can handle, cognitive overload results. Due to fears of cognitive overload, leaders may be tempted to avoid learning altogether. Rather than memorize complex material, leaders will likely use cognitive off-loading, relying upon information from manuals, technology, and other sources rather than keeping this knowledge stored directly in memory. For example, do you rely on your smartphone to record phone numbers rather than memorize them? Do you use features on your automobile that allow for more autonomy, such as GPS, lane change warnings, or back-up cameras? Then, you are engaging in cognitive off-loading, which is an expected, even helpful, response to modern life. It helps overcome the changes associated with too much information and distraction. But when we fail to understand essential procedures and are called upon to act as if we did remember them, we fall prey to the dangers of cognitive off-loading.

I became interested in cognitive off-loading while studying the psychology of organizational resilience. Organizational resilience focuses on the systematic activities that an organization can use to build resilience into the organization itself. I ranked learning as the top factor supporting organizational performance. When organizations integrate learning into their processes, they improve performance. I studied several cases where learning broke down and considered the impact of this breakdown on performance.

I reviewed an airline disaster, Air France Flight 447. Failures of learning contributed to the disaster. Two of the three pilots were unfamiliar with responding to a common problem experienced during flight. The failure of an airspeed sensor led to a warning signal in the cockpit, which in turn led to the disengagement of the autopilot system. The pilots were unfamiliar with the problem, even though airspeed indicator failure was a common problem experienced midflight. The aircraft manufacturer, Airbus, had even issued a memo warning of the possibility of this failure.

What was shocking about the pilot response? The two pilots commanding the cockpit needed to execute well-established maneuvers to keep the aircraft in flight. The third pilot, asleep in the cabin until the flight's last minutes, may have had an answer but remained unaware of the impending disaster. The commanding pilots seemed unfamiliar with the necessary procedures. In addition, the increased stress and the constant buzzing of the warning signal contributed to their panic. They were unable to communicate and respond appropriately. Contributing to the failure of the pilots to react adequately was the process of cognitive off-loading. The pilots had likely never encountered the situation before, and because they were not trained or forgot how to respond, they could not solve the problem. The problem, however, was about more than just the pilots. Modern aviation has removed the need for pilot intervention as never before. Modern aircraft are designed to correct many mistakes without pilot input. Onboard computers fly the plane, while pilots have become computer operators. Many pilots, including those in the Air France disaster, have never learned many of the procedures necessary for responding to inflight emergencies. These activities have been off-loaded to onboard computers. Pilots may learn procedures in training, but training is infrequent. Onboard manuals codify procedures but need to be easier to follow during the time crunch of most emergencies. As a result, even common problems such as these are seen as rare.[13] To manage your cognitive load, schedule reflective time into your day to address these challenges and spread learning over time. Eliminate existing activities when you add new responsibilities. Identify technology or other methods to organize your work and time. File and keep your resources organized with intuitive filing systems. Learn the underlying theories and logic of regular activities. This will help you match specific data to underlying theories and themes, limiting the need to remember precise details. Keep checklists for routine tasks to track activities you have already completed.

Stress

Stress is another factor that can decrease performance, and stress relief is often a challenge for many leaders. Many stress-releasing strategies successfully relieve stress in the short term but do nothing to reduce the underlying source of stress. Furthermore, these strategies give us the illusion of control. We gain control over the immediate situation but must address the underlying stressor. These short-term solutions resolve these unpleasant emotions and relieve the stress, but the long-term source of stress remains.

Leading outside your comfort zone requires identifying the right amount of stress to support learning and growth while not destroying your short- and long-term well-being. Stress plays a complex role in learning. Too little stress will make you unmotivated to learn, while too much stress threatens learning. Robert Sapolsky is a professor of psychology who spent years studying stress and other factors in primates. His popular books on stress, such as *Why Zebras Don't Get Ulcers*, are based on decades of studying animals in their natural habitat and then translating his findings to humans. For Sapolsky, stress is a driver of some of the most profound acts in humans, so stress is not bad. However, too much stress can lead to mental, social, and physical challenges. Focus requires identifying ways to manage stress and fatigue that work for you.[14]

Moving outside your comfort zone is inevitably stressful, but some leaders respond to stress more positively than others. One leader may experience significant stress and feel overwhelmed and out of control. In contrast, another leader may become energized by stress and find that they can learn more while under this heightened state of stress. In this book's conclusion, I offer three fundamental activities that reduce stress for most people: moving, sleeping, and learning.

In addition, Sapolsky believes that stress is not just about individual differences but also how leaders feel about themselves relative to others. Their place in the organizational hierarchy or status among peers can also dictate their stress level. Leaders with control and status may be more likely to learn and grow. Moving beyond your comfort zone may be easier if you are already established in the hierarchy, leading to the conclusion that new and emerging leaders may have a more challenging time moving outside their comfort zone than established leaders.

IMPROVING FOCUS THROUGH REFLECTION

Many learning strategies described in previous chapters can also help with focus. For example, positive emotional engagement is a way to improve focus on a particular task. Several factors predict focus and attention, many of which align with learning. Factors that inhibit focus are boredom, sleepiness, stress, and disliked activities. Excessive stress and anxiety make focus more difficult, while feelings of happiness, confidence that you can complete activities, and enjoyment all support focus.[15]

One surprising technique for improving focus is to do nothing. One study tracked individuals with attention deficit hyperactivity disorder (ADHD). People with ADHD have trouble focusing and often cannot focus on any activity for even a few seconds without distraction. The study attempted to find out how to improve concentration and found that when people with ADHD did nothing for about twenty minutes, they improved their attention. They took simple steps to clear their mind. They might stare into the distance or meditate with their eyes closed or think about nothing in particular. Individuals with ADHD represent extreme examples of the kind of struggles we all have with focus, but leaders can learn from studies on ADHD because everyone struggles with concentration to one degree or another. Other research suggests that less than a minute of meditation can improve focus.[16]

Earlier in the chapter, I described the problem of white bears, which told how two parts of the mind compete for your attention. One aspect of the mind hopes to suppress a thought, while another part of the brain keeps checking in to see if the idea is under control. In this situation, we are of two minds. Wegner recommends refocusing on something else to get these two minds in sync. For example, if you are worried about making an error in missing a putt at golf or missing a shot in basketball, focus on another aspect of your game. If you are concerned about being unable to answer a question during an interview, focus on developing phrases supporting your viewpoint. The goal here is to focus your two minds on the same thing and move your mind from competing to redirecting thoughts.

As demonstrated by the white bears experiment, it is not just about where we try to focus attention; attention is also about finding other engaging activities. Cal Newport, a professor who studies attention, suggests finding something meaningful to focus on, not just eliminating distractions. For example, don't try to limit your use of social media but rather find other activities that support your well-being. The purpose is not just to avoid something we don't desire but also to find an engaging and enjoyable activity to replace it.[17]

FOCUSING ON PEAK GROWTH AND WELL-BEING

Leaders can improve focus by taking several steps. Begin by addressing overload. Take stock of what is important to you as a leader and seek to eliminate unnecessary activities or training. Taking on too many activities can be counterproductive to performance. Management scholar Bob Sutton at Stanford University has argued that today's workplace has created impossible jobs because they demand more than can be delivered. The list of why leaders are overwhelmed includes having to be available twenty-four hours a day, being held responsible for ambiguous outcomes, lacking support, and operating in organizational cultures that only reward outcomes, even when those outcomes are farfetched.[18] Many leaders experience activity creep. They continue to increase their workload but make no provisions to drop less relevant activities. Leaders are led to believe they need to increase their goals but fail to evaluate why they are doing them, and goals are then added to existing goals that were already difficult to achieve. The result is more activity but fewer *valuable* activities. Again, focus, as a limited resource, spreads thinner and thinner throughout the day.

One approach to improve focus on the here and now is looking at a situation as an outside observer. Noted sports psychologist Alexis Castorri described an exercise where she teaches athletes to imagine themselves outside of a situation and explain what is happening in detail. The goal is not to judge the situation but to describe it while you are there. This helps put perspective on the problem and releases athletes from the potentially unpleasant emotions that may hinder their performance. Consider yourself a witness, not a judge of the case, perhaps as a play-by-play announcer rather than a participant.[19]

In addition, organize large amounts of information to be quickly and intuitively accessible in the future. Practice accessing this information under different conditions, both stressful and less stressful. Understanding the underlying theories, models, and assumptions behind different ideas will allow you to organize more information mentally. Theories and frameworks serve as mechanisms to cluster information in intuitive ways. The US Naval Academy is reintroducing primary navigation to cadets so they understand the basic underlying logic of navigation. Officers were losing their ability to understand basic navigation because they did not understand underlying nautical principles. Similarly, for decades, the US Air Force Academy has taught cadets how to fly gliders so they know the basic aerodynamics of flight. Knowing these underlying principles improves the probability of operators responding to emergencies successfully.[20]

Improved in-the-moment performance often requires settling the mind, focusing intently on one specific, narrow activity. This usually involves meditation, focusing on breathing or thoughts, calming, hypnosis, or activities like yoga. For many active and goal-directed leaders, these activities are complex. Many individuals I have worked with have found that meditation and deliberate breathing are not relaxing but provoke stress and anxiety. After all, they are not doing something. Suppose you have found it hard to meditate. In that case, you may want to try other activities instead, such as visualization, coloring, drumming, cloud gazing, morning pages, walking, or watching paint videos; these provide the same benefits but are more active.[21]

Finally, distinguish between stress and burnout. Stress is caused by too many obligations or challenges and feeling as if your resources are inadequate. In contrast, burnout results from too many emotions and feeling overwhelmed with our inner experiences. Exercise 9 will help you identify sources of stress that deplete focus.

Leading outside your comfort zone will deplete your attention and focus. Taking a few measured steps to make the most out of your limited attention will help you thrive outside your comfort zone. The chapter introduced several threats to focus—shifting between activities, multitasking, mind-wandering, rumination, limited resources, cognitive overload, off-loading, and stress/pressure. The chapter also outlined several routines leaders can adopt to manage the precious resource of focus.

Exercise 9: Stress Test

Stress comes as part of leading outside your comfort zone and can be positive or negative for focus. Too much stress leads to being overwhelmed and detracts from focus and learning, while the right amount of stress can support focus and learning. Leading while highly stressed can impair your ability to lead effectively. On the other hand, some stress levels are necessary for leading and getting work done. Stress can increase effort and improve attention. Awareness of your stressors and identifying how you address stress is an essential first step in increasing focus.

Step 1

Consider the questions below as you reflect on how stress may positively or negatively impact your leadership capacity.

1. Describe an experience where you felt pressure to perform that resulted in stress or anxiety. For example, playing a sport, giving a public speech, taking a test, or interviewing for a job.

2. Describe your feelings. Were your emotions helpful or not in your performance?

3. What mechanisms did you use to address the stress?

4. How can you address this type of stress in future situations?

Step 2

1. Review the threats to focus presented in this chapter. Which of these threats to focus are you experiencing, and which threats have the most significant impact on your performance?

2. Identify routines to help you preserve and improve your focus when stressed. Talk to others about the mechanisms they use to improve focus.

3. Identify specific ways to apply the routines to enhance focus during regular leadership activity and self-improvement.

TEN

Leading Teams

_____

Leading a team can reap significant rewards. Despite their many benefits, teams pose a unique challenge for leading. Emotions among team members run high, and leading a team requires recognizing and appropriately responding to these emotions. As a leader, you will play a crucial role in managing team members' emotions. Whether you are a CEO meeting with your board of directors, a pilot navigating with a cockpit crew, or a manager introducing a new product with a product development team, leading teams is necessary work.

This chapter offers strategies and tips for leading through these emotionally charged team situations. Entire books have focused on the dysfunctional interactions that arise in teams, but your team doesn't have to be a place where dark emotions prevent you from being an effective leader. Learning to lead a team should be at the forefront of your leadership development agenda.

THE OUTSIZED ROLE OF EMOTIONS IN TEAMS

Start by understanding the outsized role that emotions play in a team. Teams invoke uncertainty, which, in turn, heightens emotional activity. Team members may feel uncertain about their skills, and because they may need clarification about their role, leaders need to consider ways to make teams more hospitable.

Teams involve high levels of social interaction, increasing the potential for emotional conflict. Since teams serve as breeding grounds for emotions, leading a team quickly moves leaders out of their comfort zone. When teams first form or new members join, uncertainty is at its highest. Team members feel uncertain about their goals, what roles they are to play, and what responsibilities must be taken—concerns about success mount. Anytime we experience intense interaction with other people, the opportunity for conflict increases. Leaders must learn to accept this and assist the team in managing their emotions.

Teams provide a way to organize individual skills and capabilities. Steve Jobs, the former CEO of Apple, created many revolutionary products, including a home computer in the 1980s and the attention-transforming iPhone in the mid-2000s. When asked which products he was most proud of, he named none of these products. Instead, he said his greatest accomplishment was assembling the teams that designed, built, and marketed these products. Jobs was aware that no great accomplishments occur without great teams.[1]

Teams play a central role in how organizations function, are crucial to designing and delivering new projects, and are essential for managing complex activities. Teams are key in resilience and have been the central feature for building and sustaining resilience for centuries. Around the world, commercial aviation relies on teams of pilots, air traffic controllers, and ground crew to coordinate complex air traffic systems. Teams are a central feature of programs supporting personal development and change. Programs such as Alcoholics Anonymous rely on the power of groups to initiate and sustain individual change efforts.

Despite the widespread use of teams across organizations, leaders find leading teams is rarely intuitive. Leading a team requires specific skills that many organizations assume leaders already have. Organizations often overlook that leading a team requires training and organizational support. Further, teams bring human power dynamics to the forefront of team members' experience. In teams, interpersonal power struggles increase because members often meet in small numbers. Team meetings may provide opportunities for team members to test the ongoing group power dynamics, and this test of power dynamics often turns toward the leader. Leading a team requires recognizing and being able to negotiate acceptable levels of power among group members.

For many leaders, a team provides the first opportunity to assume a leadership role. Because of this, teams offer an early test of leadership capability, and the stakes increase when it is your first opportunity to demonstrate leadership skills. Leading teams and teamwork are among the most critical skills top companies look for when hiring. Team skills are not just for those at the top of the organization; working in a team is highly consequential at all levels of the organization, increasing the stakes of success even higher. But even experienced leaders can quickly get caught up in a heightened emotional situation.

LEADING WITH EMOTIONS

Because emotions run so hot in teams, many view teams as a source of dysfunction. However, seeing the high level of emotions as a source of dysfunction overlooks the overarching opportunities teams offer for building resilience. Far from being dysfunctional, these team emotions are a natural part of human interaction. A better understanding of how emotions play out in teams and how to support the emotional dynamics in teams provide a unique opportunity to apply leadership skills. Consider the following characteristics of emotions in teams.

First, emotions are contagious. This means that when one person expresses an emotion, others will easily experience that same emotion. Segal Barsade used the phrase "the ripple effect" to describe how emotions flowed through a team. When one team member expresses pleasant emotions, the team becomes more cooperative and experiences less conflict. When a team member expresses an unpleasant emotion, groups experience more significant conflict, less cooperation, and are less impressed with their performance as a team.[2]

Leaders can be influential by recognizing how emotions are transferred to others. Acknowledge unpleasant emotions but not dwell on them. Expressing unpleasant emotions can lead your team to develop negative attitudes toward their team. Not recognizing emotions can result in suppressing these emotions, and so the underlying issues may not be addressed. When leading a team, realize that simple actions, such as facial expressions and how you express your feelings, can influence the emotions of others. By observing your behavior, your body language can influence others, or they may make assumptions about your current mood.[3]

Another reason emotions are difficult in teams is because emotions easily spill over from one situation to the next. Moving throughout your day, you will experience various emotions across different meetings, events, and activities. Say you met with a peer about solving a problem; the meeting got heated, and you became tense. That tension can carry over to your next meeting, even if that meeting should be enjoyable. Perhaps you had a power struggle over who was responsible for what activity in your organization. Does that same power struggle continue to an unrelated meeting later in the day with your boss? Or does your frustration over a project continue as you move to dinner with a friend in the evening?

Emotional spillover can function positively. Pleasant feelings, say having a relaxing walk in the park during lunch, can lead to a happier and more fulfilling afternoon. Emotional contagion and carryover are not bad things, but they require being aware of your emotions and making sure that you do not let the emotion generated in one environment carry over to another area in an unproductive way. These tendencies do mean that team leaders may need to play the role of emotional regulator on the team, ensuring that emotions are motivating and can be expressed in productive ways, but also ensuring that emotions do not run too hot or lead to dysfunction and complaining. Helping the team set its emotional temperature is critical to being influential.

STRATEGIES THAT SUPPORT LEADING TEAMS

As a team leader, you can positively impact the team's performance by setting the tone and supporting your team members as they work together to solve problems and accomplish goals. Drawing on the five learning strategies introduced earlier in the book, you can keep your team moving outside its comfort zone. Begin by helping the team improve awareness of their immediate experience by asking:

What emotions am I feeling, and how are emotions preventing me from learning?

What am I experiencing in this team?

What are my frustrations and excitement?

What makes me feel good about being on this team?

Cultivating Positive Engagement
Generate positive engagement in the team. Build positive emotional engagement by considering the team as a source of growth and change for its members. Leading the team requires taking stock of successes. Help the team recall their positive contribution as a team and help each team member consider how they can contribute positively as an individual. Leaders can designate a few minutes

of each team meeting to allow team members to acknowledge important aspects of their work and life that they may be putting aside for the moment to work in the team.

Leading a team requires recognizing many unpleasant emotions, such as anxiety, frustration, or anger, and working to channel these emotions toward learning and growth. When teams are dedicated and focused, even unpleasant emotions can be motivating. While sometimes a source of conflict, these unpleasant emotions can also provide opportunities to reflect and assess current processes, and serve as the source of change and learning. Lead the team to understand that these emotions may reflect involvement and investment in the team and its product. Team members feel anxious because the team's purpose is valuable, and success is seen as a reflection of themselves. Questions to help the team recognize positive emotional engagement include:

What activities are you leaving behind to attend this meeting?

What are you learning about yourself or your job that you want to share with the team?

What makes us curious about working on this team?

What can we learn by working on this team?

Solving Problems Creatively

A second strategy is to solve problems creatively. Engage the team in creative problem-solving by having them generate new ideas about operating as a team or seek ways to improve current processes. Also, consider revising or updating the purpose of the team. As a leader, it is tempting to provide answers and solve problems; after all, don't strong leaders take charge and make decisions? These are the traps of heroic leadership discussed in an earlier chapter. The best team leaders are decisive in moments of crisis and time-critical situations. Still, under normal circumstances, they take a different path by allowing the team to work through problems with little intervention from the formal leader. Consider helping the team through challenging situations, keeping the team just outside its comfort zone so it can learn and grow. Your role becomes that of a facilitator, a conflict manager, or a role model. Guiding the team in making difficult decisions will not only support the growth of team members but also support their feelings of inclusion and ownership of the process.

Questions that guide a team to creative problem-solving include:

How can we go about solving this problem?

What are new ways to approach this situation?

What have we done before, and how can we reach our goals differently?

What is the purpose of our team, and how are we doing relative to achieving that purpose?

Building a Team Identity

Teams develop learning identities, too. Like learning identity in an individual, learning identity in a team means that the team is focused on taking calculated risks, trying new things, working together to learn and grow as individuals and as a team, and identifying new ways of doing things. As the team continues its work, recognize the positive gains that the team has already made. Acknowledge the fact that the team had a productive meeting or celebrate the achievement of an individual member.

Developing a successful learning identity in a team rests on building psychological safety, a team culture that supports bringing up complex topics, respectfully challenging the dominant viewpoint in a group, and ensuring no retaliation if disagreement or dissent emerges. Psychological safety is a prerequisite for learning.

Another way to increase the team's learning identity involves helping the team realize it already has the talents and capabilities necessary for success or can learn the required skills. If it is a new team, have team members discuss successes they have had in prior teams and have them describe what characteristics were present in these previous successes. If the team is established, have the team discuss initial achievements. Remember that many leaders become responsible for inherited teams and often have no option of changing team members. Even more unsettling, team leaders must often assume leadership of dysfunctional or challenging teams. Team members may find it difficult to recall positive elements or prior successes. This presents a real leadership challenge. Building a learning identity in this situation will seem like an uphill battle, but with time, many leaders can turn these situations around and build strong teams. Questions to create a learning identity include:

What behaviors do we want to promote in this team?

What behaviors do we consider unacceptable, and how will we address undesirable behavior from team members?

How can we create an environment on our team that allows for diverse and dissenting viewpoints?

How can we identify counterpoints to team decisions that help us understand different perspectives as team members?

Encouraging Flexibility

Another learning strategy in leading a team involves being flexible in addressing problems and doing your work. Setting standards and clear expectations helps create boundaries and expectations in the team, but the most successful teams understand that flexibility is necessary to address changes and new insights. A flexible team can address new problems that arise and understand that further information often requires a shift in thinking. Your role as a leader is to ensure that the team remains flexible and can accept new opinions, change directions, and reevaluate its processes. To build flexibility, keep alternative courses of action at the forefront of discussion. Improve flexibility by asking the following questions:

What alternatives do we have available to us?

How has a problem been addressed before, and what needs to be updated based on the changing situation?

What new ways can we go about addressing issues and problems?

What new information do we need or would help solve these problems?

Supporting Team Members

Social support is at the core of teamwork. Team members working together can surpass the work of individuals working alone. When team members coordinate their behavior and support one another in achieving their purpose, the team increases the chances of reaching their full potential. Consider the various ways you can support your team as a leader. You can provide some emotional support by understanding the unique needs of each team member, and you can work with the team members to support their development as individuals. Looking out for the well-being of team members becomes paramount in high-stress situations. You can ensure that teams have the information they need, and you can work to ensure the team has the necessary resources. Questions that generate social support include:

How can we support each other and improve how we work together?

What information and resources do we need to be effective?

How can we support one another as we move through this process?

BALANCING LEARNING AND PERFORMING IN TEAMS

Like all leadership situations, leading beyond your comfort zone in teams involves managing the demands of learning and performance. The dynamics between learning and performing were discussed earlier in the book. Managing these team dynamics requires nuance because leaders and lead members must understand the unique demands that the team faces and move between the various dimensions of learning and performing as a team. Recall that the learning and performing grid involved four dimensions—stagnation, peak/plateau, deliberate learning, and optimal improvement. For teams, each dimension has a unique role.

Stagnation

Stagnation is when the team is not learning or performing. This is reflected in a lack of enthusiasm among team members and is demonstrated by poor attendance and participation, regularly showing up late for meetings, or the failure of multiple individual members to deliver on responsibilities. Excessive conflict or disagreement also indicates stagnation. The unproductive interactions prevent the team from leveraging resources and knowledge. The result is that learning and progress suffer. The remedy for stagnation includes changing course, trying new things, recognizing new goals, or reenergizing the team's purpose. In extreme cases, the team may need to be reconfigured or disbanded.

Peak/Plateau

A team experiences a peak or plateau when it consistently performs at the top of its abilities for some time. All members contribute some or all the time, and the team utilizes all its available resources. The problem for the team is that the potential for burnout may be high because the team is functioning at a high level and may be draining its limited resources. The remedy is to find time for learning and trying new things. If the team is in a competitive environment, the team may need to consider how the competition is adjusting. In a changing climate, the team may need to consider new strategies to adapt.

Deliberate Learning

Deliberate learning describes when a team seeks strategies for continuous improvement. The problem is that the team needs to be challenged in a performance situation. The team can try to identify ways to simulate a performance environment. For example, if a team is working on a presentation or the delivery of a proposal, it can stage a mock proposal delivery.

Optimized State

The optimal state is when a team is both learning and performing, moving between the modes of learning and developing while also putting their abilities into practice in performance or by delivering on goals. The team has a vital purpose and is continually revising its objectives, procedures, and challenges, being careful to address how it coordinates its task, and having an acceptable level of conflict among team members.

DR. MARTIN LUTHER KING CHANGES THE SCRIPT

For a team to work correctly, members must be open to expressing new and different viewpoints. When teams agree on everything, they keep conflict to a minimum, but they may fail to take risks. One example occurred during Martin Luther King's "I Have a Dream" speech on the National Mall during the March on Washington in 1963. Today, few people remember the difficult road King walked as he created a coalition of groups with different views about how the civil rights movement should go forward. He resolved these differences and formed a fragile coalition among civil rights leaders.

During the culmination of the march, King made his famous speech on the steps of the Lincoln Memorial that included the words, "I have a dream . . .". In his written notes, he planned to conclude his speech with a call to action. He planned to instruct the audience to express dissatisfaction when they returned to their hometowns. But just as he approached the conclusion of his speech, Mahalia Jackson, one of the coalition members, shouted to him, "Tell them about your dream!" One of US history's most moving and memorable speeches followed. King was a coalition builder and team leader. He also knew when to take advice and listen to his team.[4]

LEADING TEAMS OUTSIDE THE COMFORT ZONE

Keep in mind these key elements of leading a team.

The Crucial First Two Minutes

The most crucial time in any team meeting occurs in the first two minutes, which can set the tone for the rest of the meeting. When a leader approaches the first two minutes with a positive tone, this becomes contagious. Alternatively, the first two minutes can also acknowledge bad news. Still, the team leader must ensure that the unpleasant tone set by delivering bad news doesn't bring the group into sustained unpleasant emotions. Instead, the leader should help the team acknowledge the unpleasant emotions and tone and foster acceptance. Comments might include statements such as "This is a difficult subject for all of us," or "Let's recognize that this isn't where we want to be and use this to adjust how we address these problems." The leader can then use the unpleasant emotions as a form of reflection to motivate evaluation of the current team processes and use the moment as an opportunity to foster change.

Ongoing Reflection as a Team Leader

As a team leader, you will be responsible for things that will often feel beyond your control. This is what it means to lead beyond your comfort zone. Preparation for leading involves understanding your values, strengths, and areas for improvement and requires an ongoing process of reflection and adjustment as a leader.

In addition to reflecting on yourself, consider these questions about the team's process of working together:

Is the team moving together, or are individuals still struggling with the team?

Are there disruptive or challenging members that limit the team's effectiveness?

Managing Stress in Yourself and Your Team

Effectively leading a team requires leaders to manage stress for themselves and their team. A technique for managing stress is visual shifting. Visual shifting is based on research that shows we are more stressed when threats are physically closer. We may not even be conscious of the threat, but our body reacts to it nonetheless. Visual shifting is a simple technique. When you feel stressed, overwhelmed, or experience unpleasant emotions, stop looking at the other team members directly and shift your focus to the distance. If there is a window, look out the window, but looking at a distant wall will do as well. The idea here is that you are shifting your field of view from a close-up threat—at least, that is how your body is reacting—to a lower threat situation, which your perception tells you is less threatening. For the team, when things get heated, and the team seems stuck and feels they cannot make progress, stop the session for a few minutes and take a break; tension and high emotions will not last very long. Movement leads to relaxation and shifts the visual and psychological focus of the team.

Leading a team requires tuning in to the stress and mood of the team. Assess the team member's workload. If the team is stressed and overworked, consider if certain aspects of a team's work can be delayed or shifted to work that may be less stressful. Remember, as a team leader, one of the factors that encourages purpose, motivates learning, and initiates action is progress. Leaders need to balance the need to relieve stress with the need to continue to progress and move forward.

Finally, leaders should consider that not all team members will respond to challenges similarly. Many team members will thrive within the team, manage the emotional challenges endemic to teamwork, and even move beyond their comfort zone. However, other members may be unable to deal with these emotional challenges.

THE EMOTIONAL DYNAMICS OF TEAMS

Lexy and Silvia illustrate the emotional dynamics associated with leading a team. While each faced a similar situation—deep team conflict—each addressed the challenge differently. How leaders recognize and handle their emotions helps them navigate beyond their comfort zone.

Lexy and Silvia both worked within a consultancy, and each faced the challenge of dealing with team conflict. Each had taken the team leader role and had employees reporting to them for the first time. The teams they inherited were in deep conflict. Neither Lexy nor Silvia saw themselves as "good at conflict," but each knew their team was headed for disaster. Neither caused these conflicts, but as leaders, they were now responsible for solving the disputes. In each case, the situation had deteriorated so quickly that their team members could hardly sit in the same room to discuss their work.

Now in formal leadership roles, Lexy and Silvia knew they were closely watched by upper management and felt the pressure to succeed. Being self-aware, Lexy and Silvia thought about their anxieties. Each had a fear of failure. Each felt discomfort with confrontation and were concerned they might worsen the conflict. Each felt a general uneasiness about their capabilities to lead these teams to success. While harboring these feelings, each leader also had a sense of confidence; after all, they were chosen for these jobs because upper management had believed in their abilities and had observed their successes in past teams. Further, each had navigated conflict in teams before, albeit as team members.

Lexy and Silvia addressed the conflict differently. Lexy faced it with trepidation; she felt unable to activate the conflict management skills she had developed as an individual contributor. She was anxious when working with her team, and because of this, she never dealt directly with the conflict. Lexy didn't want a difficult conversation with her team because she anticipated it might further fuel the conflict. Yet, she needed to initiate that conversation with her team anyway, even though she knew it would generate new unpleasant feelings.

Silvia felt anxiety, too, but she saw this as an opportunity to learn. She was cautious and introduced change slowly. She knew that the feelings of anxiety meant she cared deeply about the changes she was making. The critical difference is that Silvia did not let her unpleasant emotions dictate her steps or how she would act. She concluded that emotions were not set in stone and did not always direct her behavior. As Silvia stated, "My emotions are not the thing." She did not let her emotions get the best of her. Her stance was that she should be aware of her emotions, but she would move forward despite any unpleasant emotions she felt.

This chapter summarizes key strategies, tips, and questions essential for leading through the emotional world of teams. Leading a team is a core leadership competency, and learning to understand and manage team members' emotions is critical to successful leadership. Applying the five learning strategies discussed earlier and the improvement grid framework to teams provides a starting point for understanding how leading a team can support you and your team's resilience, growth, and well-being.

Exercise 10: Team Learning and Performing Checklist

Teams go through learning and performing cycles. Leading your team through these cycles can help the team improve. Lead your team through the following exercise to identify dominant cycles. The team must answer these questions together, not by individual members. Team members should agree on each response before it is recorded. Rank each sentence based on whether your team agrees, disagrees, or is neutral with each statement.

Stagnation

1. Our members hold an acceptable level of enthusiasm for being on the team.

2. Attendance and participation on this team is acceptable.

3. Members of the team regularly show up late for a meeting.

4. Members fail to deliver on their responsibilities.

5. Our team has high levels of conflict.

6. Our team needs to grow and progress toward its goals.

Peak/Plateau

7. The team has consistently performed at the top of its abilities for some time.

8. All members contribute some of or all of the time.

9. The team utilizes all its available resources.

10. Our team is thriving.

11. Our team has the necessary resources to meet challenges.

Deliberate Learning

12. The team seeks strategies for continuous improvement.

13. The team still has several challenges to meet.

14. The team shares new information and seeks new ways of doing things.

15. The team is sure it will be successful.

Optimized State

16. The team is moving between the modes of learning and performing.

17. The team is both learning and performing.

18. The team is practicing its abilities in performance or by delivering on goals.

19. The team has a vital purpose and continually revises its goals, procedures, and challenges.

20. The team addresses how it coordinates its task and has an acceptable level of conflict among team members.

Review the team's response to answer the questions below.

1. What does the response tell you about your team and its current performance and learning?

2. What actions can the team take to improve its learning?

3. What actions can the team take to improve its performance?

ELEVEN
Leading Organizations

Leading an organization requires translating personal leadership lessons into a larger organization. This requires moving beyond the individual and team to consider how the factors associated with leading outside your comfort zone support organizational level resilience, growth, and well-being. The chapter begins by outlining how the lessons of leading outside your comfort zone apply to strategic leadership; this includes building a learning culture, a well-being strategy, and policies that support resilience and growth throughout the organization. Five strategic learning strategies and a discussion of policies that support resilience, growth, and well-being are offered. The chapter discusses the role of focus on strategic thinking. Finally, the chapter suggests that many organizations already support resilience, growth, and well-being through existing competency models.

SUPPORTING EMOTIONAL SELF-AWARENESS IN ORGANIZATIONS

Throughout the book, you have learned to utilize pleasant and unpleasant experiences. This allows you to act while leading outside your comfort zone. Unpleasant emotions are challenging because they are often difficult for many leaders to recognize and accept. The perils of relying on only pleasant emotions can devastate organizational well-being, just as it does that of individual leaders.

161

Nokia, a technology leader, provides a cautionary tale of the consequences associated with a culture that fails to recognize and accept unpleasant emotions in its workforce. In 2006, Nokia, a telecommunications company headquartered in Finland, made over half of the mobile phones sold in the US. However, the leaders at Nokia were slow to adapt to market changes with emerging smartphones during the mid-2000s, and companies like Apple and Samsung began gaining market share over Nokia. Leaders feared the company was falling behind, but its culture was not conducive to sharing those fears, and leaders were reluctant to express their concerns openly. Unpleasant emotions were not part of the company culture. The company could have responded to the competitive challenge. They might have taken the necessary action to address the changing marketplace and thrived. Instead, leaders appeared stifled by a corporate culture that could not openly discuss problems. Voices that expressed alarm or concerns that were deemed unpleasant were suppressed or ignored. As its market share eroded, Nokia needed help to develop products to compete with the growing smartphone market. The company nearly collapsed as its market share approached zero. Nokia was eventually sold to Microsoft at a rock-bottom price in 2014. The inability to acknowledge problems associated with fear, anxiety, and other unpleasant emotions likely contributed to the company's downfall.[1]

Nokia represents an organization that had yet to learn to accept and address unpleasant emotions as part of its culture. Yet, research shows unpleasant emotions play an essential role in learning and resilience in organizations, just as they do in individual leaders. One study found that unpleasant emotions improved performance on a highly quantitative task, increasing knowledge and adaptation to change and mistakes. The study used a simulated stock market game to identify the role of unpleasant emotions in decision-making. Each participant was given a fictional $25,000 to invest across twelve companies. Each day, for twenty days, the investment decisions and their intensity were recorded, along with emotions ranging from pleasant to unpleasant. The final performance of each investor was ranked on a short- and long-term basis, including adjustments for the level of risk. In the end, the investors who were aware of their emotions, instead of avoiding them, were more likely to act and respond with better decisions. The lesson: those who focused on their emotions performed better. Performance was more pronounced in investors who were aware of their unpleasant emotions, and those who regulated unpleasant emotions made better decisions. The study concluded that unpleasant emotions contributed to better decision-making. Still, pleasant emotions did not negatively impact decisions.[2] This study shows how unpleasant emotions do not always have to be debilitating. Pleasant and unpleasant emotions can be both negative and positive motivating forces.

ORGANIZATIONAL LEARNING STRATEGIES

The five individual learning strategies discussed earlier in the book can be translated into organizational strategies. Leaders can draw on these strategies to motivate those they lead, ultimately building sustained learning in the face of common setbacks, frustrations, and challenges.

Fostering Positive Emotional Engagement
Several years ago, when my colleagues and I started studying resilience in leaders and organizations, we focused on fostering pleasant emotions. Pleasant emotions support increased initiation and sustainment of work and increased effort. In addition, pleasant emotions have been linked to learning and improvements in memory and recall. Upon further study and observation, we changed our view on pleasant emotion and focused not just on the importance of positive emotions but, more specifically, emotions that generate engagement.

Our work suggested that slightly unpleasant emotions, such as frustration, may be among the most engaging. Leaders should seek to generate engaging emotions such as curiosity and interest and encourage openness to experience. This means fostering an environment that supports employees' interests and creates work settings that support individual employee development. Strategies to increase engagement include the following.

Assign tasks based on the employees' curiosity. Related to curiosity is interest. Interest in something differs from passion. To generate interest, consider the advice of Katherine May, author of *Enchantment: Awakening Wonder in an Anxious Age*. She suggests approaching an old task in new ways. This requires finding something about the activity that creates awe and makes you feel good about it. Making the new approach work may take several tries, but the point is not to judge or criticize your attempts. Instead, you may need to slow down to notice new and exciting things about your work.[3]

Help employees become more open to experience. Openness to experience is often considered a fixed personality characteristic that cannot be cultivated and is considered one of the Big Five personality dimensions. Yet, openness to experience can be developed. Being open to experience is not anxiety-free. New experiences involve moving into unknown territory and taking on new challenges; this is the domain of the resilient leader. Resilient leaders still have anxiety and stress, but they understand that these unpleasant emotions can motivate and are often necessary for improvement and learning. Encourage those you lead to be open to new experiences and understand the internal unrest associated with these steps. Help followers understand the nature of their anxiety, find ways to buffer and draw on the motivating power of this unpleasant emotion, and allow them a safety net for when their feelings are no longer productive.

Encouraging Creative Problem-Solving

Another strategy is encouraging employees to approach problems by critically thinking and improving judgment skills. Allow employees to make their own decisions and plan work independently or as a group, with less involvement from the leader. Support employees as they develop multiple strategies to accomplish tasks and constantly seek new and better ways to get things done. Encourage the adoption of new technologies and techniques and hold regular sessions designed to surface new ideas and address ongoing challenges, even if these sessions do not result in concrete actions.

Supporting the Learning and Development of Employees

As a leader, ask yourself: What am I doing to support and enhance the learning of others? To answer this question, begin by exploring the learning opportunities available to employees through formal training, online programs, and readily available seminars. But traditional training programs are only the start. Larger organizations can invest in peer coaching groups where employees meet regularly to support individual, organization, and career goals and which serve as a form of peer mentoring. Also, it is essential to build a learning culture where risk-taking (within reason) is supported and mistakes are recognized for what they are—a normal part of learning and performing. Finally, as discussed in the previous chapter, learning is a mindset as much as a process. How are you fostering a learning mindset in those you lead?

Too often, leaders concentrate only on the skills they need to get promoted. However, learning can take the form of personal growth, too. Consider instituting "Invest in Yourself" days once a month, a popular approach where employees determine their needs and take responsibility for their learning. Even when using this approach, provide participants with some structure or choices for how to spend their time by offering speakers, seminars, and organized activities.

Enhancing Flexibility

This means helping find assignments that require learning and encouraging employees to see new ways to approach old tasks. This may include rotating or reworking assignments to add interest. Job expansion and generating new interesting and motivating responsibilities may be appropriate. Often, employees are motivated by having more responsibility. Another factor is autonomy, helping employees so that they do not need direction but can manage projects without oversight.

Creating Social Supports

Support employees across career, job, and life transitions. This effort includes institutional support such as employee assistance programs, one-on-one coaching with trained professionals, and paid time off. The most resilient organizations will go a step further and offer four-day work weeks, flexible scheduling, support for childcare, and access to a broad range of medical care. Institutional support is necessary, but resilient leaders go beyond and create a culture of support. Resilient leaders promote a culture of high psychological safety, where all employees feel included and heard and where challenging issues are surfaced, discussed, and addressed. Resilient leaders empathize with those they lead and provide technical and logistical support so employees can get their work done effectively.

Resilient leaders create supportive processes by regularly meeting with their team to discuss process improvements and surface potential problems. Even more important is to acknowledge successes and build upon what is already going well. Employee recognition programs remain popular, but many have lost their power. Employees who are burned out, looking for better employment, or just happy doing their jobs are not likely to change their attitudes or become more resilient due to a one-time recognition programs. Further, awards such as Employee of the Month or a Manager's Choice Award have not been shown to have a lasting impact on motivation. A better approach to building effective organizations is supporting strategies focusing on resilience, growth, and well-being.

FOCUSING ON THE ORGANIZATION

Psychologist Johann Hari conducted hundreds of hours of research on focus and concluded there are two types of focus. The first type involves the trees—focusing on a specific topic or aspect of a task. The second type consists of the forest—seeing the activity in context. Both types are essential for leaders to focus on the here and now and place the current situation in context. Leaders regularly get caught in the trees when they focus on doing an activity well, but the activity doesn't fit within the organization's strategic vision. From an organizational perspective, improving focus requires not only that we give our attention to one thing but also that we do *not* focus on other activities.[4]

One way to be more productive is to redefine what it means to be a leader and focus on learning. At the organizational level, regularly assess the importance of different tasks and look to eliminate processes that do not add value. Structural changes also help make the job of the leader more manageable. Four-day work weeks have become a structural way for organizations to improve mental health, morale, and working conditions in general. Organizations have become more productive by shifting from a forty-hour to a thirty-two-hour work week.

Leaders can create an environment that minimizes distractions and allows employees to improve their focus. This can be accomplished by encouraging employees to designate specific, uninterrupted work times and building time for reflection and mindfulness. In addition, employees should break down learning tasks into usable, accomplishable tasks. Leaders can increase motivation by recognizing progress—helping employees develop perseverance by encouraging them to progress in small but essential tasks and focusing on progress toward goals, not goal completion. Also, remain optimistic that success is possible and take stock of successes already achieved. As a leader, help others focus on what is important to the organization.

Neuroscientist Amishi Jha explained that the pressures of leading often result in misdirected focus. She recounted the short life of the Segway as an example of how we can focus on trying to achieve the wrong outcomes. The Segway was the brainchild of inventor Dean Kamen, and he focused on developing a personal vehicle at all costs. However, according to Jha, Kamen concentrated on engineering and technology, never considering that most people would not pay upward of $5,000 for a personal transportation machine to ride around their neighborhood. While Kamen dreamed of a Segway in every driveway, the reality was a lack of a market and a need for more space on sidewalks for all these two-wheeled personal machines. Ultimately, the Segway was primarily adopted by police forces and tourist companies rather than the mass consumer.[5]

To overcome the challenge of misdirected focus, consider ways to improve strategic thinking in yourself and those you lead. Consider multiple perspectives and consider both details and the larger context of problems. This prevents the myopic focus that may stifle understanding of the big picture. A myopic focus can lead to performing well but performing the wrong activity.

POLICIES AND PROCESSES FOR A RESILIENT WORKFORCE

One of the most pressing challenges for organizational leaders is attracting, developing, and retaining a trained workforce. The pandemic caused a movement of workers out of and across organizations that was not seen in a generation. The so-called great resignation, an unprecedented number of workers quitting and changing jobs, may have slowed down, but the underlying psychological and structural forces remain intact. Workers remain skeptical of their employers, fear that economic downturns will threaten their jobs immediately, and feel that corporate structure fails to meet contemporary demands associated with family care, lifestyle, and traffic. Leading an organization for resilience means identifying ways to support the diverse needs of employees and generating policies and procedures that support well-being and growth. Following are a few key considerations.

First, a resilient workforce includes identifying new demographics of workers, including older workers, workers educated differently, and those looking for new and flexible work arrangements. While diversity, equity, and inclusion (DEI) efforts in organizations have come under criticism, it is precisely programs like these that organizations need to adopt to identify, develop, and retain the best talent across job categories. As one leader mentioned, DEI efforts provide a competitive advantage in an environment where a high-quality workforce is in demand.[6] The demographic factors will not change, and organizations will face an aging and more diverse workforce; unless there is a significant overhaul in immigration policies in Western countries, immigration will not be a substantial source of new workers. Leaders who create an inclusive environment will reap the human capital benefits of these shifts.

To meet the needs of a changing workforce, organizations need to consider expanding the work arrangement options, including accommodating temporary workers, flexible work schedules, and shorter work weeks. As four-day work weeks become more prevalent, organizations will be forced to find ways to keep up with progressive work policies. Work from home will continue to be the only option for some highly sought-after workers and those who require flexibility in child, elder, or family care. Some organizations have offered to house workers in remote or overpopulated areas where high housing costs wipe out the benefits of relocation or housing is unavailable.[7]

Changes should include new ways to recognize and support workers. In the most forward-thinking companies, performance reviews are becoming a thing of the past or deemphasized as a source of rewarding employees. Developmental feedback is becoming the norm, especially among organizations where performance, such as consulting, analysis, and support, is more challenging to measure. Unfortunately, leaders have long embraced approaches to leading that run contrary to building resilience, which may worsen the situation. Research shows that popular leadership systems like pay-for-performance compensation need to be fixed. Once touted as the key to organizational productivity, pay-for-performance systems link established goals and the ability to achieve those goals to the ultimate compensation an employee receives. On the surface, this seems like a justifiable process. Yet, compensation programs like performance pay have been linked to increased anxiety and stress as organizations pressure workers to meet goals that are increasingly out of reach. These programs create a downward spiral. Soon, the employees become detached from the day-to-day work; motivation decreases, further alienating workers from their organizations.

Compensation systems based on measuring time working on a task prove just as problematic. Exchanging hours for dollars also leads to higher stress levels, suggesting that once sought-after professions such as law, consulting, and healthcare offer no refuge from the detrimental impact of contemporary work culture. On the one hand, leadership approaches such as these carry essential benefits. They create a sense of fairness and make strides in equating employees' efforts with measurable outcomes, but they fail to address the primary challenge that leaders face today: finding a sense of purpose and direction at work. As a result, many organizations have abandoned these age-old assessment methods but need help finding adequate replacements.[8] Some organizations, for example, have done away with traditional performance evaluations, instead focusing on employee development. Developmental opportunities are forward-looking and generate meaningful opportunities for learning and renewal.[9] When annual employee reviews concentrate on learning and development instead of performance and compliance, leaders can reimagine their leadership.

Policies and procedures should be designed to support the overall well-being of employees. This requires recognition that traditional worker-employer relationships, in many cases, have changed. Workers no longer view their employer paternalistically as a source of financial support from cradle to grave. Perhaps even more interesting, workers no longer see work as a psychological contract where loyalty and fulfillment can be achieved through work. Instead, workers see work as a means to pursue other, more enriching work outside the workplace. Yet, many organizational policies need to recognize these changes.

The changes in the worker-employer relationship are demonstrated by the breadth of union activity seen across the US and Western Europe. A handful of organizations have taken steps to prevent unions from forming. Still, the most enlightened companies realize that union activity often results from a need for a strategic focus on employee well-being. Retail store Costco, often cited as one of the best companies to work for, saw the unionizing vote as a wake-up call, not a threat. The CEO's reaction was not to disparage the union vote or dodge the issue but rather to state the need to grow as a company. To paraphrase the CEO's letter, the fact that employees voted to unionize means we must do better![10]

BOB IGER ASSESSES HIS SHORTCOMINGS AS DISNEY'S CEO

Bob Iger had just completed what most observers considered a successful fifteen years as CEO of Disney. Disney stock grew exponentially, and Iger introduced innovative new outlets for the world-renowned entertainment company. He brought successful franchises like Marvel and Star Wars under the Disney name and introduced the company's first streaming service to compete with Netflix and Amazon Prime. Iger, ready to retire from the pressures of running a high-profile company, appointed his successor, Bob Chapek. Chapek's tenure was short-lived. He alienated employees and fueled a losing battle with Florida Governor Rick DeSantis, who chose to pick a fight with Disney as a keystone to his bid to run for president.[11]

Iger's short hiatus from Disney reflected more of a sabbatical than a retirement. Chapek stepped down in under two years, and the Disney board reinstated Iger as CEO. But Iger returned to Disney with a different mindset. He recognized that his assumptions left him vulnerable as a leader at the end of his prior tenure. Reflecting on his first fifteen-year tenure, Iger described how he became overconfident and insulated from the frontline employees. He even became arrogant, dismissing the opinions of other leaders throughout the organization.

Iger found himself following the same pattern as many leaders. He remained enthusiastic and conscientious about what he could accomplish but lost his leadership edge. Iger shares a common experience among leaders. A string of successes generates accolades and recognition as a leader. However, this exact string of successes can leave the leader vulnerable to new and higher expectations. The leader may acquire counterproductive attitudes. The leader strives to learn and adapt productively, but frustration sets in. Burnout and other unpleasant emotions follow. The expectations become overwhelming and result in a loss of confidence in themselves—the struggle to meet these high expectations results from a fear of not meeting increasing performance expectations. In the end, the leader focuses on finding ways to reinforce their value as a leader rather than learning, growing, and changing. They concentrate on reassuring themselves and their stakeholders of their value rather than seeking new opportunities for the organization.

Fortunately for Disney, Iger reassessed his leadership approach and reevaluated his situation. He demonstrated strong self-awareness by contemplating what he could have done better during his prior run at Disney. He used his short time away to productively assess his leadership mindset. He reinvigorated his sense of self-worth and redefined his role as CEO. Through these actions, Iger addressed the expectation gap that plagues many leaders. He returned to Disney, confident he could learn again as its leader.[12]

RESILIENCE, LEARNING, AND WELL-BEING COMPETENCIES IN ORGANIZATIONS

One place to start building a workforce that can lead outside its comfort zone is to focus on training and development. As the psychologist Tchiki Davis has suggested, well-being is not just a state of being but requires skills. These skills help us respond to daily challenges at work and in life. These skills need to be learned and lead to developing long-term strategies that support a sense of purpose and direction. In short, well-being arises from the learning that comes from our everyday pursuits. In organizations, learning supports well-being by providing individuals with the resources necessary to excel in the face of work demands, conserve resources that lead to replenishing motivation, and recover from stress and other workplace situations that may threaten well-being.[13]

Many organizations already hold competency models that encompass resilience, growth, and well-being. These competencies focus on (1) engaging employees in processes that involve being open to experience and generating curiosity, positive emotions, and interest; (2) supporting a learning identity that leads to flexibility and adaptability; and (3) leading employees to seek social support. Competencies associated with resilience, growth, and well-being are likely already part of the overall organizational competency clusters such as cognitive, relational, emotional, and strategic competencies.

Cognitive competency supports making sense of experience through data and communicating this understanding effectively through stories, anecdotes, and personal examples. As a result, leaders often become the embodiment of their leadership values. Michael Mumford has identified the core cognitive skills of leadership, which he considers among the most potent predictors of leadership performance. Leadership, he argues, is a process of solving problems and making judgments. He identifies nine cognitive skills; four of these skills are related to resilience and judgment. The first related skill is goal analysis: choosing which goals to pursue among an extensive set of choices and recognizing which plans are viable and likely to succeed. The second skill is constraint analysis, which focuses on understanding the factors that can limit the successful accomplishment of goals. Leading requires understanding constraints, including individual, organizational, and social constraints, while remaining able to act in the face of those constraints.

Further, leadership requires not only selecting which goals to pursue but actively updating these goals, accepting that goal pursuit may not be successful, and knowing when to abandon goals. Forecasting, the third cognitive skill, involves simulating future possibilities and outcomes. To fully consider well-being in leadership requires forecasting and imagining multiple possible outcomes. The fourth cognitive skill is idea evaluation, which consists of setting standards under which success can be determined. Cognitive competencies are essential for resilience because setting reasonable expectations and knowing what to do when outcomes fall short of expectations are critical.[14]

A second and third set of competencies involves relational competency, which describes a leader's ability to judge and act in various social and cultural contexts. Although the original formulation of cultural intelligence focused on an intercultural context, resilience is also necessary for different organizational, regional, and social-cultural contexts. Relational competencies include understanding how others are motivated, influencing teams and groups, communicating a message, and using impression management techniques.

Richard Boyatzis, Melvin Smith, and Ellen Van Oosten have outlined how relational competencies can be developed and implemented for leaders.[15] For these authors, social competencies are tied to emotional competencies, which include emotional self-awareness. Emotional competencies help leaders develop a clear view of their strengths and weaknesses; importantly, they also know how others view them. This sense of self-awareness supports realistic expectations of themselves and others and leads to a rich understanding of their inner emotional life. A plan for developing social and emotional competencies should involve a comprehensive approach to self-discovery and self-development where leaders commit to learning about themselves, their capabilities, and where they may need to improve as leaders. Self-awareness is critical because leaders no longer have the privilege of hiding their emotions, nor are they expected to suppress emotions. Still, they are expected to know how to express them appropriately.

A fourth set of competencies are associated with strategic change and help leaders implement change and organizational strategy. Resilient leaders work in the face of challenges, even when the outcome and gains are unclear. One of the most enduring strategic leadership models is set out in *The Leadership Challenge*.[16] Leading strategically involves clarifying values, inspiring a shared vision, challenging the process, enabling others to act, and encouraging the heart. Each of these five factors is essential for well-being, as each requires the ability to respond and work through challenges as leaders set out to put these strategic actions into practice.

The four clusters of competencies—cognitive, emotional, social, and strategic—form the basis of resilience, growth, and well-being.

THE LEAD MODEL: LEARNING FROM HEALTHCARE ZERO-HARM GOALS

Healthcare organizations represent some of the most complex and challenging organizations to lead. Staffing shortages, escalating costs, and poor morale run rampant. Sprawling regulations confound these challenges. Medical professionals must learn long lists of care protocols designed by professional committees. In addition, the work involves life-or-death situations, which make the stakes high and safety a top priority. However, creating a safe environment for patients and healthcare personnel can be difficult. Competing priorities between professions, medical care providers, and healthcare executives, as well as sometimes conflicting standards and regulations, add to the challenge. I met with two researchers working to solve the patient safety problem. These researchers are physicians, giving them a unique view of patient safety from the front lines and the C-suite. They had no illusions about how difficult it is to improve patient safety, but they were also optimistic that they could identify small changes that could have a significant impact.

My colleagues, David Stockwell and Eric Thomas, both physicians, are on the front lines of healthcare and see firsthand the challenges of leading in complex organizations. I share their concern that, although there is a significant desire to improve healthcare in areas such as patient care, safety, and accessibility, there are often unrealistic expectations that further pressure organizations. These pressures fuel organizations to take undue risks and shift priorities away from the organization's primary purpose.[17]

We discussed ways that healthcare organizations are forced outside their comfort zone. We identified a few specific goals organizations can strive for when they find themselves outside their comfort zone. One factor of increasing concern involves efforts to improve patient safety through measures such as zero-harm targets. Zero-harm goals suggest that all healthcare organizations should set a goal of committing zero errors. Rather than set a tone for positively addressing patient care, we argued that zero-harm goals present a problem. They set unachievable goals that drain valuable resources from their institutions. All the while, these goals do very little to limit errors.

Zero-harm goals rely on misconceptions about how organizations work. Poor patient safety arises from a mixture that includes a lack of resources, a lack of measurable outcomes, misdirected attention of leadership, and poor management, among other things. Like many organizational goals, achieving zero-harm goals relies on more than clear aspirations; they require factors beyond healthcare organizations' control. Insurance providers, third-party payers, licensing and accrediting bodies, and fundamental economic realities must be considered as part of the zero-harm equation. Yet, most discussions of zero-harm seem to reflect the old phrase, "where there is a will, there is a way," with little consideration for these external forces.

The potential downside of setting zero-harm targets goes further. It does not take long to find examples of companies like Circuit City, Wells Fargo, Boeing, WeWork, and others that tried to achieve organizational moonshots such as zero-harm targets. These organizations either declared bankruptcy or paid significant fines, partly because they drained resources to accomplish short-term gains at the expense of long-term resilience.

We also brainstormed ways to help organizations move from narrowly targeted goals to more comprehensive strategies that embraced learning and worked toward resilience. Guided by research, our collective experience suggested a program we labeled the LEAD approach. LEAD is an acronym for level targets, equal emphasis goals, accurate and data-driven learning, and developmental goals.

First, we recommend that organizations set realistic goals that reduce fear and anxiety. Too often, setting excessive goals fails due to a lack of resources and know-how to achieve these high targets. After all, if these high targets were, in fact, easily achievable, all organizations would be successful. Most are not, leaving only a legacy of stressed and burned-out employees and high turnover among workers stretch too thin. Unfortunately, many organizational leaders have convinced naive boards to pursue these improbable scenarios.

Second, equal emphasis goals recommend a grassroots approach to organizational resilience. This means supporting and listening to those organizational members on the front lines. In the case of healthcare, workers in direct contact with patients are likely to have the most valuable insights. The goal is to take stock of the resources needed at the micro level and match the resources at the macro level. This means that patient care units would drive the goal-setting process in healthcare, and the organization would be responsible for providing resources—the goal-setting level shifts from the broader organization to the unit. Not only would equal emphasis goals improve employee well-being, but they would also engage learning as employees would become more aware of outside stakeholders and could make connections between their work in a larger strategic context.

The third and most challenging factor is accurate and data-driven learning. Despite the data revolution, the need for improved data capture, reporting, and analysis remains surprisingly high in organizations. Improved data-driven learning relies on resources and often requires a substantial investment in start-ups and operations.

Fourth, the emphasis should be on developmental and not just performance goals. Formal feedback processes were one way we imagined developmental goals could improve learning in the patient safety setting. We speculated that emphasizing developmental goals would result from and enhance collaboration, leading to better handovers, care, and improved safety.

These ideas may prove unreachable in the current environment, but improving organizations' resilience, growth, and well-being is no longer tangential to organizational success. The challenges at Boeing introduced in the preface to the book are representative. Boeing faced recalls and safety breaches on its 747 Max planes. These challenges included poor employee morale, turnover, and an inexperienced workforce. The challenges in healthcare and aerospace are representative of challenges faced by organizations in other industries. Adopting some or all the LEAD elements can address the problems of stress, burnout, and other obstacles to resilience, growth, and well-being experienced by organizations.[18]

Leading outside your comfort zone often requires leading at an organizational scale. The goals remain the same: to build resilience, growth, and well-being. Organizational leadership requires strategies, policies, and processes that support learning. One path forward for leading outside your comfort zone involves building learning strategies into everything the organization does and across levels of the organization. However, many organizations' competency models already support resilience, growth, and well-being, and organizations can emphasize these competencies in leadership training and development programs.

Exercise 11: Organizational Check-Up

The organizational check-up involves two sets of questions. The first set of questions considers your organization and how your work contributes to the organization. The second set of questions focuses on your sense of purpose and meaningfulness within your organization.

Consider formal and informal ways your organization supports resilience, growth, and well-being through the following questions:

Organizational Contributions

- How can my organization create an environment where members can talk through difficult problems?
- How can we encourage different viewpoints to be heard?

- How can we create an environment where individual members are aware of the particular challenges that others face?

- How does my work in my organization contribute to the organization's mission and overall success?

- How can I assist others when problems arise?

- How can I improve how I share information with others in the organization?

Purpose and Meaning at Work

- How does my work contribute to my overall purpose in life? Does work serve as a (financial) means to a happy life, or does my work provide my fulfillment?

- How can I improve my energy toward work?

- Do I regularly speak with my supervisor about how I can contribute at work?

TWELVE
Tiered Goal-Setting

OVERCOMING THE LIMITS OF GOAL-SETTING
THROUGH TIERED GOALS

Leading outside your comfort zone requires constant improvement and refinement of current skills. This push for improvement relies on setting higher goals and facing new challenges. Unfortunately, common goal-setting approaches fail to provide the necessary structure for most leadership challenges. They may be doing more harm than good because they fail to respond to the multiple challenges associated with leading. Leading requires taking advantage of the benefits of goal-setting and finding methods to address some of the pitfalls related to standard approaches to goal-setting.

This chapter introduces tiered goal-setting, which offers a way to adapt traditional goal-setting techniques such as SMART and stretch goals to overcome the limitations inherent in these processes. Tiered goals address the dual demands of learning and performing and offer a way to build resilient goal-setting that supports well-being.

THE UNINTENDED PITFALL OF SMART AND STRETCH GOALS

SMART goals, an acronym for (specific, measurable, achievable, relevant, and timely), are everywhere in organizations. SMART goals are used to improve job performance, address workplace deficits, inspire achieving new performance levels, engage in personal change, and increase productivity. SMART goal-setting and pursuit are also central in leadership developmental efforts. In many cases, SMART goals have become the go-to goal-setting tool. Stretch goal, which are goals that push you beyond your current capabilities, have received significant attention as well. Stretch goals have become a popular mechanism to set increasingly higher goals that stretch the leader to move beyond their current performance levels. SMART and stretch goals are essential to successful leadership development efforts but have limitations.

First, SMART goals have emerged as a critical leadership development tool for good reason. At the organizational level, goals create a common language and focus collective attention on small areas for change. Progress toward SMART goals becomes visible and results in feelings of successful progress toward a future desired state. Leaders show they are meeting their goals, and others in the organization can share in the success. The same emotional dynamics exist at the individual level, too. SMART goals are the basis for generating positive feelings and progress.

But lurking underneath the seeming success of SMART goals is a problem. SMART goals don't address the common pitfalls of leading outside your comfort zone. SMART goals may help leaders achieve visible victories, but the results are often too short-term and narrow. The amount of available effort exerted toward reaching goals is limited. Directing too much effort to limited goals can leave other important goals unattended. Further, the shifting nature of contemporary organizations means that achieving goals often requires adjustment and change after the goals are set.

Second, stretch goals have become important as leaders stretch themselves and their organizations to new heights. But stretch goals, too, present a problem. The staying power needed to continue pursuing the stretch goal can be overwhelming. Stretch goals can generate unpleasant emotions such as fear of failure or anxiety due to a lack of skills, leading to procrastination and early abandonment of the goal. SMART and stretch goals may have a place in leading, but they are just as likely to result in unintended consequences. This chapter suggests that leading requires adopting new methods of goal-setting and pursuit that are better aligned with the psychological and leadership demands of leading outside your comfort zone.

SETTING TIERED GOALS

One technique to address these pitfalls involves setting and pursuing tiered goals. Tiered goals were initially developed in sports training and were used to improve participation in new activities and push new levels of achievement.[1] Tiered goals expand the range of possible successful results achieved while pursuing a goal. They manage the unpleasant emotions that arise from initiating and sustaining goals over long periods. Tiered goals involve simultaneously setting multiple progressive goals and revising the goals during each step of the way. Using tiered goals in leadership development programs shows that tiered goal-setting improves the psychological underpinnings that counter these pitfalls. Participants in our programs report substantial increases in helpful insights after using tiered goals, such as understanding the emotions that support goal achievement.

Jake was like many of the participants in our executive education programs. He wanted to move up the ranks in his organization, so he met with coaches, his boss, and the talent development manager of his organization, a large multinational bank. They all recommended that he set SMART goals. At first, SMART goals seemed valuable, as the process helped Jake set his ideal goal: to be an executive VP in five years. However, the uncertainty associated with action, which involved the possibility of failure, came with significant emotional risks.

Jake's situation is representative of many leaders. The emotional challenges of leading prevent leaders from taking risks. The negative actions that result from these emotions range from procrastination to burnout. These pitfalls arise because common goal-setting approaches can generate unpleasant emotions due to uncertainty, fear of failure, and the stressors associated with change. To overcome these unpleasant emotions, we developed a goal-setting process that starts with tiered goals, which expand the range of possible successful performance outcomes and celebrate adaptability, generating more positive experiences when starting and pursuing goals.

Tiered goal-setting involves setting three progressively challenging goals for each session, practice session, or goal attempt: initiating, enhancing, and optimizing goals.

Tier 1: Initiating Goals

The initiating goal turns traditional goal-setting logic on its head and sets a lower bar to generate the positive emotions associated with the activity. It lowers the bar to engagement, thus encouraging participation in goal-directed behavior and addressing barriers like procrastination. This seems counterintuitive because most goal-setting techniques encourage setting challenging yet achievable goals.

An initiating goal helps generate positive emotions toward an activity by answering the question, did I do something toward achieving my goal? For example, Jake's tier-one goal involved speaking to his manager about new assignments and responsibilities that might lead to his developmental growth as a leader. He realized that he needed to have the conversation despite his fears of being rejected in his request. The tier-one goals lowered the perceived consequence of starting the goal-setting process.

For example, tier-one goals can address overcoming writer's block. For many writers, the biggest problem is getting started on the writing project and then continuing to write day after day. Looking at the blank page is a significant obstacle to writing. One piece of writing advice is to set a small goal to overcome any unpleasant emotion associated with the writing process. An active mind can disrupt any activity. My writing isn't good enough. I don't have anything to say. I don't know where to start. These and other thought intrusions can prevent you from beginning any problematic writing project. However, you become less likely to procrastinate when the set goal has little negative consequences and requires little effort. Thus, setting an initiating goal to write for one minute sets the right level of tension. But once you start writing, something magical often happens. You continue to write after the one minute is over. Writer's block fades away as you can continue to write even longer. The one-minute goal offered a low threshold that removed the often intimidating first sentence. Other examples continue to show up in our research. For instance, a tier-one goal might be starting to run with no distance requirement, meeting with a new person with no objective to accomplish anything other than build the relationship, or starting a new project with no focus on any performance outcome. When you initiate a goal, the learning mindset puts you on the right course.

Tier 2: Enhancing Goals

Tier two, or an enhancing goal, is where SMART goals usually begin, with the desired outcome. Enhancing goals pushed Jake to increase effort and duration. Jake needed to go beyond speaking to his manager and take on new responsibilities—what he would achieve if he reached tier two. If everything went as planned, Jake would reach his enhanced goal of getting the opportunity to lead. Enhancing goals include running for three minutes at a designated pace, meeting with five new network contacts to learn about a new job, or completing homework by a specific time each day.

Sustaining the goals is even more challenging than starting them. Research suggests that goals take time to obtain and maintain. Many of the traditional approaches to change behavior require revisions.[2] Goals that require significant behavioral changes, such as weight loss, reducing or eliminating harmful habits such as smoking, eating healthier, or overcoming addiction, prove even more challenging to maintain. The reason for the poor performance lies in the fact that goals often rely on external rewards instead of engaging in intrinsically motivating activities. This is essential information for setting enhancing goals. Enhancing goals should reflect a level of activity that is enjoyable (or at least tolerable), generates curiosity, and that can be sustainable over time.

Tier 3: Optimizing Goals

Optimizing goals resemble stretch goals. They imply setting and pursuing goals beyond our reach that we might achieve if every variable fell nicely into place. Success at optimized goals happens when the conditions are nearly perfect. A well-known endurance running coach noted that an optimized goal is a peak performance outcome and might be slightly unrealistic. For example, a top performance in a race might occur only when perfect weather, health, and mental conditions align. The value of an optimizing goal is that it provides a long-term perspective. This long-term perspective offers the framework for developing strategies and approaches to reach the optimized outcome.

The tiered goal-setting process encourages reflection, encourages continued engagement, and enhances learning by adapting the goal-setting strategies and reconsidering the goal based on new information. Each time a person engages in an activity targeted toward reaching the goal, the tiers are revised after each attempt. For example, after each practice session, the goals are adjusted for the next practice session.

THE SURPRISING PSYCHOLOGY OF TIERED GOALS

Tiered goals strike many leaders as counterintuitive. After all, most leaders have been trained to set stretch goals and pursue these goals with passion. SMART goals provide the primary language for leaders to set and pursue goals. Tiered goals are counterintuitive because they draw on psychological principles differ-ent from traditional goal-setting. They provide four critical steps to achieving outcomes that support improvement.

Initiation: Starting Sooner and with More Confidence
Leaders commonly need help with starting a new initiative. When starting new goals, have a positive response to the question, did I begin progression toward the goal? Psychological research, such as activation theory, suggests that getting started in an activity is often the most challenging element of improvement. We don't generate positive experiences until we begin working on the project, but we don't anticipate that we will enjoy the activity before engaging in it.[3] For many individuals, starting an activity remains difficult; the initiating goal addresses this challenge. For individuals with attention challenges, starting an activity is difficult because they have difficulty activating parts of the brain that require shifting from one activity to another. Removing the fear, anxiety, or concern for unpleasant emotions makes engaging in the activity more likely.

Enhancement: Increasing Effort
Achieving a goal requires increasing and varying effort toward reaching the goal. Enhancing goals address the question, did I put in adequate energy and effort? Psychologists have found that the brains of zebrafish are remarkably like the brains of humans. Young zebrafish are especially useful for studying how the brain works because their bodies are transparent for a short period after birth, and researchers can observe the brain and body function as if they were looking through a piece of glass. Observing young zebrafish offers insights into the rela-tionship between goal-setting and resilience.

In one study, researchers wanted to see how zebrafish respond to external stimuli, such as perceived progress when swimming. They found that when a fish is swimming, putting in effort to swim, and making progress, the young fish is more likely to produce chemicals and use brain areas associated with perceived happiness and joy, such as dopamine and serotonin. The experience of progress pushed them to continue swimming. The reward for swimming and making progress is the experience of movement through the water.

In another version of the experiment, the scientists created a tank that made it appear to the fish that they were not making progress, even when they were working hard to swim forward. In this case, when fish perceived they were putting in effort but not making progress, they burned out quickly, and the brain activity associated with joy and engagement was never present. The scientists concluded that the fish that had not experienced progress stopped putting in the effort.[4] One thing we can learn from the experiment with zebrafish is that in order to successfully pursue goals, there needs to be a direct relationship between the effort we put toward goals and the outcomes we are achieving.

Making Progress

We increase the likelihood of continuing to pursue goals when we are making positive progress toward achieving the goal. This addresses the question, did I enjoy the activity? Strictly following conventional wisdom on goal-setting can result in frustration, often resulting in dysfunctional persistence. Setting traditional goals can even hasten failure. In many cases, you may end up abandoning the goal, which leads to feeling more powerless to invoke the desired change. One reason goals are challenging to achieve comes from how we meet them, called the depletion effect or the "pre-goal attainment error," it describes how we often burn out as we approach our goals. This is because our brains celebrate success too early—and deplete the energy needed to push ourselves to the finish line or continue our pursuit. This means we increase the risk of missing valuable information necessary for reaching the goal because we have anticipated achieving it and have not focused on addressing the obstacles required. The feelings of exhaustion and depletion occur by expending too much effort early in the goal-setting process. The tiered goal-setting process helps overcome the depletion effect by shifting the focus from performing to learning and focusing on strategies that increase engagement through curiosity, interest, and genuine openness to experience.[5]

The study on zebrafish provides a parallel to effort and enjoyment. When we feel we are making progress toward our goals and making progress in our efforts at leadership, we are more likely to both initiate and persist at our goals. When we stop feeling that we are making progress, we are more likely to feel burnout and abandon or halt our engagement.

Tiered goals address the problem of effort and reward by balancing effort and renewal. Stress accompanies efforts, while pleasant emotions accompany renewal. The ability to initiate, sustain, and increase effort toward a goal may be embedded in the very makeup of our biology. Too much effort and little progress can result in burnout, decreased effort, and even complete withdrawal.

Learning

The fourth element returns to another central theme of leading outside your comfort zone: learning itself is motivating. The role of learning as a tool to both inspire and educate has been discussed throughout the book. Tiered goals add to this point by providing a concrete set of steps that leaders can take to improve their goal-setting as well as improve the goal-setting of those they lead.

Overcoming Procrastination and Perfectionism

Tiered goals address two common problems with goal-setting. The first problem is procrastination, which occurs for two reasons. The first reason plays on the recurring theme of avoiding unpleasant emotions. Procrastination occurs because you are trying to avoid the unpleasant emotions you anticipate when carrying out the task. These emotions entail an enormous range. It might include boredom over anticipation of doing something repetitive and uninteresting, like reviewing a budget. It might entail avoiding the potential conflict of doing a performance review or delivering bad news. It might involve anticipation of fear, which might arise from not completing the task because you perceive it will be difficult. Procrastination allows us to avoid these unpleasant emotions. Another likely reason for procrastination is that you imagine the task will be easier if you wait to complete it. You can trick yourself into believing that your focus will be stronger, that you will be well-rested, that you will have more information, or that the problem might even go away if you wait.

Another barrier to leading outside your comfort zone is perfectionism—the belief that you must always be successful, holding outsized expectations about your performance, and pushing yourself into critical self-evaluation if you don't perform well. Perfectionism can challenge growth because when you are overly focused on not making mistakes, you fear being seen negatively by others; you are less likely to try new things when you cannot execute them flawlessly.[6]

Tiered goal-setting positively responds to procrastination and perfectionism by changing expectations from performing to learning. A tier-one initiating goal resets the barrier to entry by design to encourage engaging in the activity. The emotional consequences of failure are lowered, while the chances of generating a positive encounter with the activity increase. At the same time, tier-two goals drive higher performance, which is consistent with the motivating power of traditional goal-setting. We tracked some of our participants over time and found that the tiered goal-setting process increased their initial engagement with the activity and the effort and enhanced perceived success.

The problem with goal-setting is also one of its greatest strengths. Goals inspire positive feelings about the desired future state but also lead us to ignore the unpleasant feelings associated with their pursuit. Gabriele Oettingen at New York University has studied mental contrasting. In mental contrasting, people imagine their current circumstances and then imagine an idealized future situation. You may generate mental contrasts between your current and imagined future leadership roles. For example, a leader might recognize their current role as a team leader, with fifteen direct reports and a $5 million dollar budget, but imagine that they would be CEO with over 1,000 reports and a budget of $100 million in the future. The contrast is between a fantasy (being CEO) and reality (being a team lead).

While many might view the process of mental contrasting as valuable, even ideal, Oettingen sees it as a barrier to growth. Imagining an idealized future may even be indulgent because it can lead to positive feelings, but it may fail to motivate you to adopt strategies that lead to goal achievement. It's almost as if imagining the outcome produces the satisfaction and enjoyment of accomplishing the task without requiring you to put in the effort to realize it. Of course, we can all understand the difference between imagining you are a CEO versus gaining the experience necessary to become one. Still, mental contrasting suggests that the gap is not always that clear to the goal-setter. The fantasy may be required to keep us interested in working through the unpleasant emotions and other challenges of getting promotions. Still, we must guard against thinking that we have accomplished the goal.[7]

Moving outside your comfort zone is about setting goals and developing intentions to implement the goal. This means identifying specific strategies (rather than just imagining future desired states) that support achieving the goal. Even more important is to imagine the potential obstacles we may encounter along the way and imagine strategies to address these obstacles. Oettingen has coined the acronym WOOP—wish, outcome, obstacle, and plan—to describe the process of achieving goals, which includes making a wish, imagining the outcome, identifying barriers, and creating a plan to achieve that wish.

EVIDENCE FOR SUCCESS

We collected data on leaders like Jake, who participated in one of our leadership programs and was part of a more extensive study under peer review on leadership and tiered goal-setting. The results reveal an improvement in pleasant emotions associated with a goal and a decrease in unpleasant emotions. The anxiety reduction notably decreased by 57 percent. In addition, participants recorded an 8 percent increase in their effort toward goals, while the number of insights achieved increased sixfold.

INITIATING GOALS CAN IMPROVE OVERALL PERFORMANCE: THE CASE OF WOMEN'S ELITE MARATHON RUNNERS

Women's elite marathon running illustrates the value of how introducing a tier-one initiating goal can improve overall performance in a competitive situation. The overall scores of women's marathon events improved when the governing body lowered the minimum qualifying time by over two full minutes in 2016. Not only did the general pool expand, but the average finishing times increased. Lowering the bar to entry may have raised the bar for overall performance.

Remarkably, lowering the qualifying standard boosted participation and overall performance. In the 35 years before implementing the change, between 50 and 150 American women ran a marathon in less than 2 hours and 45 minutes in any year. However, just two years after lowering the minimum qualifying time, the number of American women who ran at this pace increased to over 200. In 2019, over 250 American women reached this benchmark of a sub 2:45 marathon.[8]

With a lower bar to entry, more runners sought to compete because they saw the goal as more readily achievable. Rather than seeing the goal as a barrier, it was seen as a challenge. More runners could justify putting in the effort to qualify. Lowering the minimum qualifying time increased participation and the field's overall performance.[9]

Surprisingly, the changes led to an improvement among top runners as well, not just the overall average. In 2021, just five seasons after lowering the barriers to entry, Shalane Flanagan, an American, won the Women's open division of the New York City Marathon, giving Americans their first win in decades.[10] Then, in 2021, at the Summer Olympics in Tokyo, American runner Molly Seidel won a bronze medal, an event in which American women had not won a medal since 2004. Although she had competed internationally at shorter distances, it was only the third marathon she had ever run. Seidel went on to post the course record for the New York Marathon in November of 2021, which was only the fourth marathon she had ever run.

New York Times columnist Lindsay Crouse explains that an underlying psychological phenomenon may be contributing to the growing success of American women distance runners. She calls it the "Shalane Flanagan Effect." This represents a renewed feeling of camaraderie, inspiration, and resources that has come with the increased participation in women's long-distance running in the US. With a growing number of runners competing in marathons, there is a greater sense of belonging and support. Crouse cited the unfortunate situation in 2000, perhaps a low point in American women's marathons, when only one runner qualified for the Olympics—while training primarily alone on a treadmill. However, the sense of camaraderie, competition, and belonging encouraged more women to enter the field and encouraged more training and participation in competitions.[11]

As noted in the *New York Times* series, other factors may come into play in increasing participation and top performance. Improved shoe technology, changing work-life situations for women, and other factors may play a role. Even if only a tiny portion of the improvement can be attributed to the lower qualifying time, it suggests that setting and initiating goals on a broader scale can positively impact overall performance.[12] After all, nothing horrible happened when the standard for entry was lowered, which should at least stave off the critics who would argue that you are "lowering standards" by setting the bar too low.

SETTING TIERED GOALS

The tiered goal-setting map provides an easy-to-use format to improve goal-setting (see table 12.1). The map offers a structure to set three progressively difficult goals and suggests considering your progress on goals in chunks of three efforts. An effort is a trial, practice, or attempt at a larger goal. The goals can be learning or performing in nature, but all focus on learning, progress, and improvement. In addition to setting three progressively difficult goals, the map also encourages you to note your effort and your perceived level of success. Accounting for level of effort and success will increase awareness of emotions, progress, and other aspects of self-awareness.

Sherry's pursuit to improve her running allows us to continue with the running analogy. Running illustrates the value of tiered goal-setting because progress can be easily measured and effort easily documented. Sherry wanted to rekindle her love of running to improve her health, but she had not run in years. She used the tiered goal-setting map to organize her progress. She used the initiating/first-tier goal to motivate herself to get out and move. After completing her first-tier goal on day 1, she reassessed and adjusted her tier-one goal for the second running session in two days. Each time she moved and took part in running and walking, she accomplished her first-tier goal: initiating the activity. In the second tier, the enhancing goal, she pushed herself harder and strived to

TABLE 12.1 Tiered Goals Map

	SESSION 1	SESSION 2	SESSION 3
Tier 1: Initiating goal to get started			
Tier 2: Enhancing goal to push yourself			
Tier 3: Optimizing goal for best case improvement			
Describe your feelings and thoughts during the session. Describe successes you had.			
How successful were you in your session? (rank 1 = low to 120 = high)			
How much effort did you put into the session? (rank 1 = low to 10 = high)			

reach a specific duration and distance. The first time she returned to running, the goal was to run for fifteen minutes at a pace of a six miles per hour. The second tier looked like more traditional goal-setting. In the case of her third tier, optimizing, she congratulated herself by completing a 5k race.

Sherry illustrates how the tiered goal map served as a helpful tool to support participants as they track their goals across three distinct practice sessions. The goals that participants chose to work on cover a wide range of pursuits, including academic (e.g., getting better grades), professional and career (e.g., getting promoted), and personal (e.g., healthy living). The example in table 12.2 shows how one participant put the tiered goal map into action.

GOAL-SETTING FOR RESILIENCE

Along with the tiered goal-setting map, consider these tips for getting the most out of the process and overcoming some of the pitfalls associated with traditional goal-setting.

First, challenge the temptation to adopt a star-performer mentality. Organizations tend to focus on the successes of a few top performers who receive a large share of the rewards. This often comes at the expense of others in the organization. Thinking of yourself as a star performer in the top 1 to 10 percent may make you feel good about yourself and build self-esteem, but it may lead to overconfidence. Further, your star performances may not translate into other areas of leadership. Taking on a star performer mindset may cause you to ignore self-reflection and encourage you to see an effort to improve self-awareness as unnecessary. In addition, star performers often lack team skills and can generate resentment among other team members, and a toxic culture may result. Instead, as a leader, encourage an approach where more individuals can participate. Don't make participation exclusive. After all, if one star performer could do all the work, we wouldn't need an organization or organizational leaders.

Consider the techniques mentioned in prior chapters, such as adopting an optimal improvement mindset that embraces learning and performing. Engage the five learning strategies, especially seeking out the support of others. Consider adopting the five learning strategies and identifying ways to infuse these routines through the organization. Finally, identify new ways to initiate activities, even if these activities generate unpleasant emotions or pose difficult barriers. This is what psychologists call behavioral activation: start something, even

TABLE 12.2 Tiered Goal Map Sample

	SESSION 1	SESSION 2	SESSION 3
Tier 1: Initiating goal to get started	Set clear working hours: 8 to 5, no work beyond that time.	Create working hours.	Create working hours.
Tier 2: Enhancing goal to push yourself	Take work email off phone.	Take work email off phone.	Take work email off phone.
Tier 3: Optimizing goal for best-case improvement	Actually stop doing work outside of identified work hours.	Stop doing work outside of scope.	Stop doing work outside of scope.
Describe your feelings and thoughts during the session. Describe successes you had.	I had some success with working only during my defined working hours, probably 1/3 during time but not successfully reaching level 2.	I had more success time 2, but was holding myself to a higher standard in time 2. I did not remove it from my phone, but I did check it less outside of work hours. Was able to achieve tier 3 goal.	Time 3 I had success! I wouldn't say it was 100%, but it was at least 90% of the time, and that's a win! I still have not completely removed it from my phone, but I only check during work hours, or for non-work-related items (i.e., for student-related reasons) outside of work hours. I have stopped this altogether, and nothing has happened (except that work didn't get done, but it's not my work to do). So this was a win too.
How successful were you in your session? (rank 1 = low to 120 = high)	Self-score: 72/120	Self-score: 72/120	Self-score: 90/120
How much effort did you put into the session? (rank 1= low to 10 = high)	3	3	4

if you don't feel ready or don't feel like taking action at the moment. We often become motivated after we start something, not before. Regardless of the level of effort, taking action is an essential step in psychological change. Simply scheduling an appointment with a therapist has been shown to decrease depression and anxiety. Acting seems to mitigate some of the unpleasant emotions associated with a task.[13]

This chapter outlined tiered goal-setting, a method to supplement standard methods of goal-setting such as SMART and stretch goals. Tiered goals help overcome emotional obstacles to initiating and maintaining effort toward goals. Procrastination and burnout are often unintended outcomes of goal-setting, and tiered goals provide a systematic approach to overcoming these challenges.

Exercise 12: Creating a Tiered Goal Map

Use the blank map in table 12.1 as the basis for your tiered-goal map, or use a separate document. A spreadsheet also works well as a form. Tiered goal-setting starts by setting three levels of goal achievement across at least three practice sessions. The process can be repeated for as long as it is functional.

Set three tiers for each practice session:

- Tier 1: Initiating. The initiating goal should be a low bar. It should be a goal that is easy to reach and usually involves just engaging in the activity with no expectation of how much effort, how long, or how much intensity. The objective of setting a tier-one goal is to get started.

- Tier 2: Enhancing. An enhancing goal should focus on improving your performance over tier one—the goal of enhancing moves beyond just initiating to include a specific performance goal. An enhancing goal should direct you beyond your current level of performance but not too far. The enhancing goal will help you test where your performance level lies so you can determine how to set your SMART goals in the future.

- Tier 3: Optimizing. An optimizing goal should reflect a level of performance under perfect conditions. For example, if you are planning on giving a speech, consider what it would look like to present in front of an enthusiastic audience, a great introduction, and a day full of feeling positive emotions. You are completely energized before and during the speech. Consider the setting for the speech as being all but perfect. If your goal is to run a 5K, consider what your strongest performance would look like on a clear and sunny day with a group cheering you on and a full night's rest the night before.

After completing your first practice session, reflect on the process. What was your level of effort? What was your level of engagement? How successful was your process? Based on the feedback you provide, modify each tier of your goal. Finally, repeat the process of tiered goal-setting for practice sessions two and three. You can continue the process beyond the third practice session as well.

CONCLUSION

Pathways to Leading Beyond Your Comfort Zone

A SIMPLE FORMULA FOR LEADING: MOVE, SLEEP, LEARN

Completing this book is an entry point for leading outside your comfort zone. This concluding chapter offers three pathways to the future. First, I describe a formal assessment tool designed to help leaders, trainers, and coaches develop the five learning strategies at the heart of leading outside your comfort zone. Second, I present six questions that can be used to assess readiness for leading for resilience, growth, and well-being. Third, I offer a simple formula for supplementing formal leadership development activities. This formula entails moving, sleeping, and learning.

LEARNING STRATEGIES QUESTIONNAIRE

Throughout this book, you have read about and engaged in exercises to support your leadership development. Short thought pieces, activities, and extended exercises have helped you reflect on the past and plan for the future. An additional tool is the Learning Strategies Questionnaire, a more formal survey to increase self-awareness of the five learning strategies. It is available through our seminars and programs.

Paul is a good case in point of how to apply the questionnaire. He is one of over 1,000 people who completed the questionnaire, which was developed to help participants gauge their attitudes toward improvements in different conditions. Paul worked in consulting for about eight years. As a consultant, he sought ways to improve his weekly team meetings. He felt good about them and experienced them as an area he constantly enhanced. On the other hand, he thought he needed to progress more in other areas of his leadership. He wanted to accelerate his improvement toward becoming a resilient leader.

Paul completed the Learning Strategies Questionnaire, which involved two sets of questions. In the first set of questions, Paul identified a frustrating activity—getting his team to take responsibility and show autonomy without his guidance. He then ranked himself on using the five learning strategies in this situation. For the second set of questions, Paul identified his regular team meetings as a time he was progressing in his learning and again ranked himself on the five factors.

Figure C.1 shows Paul's scores. In each of the five strategies, Paul saw that he ranked higher when making progress than when frustrated. These scores represent a familiar pattern. My colleagues Phil Wirtz and Jing Burgi-Tian and I conducted a statistical analysis to understand better the patterns of individuals who had completed the questionnaire. Our research showed a pattern like Paul's in about 75 percent of the people we studied. People were activating learning strategies more often when they felt they were making progress than when they were frustrated with their progress. Yet, in 25 percent of the cases, people were activating learning strategies in frustration and when making progress. Although preliminary, an interesting pattern has emerged, but the results require more investigation. It may be that the 25 percent of participants engaging in strategies in both situations have found mechanisms to take advantage of and activate the learning benefits even when frustrated with their progress while learning.[1]

The Learning Strategies Questionnaire measures how leaders experience periods of frustration differently than they experience periods of progress. Frustration can stop progress, and overcoming frustration can be achieved, at least partially, by identifying which strategies need to be activated when learning. The more leaders can practice necessary strategies, the better they can progress. Like Paul, leaders activate some or all of these strategies at various times. The challenge is to find ways to activate these strategies in times of frustration.

The high-stakes world of athletics inspired the questionnaire. Sports psychologists Montes Ruiz and Yuri Hanin developed a method to determine which stressors are associated with poor versus top performance. Hanin shows athletes

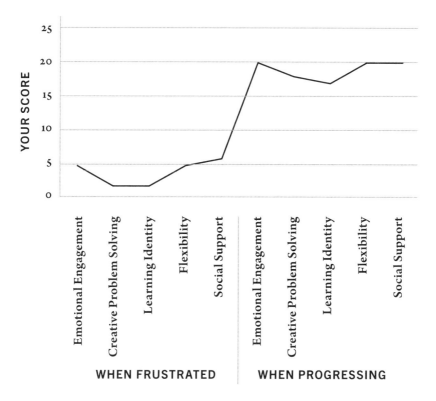

FIGURE C.1 Learning Strategies Questionnaire Sample Results

often experience their emotions and thoughts differently when performing at their best versus worst. He asked high-performing athletes to recall times when they were at peak performance and check various factors associated with their performance.[2] The factors included a list of experiences with emotions, thoughts, and physical sensations. Then, the athletes were asked to consider their worst performance and check off the same list. Not surprisingly, there was a definitive list of feelings associated with the best performance versus the worst performance. Pleasant feelings were more related to top performance, while unpleasant feelings were associated with poor performance.

The Learning Strategies Questionnaire is based on a similar idea, but I wanted to understand how individuals associated emotions during learning situations and how experiences of learning and making progress might differ from learning while frustrated. I developed this questionnaire as a developmental tool to help participants in our workshops, classes, and programs understand the five learning strategies and how they may be activated in different situations.[3]

At first, I developed an instrument to help students, executives, and leaders identify the strategies that emerged during frustration and progress. They could see what might be activated when frustrated, such as when experiencing unpleasant emotions. They could compare this to a situation where they were making progress, that is, when experiencing pleasant emotions. In some cases, like Paul's, the use of the strategies dropped significantly when frustrated. The participants would identify ways to activate the strategy during certain situations, and we had detailed discussions about learning under these conditions. A simpler version of the questionnaire appeared in the chapter 7 exercise.

Paul determined that two strategies related to positive emotional engagement and learning identity would help his team become more autonomous. He had them identify exciting and interesting projects for the team and then asked them to focus on their learning identity as a team. These helped motivate the team and made them focus on learning rather on making mistakes and proving themselves. The team took on more responsibility by building a learning identity and working on an exciting project. As a result, Paul was able to shift more daily responsibilities to his team.

READINESS TO LEAD OUTSIDE YOUR COMFORT ZONE

Several years ago, I met with an executive, Nazir, who was considering taking the next step as a leader. After nearly five years as a successful executive leading a nonprofit, she considered returning to school and getting her MBA. However, she seemed unsure of what to do and doubted her commitment to the graduate school track. I asked six questions to help her gauge the likelihood that she would get the most out of graduate school. These questions prompted Nazir to consider her resilience and well-being as she started and completed graduate school. Since she answered yes to most of the six questions, she had a good chance of success in achieving her graduate work. She appeared to be quite resilient in this situation. When Nazir answered yes, she reaffirmed that she was on the right path to improvement. But if she answered maybe or no, she could identify areas of potential frustration that might derail her efforts at getting a graduate degree.

Leaders can ask themselves the same six questions to determine their readiness to lead outside their comfort zone. These questions are the first step in assisting leaders to surface assumptions about the sources of their frustration and help them remain on course in reaching their full potential as leaders.

1. Do you enjoy the activity?

You are more likely to sustain improvement when you are curious about and enjoy the activity. This helps you assess your interest in and excitement about the improvement activity. When interested in something, you are also more likely to learn and grow in an activity. You are more likely to experience progress when you (1) enjoy the activity, even if it does not have clear rewards or outcomes; (2) believe the activity to be exciting and engaging; (3) learn new aspects of the activity; and (4) are open to exploring new dimensions of the activity.

2. Can you learn, acquire new behaviors, and improve in the activity?

You are more confident in your ability when you believe you can learn and improve. Your expectation of improvement helps you maintain your efforts. This question considers your learning identity. Learning identity reflects a positive attitude toward learning and growing and that your current levels of improvement are not fixed. The question is a barometer for how open you are to cultivating new talents, taking stock of weaknesses, believing that you can learn, change, and develop, and accepting feedback and not taking it personally. These are all elements of a learning identity. When you believe you can learn new things, grow, and improve, you are more likely to succeed than if you think you are already performing at your best.

3. Can someone provide regular feedback on your progress and support you emotionally during challenging times?

Improvement can thrive when you seek new insights about your performance. One way to increase your knowledge is to surround yourself with people with the same interests, goals, and ambitions. Finding social support is essential to getting better, whether seeking a coach, a mentor, or a helpful peer. Leaders learn from those who have mastered an activity and seek emotional support during stressful times. Improvement is a social process and occurs when people learn from the experience of others. This learning translates into individual improvement and improves team and organizational performance. By watching, listening, and working with others who have already been successful, you can learn from their mistakes and learn the accumulated knowledge of others.

4. Are you willing to take risks and experience some failures and setbacks but continue to pursue the outcome, even if it means changing direction?

You learn and improve by developing multiple strategies, realizing that many changes and adjustments need to be made, and being flexible and understanding the importance of failure; this allows you to change direction and constantly update your assessment of the situation and challenges. Can you take different strategies, learn new ways, and take calculated risks to improve?

5. Can you focus for an extended time on this activity?

Learning to achieve your full potential requires removing distractions, understanding and managing competing goals, and taking action in the face of complexity. Progress often requires dealing with greater complexity and new challenges. Suppose you are performing at or near the top of your ability. In that case, you may experience pressure to succeed continually, and focus may become difficult because other activities may seem more attractive. Ask yourself how you can keep the process interesting by reminding yourself of why you were interested in this activity in the first place.

6. Will you work through challenges, even if you feel bored and uninterested in certain activity details?

This question probes how easily you will be distracted by failure to make progress. The question gauges your potential to stay with the improvement efforts, even during setbacks and periods of frustration and boredom. You must work through challenges and find ways to keep your improvements moving forward. Accepting that progress will take time requires persistence and often results in small incremental changes or progress.

A SIMPLE FORMULA FOR LEADING: MOVE, SLEEP, LEARN

Developing leadership is about taking one step at a time. This final section outlines three essential strategies for maintaining mental and physical health. These are moving, sleeping, and learning.

Steven is representative of many leaders who show great potential, resilience, and a desire to learn but struggle from moment to moment. Steven was stressed and didn't need a lecture on resilience or another self-assessment. He needed sleep. He required movement, and he needed to improve his overall health. The evidence was clear: Steven's leadership resilience depended on healthy life habits associated with body movement, sleep, and an appropriate diet. Unfortunately, Steven was not doing well in any of these areas.

Steven approached me after the class session and looked down. A growing family, a demanding job in a high-profile government agency, and aging parents were wearing him down physically and mentally. He told me he was taking a leave of absence from our program. Throughout the last few weeks, I saw that he had diligently completed all the work in class. Although he was still developing resilience, Steven had a strong sense of leadership capabilities and values. He was optimistic about his future. Still, he struggled to meet the demands that seemed to increase daily.

Two years later, I saw him at an event. He looked rested and presented more energy than he had in the past. He told me he drew strength from his supportive family. During the COVID pandemic, he left his government job to work for a contractor that supported his agency. This allowed him a more flexible schedule. He told me that he slept regularly and reduced his stress at work. He was no longer under intense time pressure to identify threats as he was when he worked with the agency. He was now involved in long-term planning and support.

Steven accepted that his situation was not sustainable and that significant changes were needed. Leaders like Steven need to consider their own well-being and that of those around them. Therefore, well-being requires attention to these building blocks: moving, sleeping, and learning.

Body movement is the first building block of well-being. Well-being requires being in touch with your body and mind; this includes moving your body to achieve health. You can choose from many activities, but moving the body is essential—especially for those who work at a desk or work from home. Well-being is built upon a foundation of physical well-being, and moving is the foundation of this process. Consider moving away from your desk at least every hour and taking thirty-minute breaks, including walking or body movement. You can even build in doing household tasks if you are working from home. Regular movement breaks can improve your cognitive abilities and refresh your ability to pay attention, focus, and concentrate.[4]

Even a short amount of exercise is beneficial if you can't fit in a thirty-minute walk. As little as two minutes of walking to interrupt periods of prolonged sitting can positively impact your well-being,[5] but any body movement will improve the foundation of well-being. Set your own movement goals based on your situation.

Movement can support improved mental functioning, including improved heart health, memory, and cognitive functioning.[6] Also, leading requires focusing on the long haul and developing mechanisms to help you deal with the challenges throughout your leadership career and life. Make movement a part of your leadership journey. Consider walking or finding something you enjoy doing. Make the walk enjoyable, find a partner, and engage all the learning strategies as a personal development project.[7]

Make your movement more emotionally engaging. Adventurer and author Alastair Humphreys explains that you don't need to go anywhere exotic. You could stoke your adventurous side in your own neighborhood. In 2020, he pushed himself to run, walk, or bike down every street in his London suburb and discovered places he never knew existed.[8]

Sleep is a second building block of resilience. Too often, due to busy schedules and a calendar full of appointments, sleep is often the first activity we drop. Sleep has been linked to several essential leadership attributes, including better focus, attitude, concentration, patience, and overall mental health. Sleep is essential for effective decision-making and facilitates learning. Often, when I teach a late-night class, I joke that students' focus is at the lowest of the day, but the positive side is that they are likely to go right to sleep after class, and sleeping right after learning aids in memory and recall. Studies have shown that sleep is essential for memory consolidation, moving what you learned from short-term to long-term memory.

Many tricks are available to improve sleep. However, our experience is that accepting that you need more sleep is the most significant barrier to getting enough sleep. Unfortunately, many leaders are tempted to avoid sleep and use valuable sleep time to finish work or projects. Some leaders even replace their valuable sleeping time with mindless internet browsing. This approach is often embedded in the performance-based mindset that has become so prevalent in our workplaces. Instead, resilient leaders should be mindful of the importance of sleep and not fall prey to the myth that sleep doesn't matter.

Sleep is essential, but so are non-sleep restful states such as meditation, thinking, simply viewing nature, and engaging as many senses as possible. There is a growing list of aids, including apps, workbooks, and accessible online sources, that can help you identify ways to bring sleep and other non-sleep restful states into your well-being development practices. For example, Stanford Medical School Professor David Spiegel has developed a comprehensive system that leaders can use to manage stress and anxiety through hypnosis. In addition, there is a growing list of resources on using meditation and silence to support improved well-being.[9]

The third building block of well-being is this book's core focus: learning. Learning, moving, and sleeping are foundational to well-being, but learning is the most challenging. Learning requires coordinating multiple psychological, social, and biological processes. Throughout this book, you have encountered examples that illustrate learning and its role in resilience, explanations for why learning is essential for building well-being, and exercises and tips for adopting learning strategies. Moving, sleeping, and learning are mechanisms to deal with the inevitable stresses associated with leadership.

This book focuses on preparing leaders who face increasing challenges and helping them meet them with a focus on well-being. You must move beyond the self and create an environment for resilience and learning. This means building a culture that supports resilience and learning for others. This is based on the idea that no personal change or leadership development, no matter how powerful, can be sustained without a supportive environment.

A FINAL LESSON ON RESILIENCE, GROWTH, AND WELL-BEING

One striking example of resilient learning arose as I watched karate students learn to break wooden boards with just their fists. Success at breaking the board requires overcoming a natural tendency to pull their punch just before encountering it. This inclination occurs in anticipation of the first sense of discomfort, but a successful break requires moving through the punch despite the anticipated pain. The student must maintain forward motion and overcome this anticipation. However, once students learn how to move through their punch, they quickly learn that the pain is minimal, especially once they have developed the skill to hit the board in one solid movement. Learning to overcome this challenge when breaking a board provides a metaphor for resilience. While the metaphor may be brutal, it makes the point well. Well-being arises from learning to work through unpleasant experiences and solve problems despite these unpleasant experiences.

This lesson from the karate studio applies to leaders facing daily organizational challenges in business and all walks of life: face unpleasant emotions as challenges. Well-being emerges when we find a purpose and pursue that purpose despite challenges, setbacks, and fears. Continue to learn and grow despite obstacles and unpleasant emotions. Take action, accept reasonable risks, and learn from those experiences.

Ultimately, leading is about overcoming obstacles and continuing to progress toward learning and well-being, considering these obstacles. Resilient leaders keep learning despite unpleasant situations. These leaders maintain their learning regardless of their circumstances, and resilient leaders revert to the basics when learning comes to a halt. When learning stops, moving and sleeping are good places to start again.

Exercise 13: Developing Your Leadership Plan
This eight-step planning document will help you reflect upon and summarize your leadership development experiences, goals, and insights. It will help you plan for future leadership development experiences.

Step 1: What will I be doing?
Write a short description of the action you will take to improve your leadership.

Step 2: What do I hope to learn?
Identify one thing you hope to learn. This should be phrased as a process or as knowledge, not an outcome.

Step 3: What are different ways I can measure my success?
A tiered goal ranks different levels of accomplishment each time you participate in an improvement activity. Each tier is more challenging than the previous tier.

- Tier 1:

- Tier 2:

- Tier 3:

Step 4: What prior experience have I had in this area of improvement?
Consider previous experience in this area, task, or situation. Return to your responses throughout the book to guide your reflection.

Step 5: What negative emotions might I experience, or have I experienced when frustrated with progress?
Draw on your experience.

Step 6: What learning strategies will I need to use or develop to learn at my best and make progress?
Identify potential strategies you need to activate or draw upon to get the most out of this activity.

Step 7: What action plans can I formulate?
Identify at least three practice sessions that you will do. This may change, but plan for at least three practice sessions now.

    1.

    2.

    3.

Step 8: How does this contribute to my leadership?
Describe how the activity contributes to your leadership development and supports your preparation for a leadership role.

Epilogue

I can trace my first conscious awareness of the importance of making progress despite obstacles beyond my control to the tennis court over thirty years ago. I was about fourteen years old at the time. One summer, a group of friends and I decided to learn to play tennis. We met each day at the local park. Rarely did the balls we were hitting make it to the other side of the court. Sometimes, the ball went well over the fence designed to serve as a backstop.

One day, the high school tennis coach noticed us playing. He could have directed his attention to more accomplished players. Instead, he organized a class through the local parks and recreation department and invited us to join even though we were learning the sport in our early teens. Most teens in neighboring towns had played for years, some starting as early as five. On the other hand, he may have seen our potential. He knew we were passionate about the sport and willing to do almost anything to improve. The coach looked beyond the next season and considered building a sustainable program for the long term.

The coach taught us the basic forms for each tennis stroke. He gave special attention to the aspects of our skill that were particularly important, so we spent hours practicing our service game since each point always starts with a serve. We played hours of tennis each week, and over time, the balls we hit began to stay within the lines and went over the net more times than not. The once awkward teens became a successful team over the next six years of playing tennis. We captured several titles and shared many great experiences.

This was my first direct experience with the power of productive well-being.

Tennis provided a method to achieve our ambitions. Tennis taught us how to support teamwork and build individual confidence in our ability to improve. We learned how to work out problems and manage our emotions under pressure. The greatest lesson we learned was about becoming more resilient. Decades later, as I have renewed friendships with these old teammates, we all point to the lessons we learned on the tennis court as critical for our future resilience in the face of obstacles. Our team was lucky enough to have a coach willing to focus on developing our talents over the long term. Our well-being takes shape when we focus on the achievements and direction we are heading.

NOTES ON METHODS

This book was written for a general audience and used citation methods consistent with this goal. Every effort was made to cite relevant and influential research. Grammarly software was used to check for spelling, grammar, and potential plagiarism. Composite characters and other methods were used to protect the identity of participants. The use of composite characters has two primary benefits. First, composite characters present complex situations that occur across time and space into episodes, and second, they provide a method for communicating to nonacademics in nontechnical terms.[1]

NOTES

Preface

1. Peter Coy, "The Scariest Part About the Boeing 737 MAX 9 Blowout," *New York Times,* January 10, 2024, https://www.nytimes.com/2024/01/10/opinion/boeing-737-max -alaska-japan-airlines.html; Douglas MacMillan and Michael Laris, "After Midair Failure, Critics Ask: Did Boeing Learn from Max Crashes?" *Washington Post,* January 12, 2024, https://www.washingtonpost.com/business/2024/01/12/boeing-max-safety-crashes/; Sylvia Pfeifer and Claire Bushey, "'It Ain't Working': Boeing's Quality Pledges in Question after Max 9 Incident," *Financial Times,* accessed January 15, 2024, https://www.ft.com/ content/233d6387-ebof-4df1-b1e5-8ba3679fdb78.

Introduction

1. David Watson, Olga Tregaskis, Cigdem Gedikli, Oluwafunmilayo Vaughn, and Antonina Semkina, "Well-Being Through Learning: A Systematic Review of Learning Interventions in the Workplace and Their Impact on Well-Being." *European Journal of Work and Organizational Psychology* 27, no. 2 (2018): 247–68, https://doi.org/10.1080/ 1359432x.2018.1435529; information on burnout was reported at: https://www.gallup. com/394424/indicator-employee-wellbeing.aspx; World Health Organization, "Burn-Out an 'Occupational Phenomenon': International Classification of Diseases," press re-lease, May 28, 2019, https://www.who.int/news/item/28-05-2019-burn-out-an-occupa tional-phenomenon-international-classification-of-disease; low worker motivation was from a survey found at: https://www.adpri.org/insights/employee-motivation-and-com mitment-index/; the loneliness situation is described at: https://www.hhs.gov/sites/ default/files/surgeon-general-social-connection-advisory.pdf; Dante L. Mack et al., "Mental Health and Behavior of College Students During the COVID-19 Pandemic: Longitudinal Mobile Smartphone and Ecological Momentary Assessment Study, Part

II," *Journal of Medical Internet Research* 23, no. 6 (2021): e28892, https://doi.org/10.2196/ 28892.

2. American Psychiatric Association, "New APA Poll Shows Sustained Anxiety Among Americans; More Than Half of Parents Are Concerned About the Mental Well-Being of Their Children," press release, May 2, 2021, shorturl.at/tvU45; Megan Leonhardt, "44% of Older Millennials Already Have a Chronic Health Condition. Here's What That Means for Their Futures," CNBC Online, May 4, 2021, https://www.cnbc .com/2021/05/04/older-millennials-chronic-health-conditions.html.

3. Lev Semyonovich Vygotsky, *Mind in Society: The Development of Higher Psychological Processes* (Cambridge, MA: Harvard University Press, 1978). The idea of a learning zone is also associated with Robert M. Yerkes and John D. Dodson, "The Relation of Strength of Stimulus to Rapidity of Habit-Formation," *Journal of Comparative Neurology and Psychology* 18, no. 5 (1908): 459–82, https://doi.org/10.1002/cne.920180503; for a critique see Martin Corbett, "From Law to Folklore: Work Stress and the Yerkes-Dodson Law," *Journal of Managerial Psychology* 30, no. 6 (2015): 741–52, https://doi.org/10.1108/ jmp-03-2013-0085. For empirical support see Kristen Joan Anderson, "Impulsivity, Caffeine, and Task Difficulty: A Within-Subjects Test of the Yerkes-Dodson Law," *Personality and Individual Differences* 16, no. 6 (1994): 813–29, https://doi.org/10.1016/0191-8869 (94)90226-7.

4. Attributed to Peter M. Senge, *The Fifth Discipline: The Art and Practice of the Learning Organization* (New York: Currency and Doubleday, 2006).

Chapter 1

1. Steve Mollman, "Blockbuster 'Laughed Us out of the Room,' Recalls Netflix Cofounder on Trying to Sell Company Now Worth over $150 Billion for $50 Million," *Fortune*, April 14, 2023, https://fortune.com/2023/04/14/netflix-cofounder-marc-randolph -recalls-blockbuster-rejecting-chance-to-buy-it/.

2. Jordan Valinsky, "Netflix Co-CEO on Dave Chappelle Fallout: I Screwed Up," *CNN*, October 20, 2021, https://www.cnn.com/2021/10/20/media/netflix-dave -chappelle-ceo-reaction/index.html; Matt Donnelly, "'I Screwed Up': Netflix's Ted Sarandos Addresses Dave Chappelle Fallout," *Variety*, October 19, 2019, https://variety. com/2021/film/news/dave-chappelle-netflix-ted-sarandos-i-screwed-up-1235093098/; Reed Hastings and Erin Meyer, *No Rules Rules: Netflix and the Culture of Reinvention* (New York: Penguin, 2020).

3. Hastings and Meyer, *No Rules Rules*.

4. Jeffery A. Sonnenfeld, "The Jack Welch That I Knew," *Yale Insights*, March 2, 2020, https://insights.som.yale.edu/insights/the-jack-welch-that-i-knew.

5. Heidi Brooks, "Everyday Leadership," Yale School of Management, https://faculty .som.yale.edu/heidibrooks/everyday-leadership/.

6. Karl Weick was one of the first to challenge the myth of heroic leadership; see this review of his work, Dave Schwandt, "Karl E. Weick: Departing from Traditional Rational Models of Organizational Change," in *The Palgrave Handbook of Organizational Change*

Thinkers, ed. David B. Szabla, William A. Pasmore, Mary A. Barnes, and Asha N. Gipson, 1415–31 (London: Palgrave Macmillan, 2017), https://doi.org/10.1007/978-3-319-52878-6 _62. See also for a discussion of the problems with heroic leadership, Hortense le Gentile, "Leaders, Stop Trying to Be Heroes," *Harvard Business Review*, October 25, 2021, https://hbr.org/2021/10/leaders-stop-trying-to-be-heroes.

7. For details on production hell see, Charles Duhigg, "Dr. Elon & Mr. Musk: Life Inside Tesla's Production Hell," *Wired*, December 13, 2018, https://www.wired.com/story/elon-musk-tesla-life-inside-gigafactory. For a look at what it means to be extremely hard core see, Christopher Mims, "Are You 'Extremely Hardcore' or Not? How Elon Musk Is Dividing Silicon Valley's Elite," December 24, 2022, *Wall Street Journal*, accessed January 30, 2024, https://www.wsj.com/articles/elon-musk-leadership-analysis-extremely-hardcore-11671832630.

8. For more on Dorsey's approach to self-care see, Laura Gesualdi-Gilmore, "Inside How Jack Dorsey Eats 1 Meal a Day and Goes to Silent Retreat with No Phone," *US Sun*, April 25, 2022, https://www.the-sun.com/news/4168298/jack-dorsey-fast-silent -meditation-retreat/.

9. Russ Vince, "Behind and Beyond Kolb's Learning Cycle," *Journal of Management Education* https://doi-org.proxygw.wrlc.org/10.1177/105256299802200304 22, no. 3: (1999) 304-319.

10. Deloitte, "The Social Enterprise in a World Disrupted," accessed January 13, 2024, https://www2.deloitte.com/content/dam/insights/us/articles/6935_2021-HC-Trends/di_human-capital-trends.pdf; A. Ozimek, K. Fikri, and J. Lettieri, *From Managing Decline to Building the Future: Could a Heartland Visa Help Struggling Regions?* (Economic Innovation Group, 2019), https://eig.org/wp-content/uploads/2019/04/Heartland -Visas-Report.pdf; Lisa Taylor and Fern Lebo, *The Talent Revolution: Longevity and the Future of Work* (Toronto: University of Toronto Press, 2021).

11. World Health Organization, "Burn-out an 'Occupational Phenomenon': International Classification of Diseases," May 28, 2019, https://www.who.int/news/item/28-05 -2019-burn-out-an-occupational-phenomenon-international-classification-of-diseases; U.S. Department of Health and Human Services, *Addressing Health Worker Burnout. The U.S. Surgeon General's Advisory on Building a Thriving Health Workforce,* 2022; "Health Worker Burnout—Current Priorities of the U.S. Surgeon General," accessed January 12, 2024, https://www.hhs.gov/surgeongeneral/priorities/health-worker-burnout/index. html; Mayo Clinic Staff, "Covid-19: How to Manage Your Mental Health During the Pandemic," Mayo Clinic, July 22, 2023, https://www.mayoclinic.org/diseases-conditions/coronavirus/in-depth/mental-health-covid-19/art-20482731; Dante L. Mack et al., "Mental Health and Behavior of College Students During the COVID-19 Pandemic: Longitudinal Mobile Smartphone and Ecological Momentary Assessment Study, Part II," *Journal of Medical Internet Research* 23, no. 6 (2021): e28892; American Psychiatric Association, "New APA Poll Shows Sustained Anxiety Among Americans; More Than Half of Parents Are Concerned About the Mental Well-Being of Their Children," press release, May 2, 2021, https://www.psychiatry.org/newsroom/news-releases/new-apa-poll-shows-sustained

-anxiety-among-americans-more-than-half-of-parents-are-concerned-about-the-mental
-well-being-of-their-children; see also, Ece Yildirim, "Gen Z Could Overtake Boomers in
the Workforce by 2024: This Has 'Sweeping Implications' Economist Says," CNBC, https:
//www.cnbc.com/2023/12/05/gen-z-will-overtake-boomers-in-us-workforce-glassdoor
-report.html.

12. Terry L. Price, "Feeling and Dirty Hands: The Role of Regret Experienced by
Responsible Agents," in *Judgment and Leadership*, ed. A. B. Kayes and D. C. Kayes, 117–29
(Cheltenham, UK: Edward Elgar Press, 2021), https://doi.org/10.4337/9781839104107
.00015.

13. Jason Aten, "The CEO Who Fired 900 Employees over Zoom Is Back, and Now
He's Asking More to Quit," *Inc.*, April 7, 2022, https://www.inc.com/jason-aten/the-ceo
-who-fired-900-employees-over-zoom-is-back-now-hes-asking-more-to-quit.html;
Clare Duffy, "From the Brink of Bankruptcy to a 1,300% Stock Gain: How This CEO
Turned Around Her Company," *CNN*, March 26, 2020, https://www.cnn.com/2020/03/
27/tech/lisa-su-amd-risk-takers/index.html.

14. Ryanard S. Kington, "Advice: Presidents Don't Talk About Their Panic Attacks,"
Chronicle of Higher Education, accessed January 13, 2024, https://www.chronicle.com/
article/presidents-dont-talk-about-their-panic-attacks.

15. EgonZehnder, "972 Global CEOs Share Their Perspective on the Future of CEO
Leadership," 2022, https://www.egonzehnder.com/it-starts-with-the-ceo.

16. Ursula. M. Burns, *Where You Are Is Not Who You Are* (New York: Amistad, 2021).

17. Kate Beioley, "Pallas's Natasha Harrison: 'I Felt Completely like an Outsider
Going into Law,'" *Financial Times*, May 15, 2022, https://www.ft.com/content/99d7656e
-b67f-4184-97a1-f0b3383e89b4.

18. Justin Cash, "An Audience with Helena Morrissey: '100-Hour Weeks Are More
Like Slave Labour,'" *Financial News*, December 1, 2021, https://www.fnlondon.com/arti
cles/an-audience-with-helena-morrissey-mp-side-job-scandal-is-embarrassing-20211
201; Helena Morrissey, "I Wish I Hadn't Helped Create the Myth That It's Easy for
Women to Have It All," *Daily Mail*, March 18, 2022, https://www.dailymail.co.uk/femail
/article-10628799/HELENA-MORRISSEY-wish-hadnt-helped-create-myth-easy-wo
men-all.html.

19. References to weight loss: Christine Logel, and Geoffrey L. Cohen, "The Role of
the Self in Physical Health," *Psychological Science* 23, no. 1 (2011): 53–55, https://doi.org/10
.1177/0956797611421936.

20. Reference to self-affirmation and academic performance: Shannon T. Brady,
Stephanie L. Reeves, Julio Garcia, Valerie Purdie-Vaughns, Jonathan E. Cook, Suzanne
Taborsky-Barba, Sarah Tomasetti, Eden M. Davis, and Geoffrey L. Cohen, "The Psychol-
ogy of the Affirmed Learner: Spontaneous Self-Affirmation in the Face of Stress," *Journal
of Educational Psychology* 108, no. 3 (2016): 353–73, https://doi.org/10.1037/edu0000091.
Reference to anxiety reduction: Patryk Łakuta, "Using the Theory of Self-Affirmation and
Self-Regulation Strategies of Mental Contrasting and Forming Implementation Intentions to Reduce Social Anxiety Symptoms," *Anxiety, Stress, and Coping* 33, no. 4 (2020):

370–86, https://doi.org/10.1080/10615806.2020.1746283. References to general well-being: Geoffrey Cohen and David K. Sherman, "The Psychology of Change: Self-Affirmation and Social Psychological Intervention," *Annual Review of Psychology* 65 (2014): 333–71, https://doi.org/10.1146/annurev-psych-010213-115137; Philip M. Ullrich and Susan K. Lutgendorf, "Journaling About Stressful Events: Effects of Cognitive Processing and Emotional Expression," *Annals of Behavioral Medicine* 24, no. 3 (Summer 2002): 244–50.

21. Adapted from Łakuta, "Using the Theory of Self-Affirmation." Research has shown that affirming one's self-worth, skills, and past successes can help support resilience in a variety of activities such as weight loss (Logel and Cohen, "The Role of the Self in Physical Health"); academic performance (Łakuta, "Using the Theory of Self-Affirmation"); and anxiety (Łakuta, "Using the Theory of Self-Affirmation").

Chapter 2

1. Jiangmeng Liu, Cheng Hong, and Bora Yook, "CEO as 'Chief Crisis Officer' Under Covid-19: A Content Analysis of CEO Open Letters Using Structural Topic Modeling," *International Journal of Strategic Communication* 16, no. 3 (2022): 444–68, https://doi.org/10.1080/1553118x.2022.2045297.

2. Adapted from Geoffrey Cohen and David K. Sherman, "The Psychology of Change: Self-Affirmation and Social Psychological Intervention," *Annual Review of Psychology* 65 (2014): 333–71.

3. Edward H. Powley, "Reclaiming Resilience and Safety: Resilience Activation in the Critical Period of Crisis," *Human Relations* 62, no. 9 (2009): 1289–326, https://doi.org/10.1177/0018726709334881.

4. George A. Bonanno, "The Resilience Paradox," *European Journal of Psychotraumatology* 12, no. 1 (2021), https://doi.org/10.1080/20008198.2021.1942642.

5. George A. Bonanno, *The End of Trauma* (Basic Books, 2021).

6. Bonanno, "The Resilience Paradox," 5.

7. Life setbacks: Richard G. Tedeschi, Jane Shakespeare-Finch, K. Taku, and Lawrence G. Calhoun, *Posttraumatic Growth: Theory, Research, and Applications* (New York: Routledge, 2018); resilience in clinical care: L. A. Ellis et al., "Patterns of Resilience: A Scoping Review and Bibliometric Analysis of Resilient Health Care," *Safety Science* 118 (2019): 241–57, and Selina U. Platte, Ulrich Weismann, Richard G. Tedeschi, and Doris Kehl, "Coping and Rumination as Predictors of Posttraumatic Growth and Depreciation," *Chinese Journal of Traumatology* 25, no. 5 (2022): 264–71, https://doi.org/10.1016/j.cjtee.2022.02.001.

8. Richard Friedman, "You Might Be Depressed Now, But Don't Underestimate Your Resilience," *New York Times*, May 4, 2021, https://www.nytimes.com/2021/05/04/opinion/covid-brain-mental-health.html.

9. Dean G. Kilpatrick, Heidi S Resnick, Mellissa E. Milanak, Mark W. Miller, Katherine M. Keyes, and Matthew J. Friedman, "National Estimates of Exposure to Traumatic Events and PTSD Prevalence Using DSM-IV and DSM-5 Criteria," *Journal of Traumatic Stress* 26, no. 5 (October 2013): 537–47, https://doi.org/10.1002/jts.21848.

10. Graham Jones, Sheldon Hanton, and Declan Connaughton, "What Is This Thing Called Mental Toughness? An Investigation of Elite Sports Performers," *Journal of Applied Sport Psychology* 14, no. 3 (2002), 205–18, https://doi.org/10.1080/10413200290103509.

11. Jeffery LePine, Marci LePine, and Christine Jackson, "Challenge and Hindrance Stress: Relationships with Exhaustion, Motivation to Learn, and Learning Performance," *Journal of Applied Psychology* 89, no. 5 (2004): 883–91, https://doi.org/10.1037/0021-9010.89.5.883; Slessareva E. Muraven and Roy Baumeister, "Self-Regulation and Depletion of Limited Resources: Does Self-Control Resemble a Muscle?" *Psychological Bulletin* 126 (2000): 247–59, https://doi.org/10.1037/0033-2909.126.2.247; Eric. N. Smith, Michael D Young, and Alia J. Crum, "Stress, Mindsets, and Success in the Navy SEALs Special Warfare Training," *Frontiers in Psychology* 10 (2020): 2962, https://doi.org/10.3389/fpsyg.2019.02962.

12. Angela Duckworth and James J. Gross, "Self-Control and Grit," *Current Directions in Psychological Science* 23, no. 5 (2014): 319–25, https://doi.org/10.1177/0963721414541462.

13. Jesse Singal, "The Weak Case for Grit," *Nautilus*, April 14, 2021, https://nautil.us/the-weak-case-for-grit-238181/.

14. Danielle D. King, Alexander Newman, and Fred Luthans, "Not If, But When We Need Resilience in the Workplace," *Journal of Organizational Behavior* 37, no. 5 (2016): 782–86, https://doi.org/10.1002/job.2063. Suniya S. Luthar, Cante Cicchetti, and Bronwyn Becker, "The Construct of Resilience: A Critical Evaluation and Guidelines for Future Work," *Child Development* 71, no. 3 (2000): 543–62, https://doi.org/10.1111/1467-8624.00164.

15. King, Newman, and Luthans, "Not If, But When," 543.

16. Shannon Cheng, Danielle D. King, and Frederick Oswald, "Understanding How Resilience Is Measured in the Organizational Sciences," *Human Performance* 33, no. 2/3 (2020): 130–63, https://doi.org/10.1080/08959285.2020.1744151.

17. Jeremy Stahl, "Master of the Knuckleball," *Slate*, October 29, 2012, https://slate.com/culture/2012/10/how-did-r-a-dickey-get-so-good-the-mets-pitcher-reveals-how-he-mastered-the-knuckleball.html.

18. Stahl, "Master of the Knuckleball."

19. Baseball reference: "R. A. Dickey," BR Bullpen, accessed January 13, 2024, https://www.baseball-reference.com/bullpen/R.A._Dickey; Independent Film Festival Boston, "Q&A: Ricki Stern and Annie Sundberg on KNUCKLEBALL," YouTube, 2012, https://www.youtube.com/watch?v=byQJ4VvdPUc; Jeremy Rapanich, "R. A. Dickey, Tim Wakefield, Charlie Hough, and the Art of the Knuckleball," *Sports Illustrated Kids*, September 27, 2012, https://www.sikids.com/dugout-dispatch/ra-dickey-tim-wakefield-charlie-hough-and-art-knuckleball.

20. Stahl, "Master of the Knuckleball."

Chapter 3

1. The idea that leading requires a focus on learning was presented in D. Christopher Kayes, Jeewhan Yoon, and Crystal Han-Huei Tsay, "Five Routines That Help Leaders Learn," *Organizational Dynamics* 52, no. 3 (2023): 100991, https://doi.org/10.1016/j.org dyn.2023.100991.

2. Argyris, Chris Argyris, "Teaching Smart People How to Learn," *Harvard Business Review*, May-June 1991, https://hbr.org/1991/05/teaching-smart-people-how-to-learn.

3. Sean R. Zion and Alia J. Crum, "Mindsets Matter: A New Framework for Harnessing the Placebo Effect in Modern Medicine," *International Review of Neurobiology* 138 (2018): 137–60, https://doi.org/10.1016/bs.irn.2018.02.002.

4. Anders K. Ericsson, ed., *The Cambridge Handbook of Expertise and Expert Performance* (Cambridge: Cambridge University Press, 2018), https://doi.org/10.1017/9781316480748.

5. Richard E. Boyatzis and David A. Kolb, "Assessing Individuality in Learning: The Learning Skills Profile," *Educational Psychology* 11, no. 3–4 (1991): 279–95, https://doi.org/10.1080/0144341910110305.

6. Carol Dweck, *Mindset: The New Psychology of Success* (New York: Ballantine Books, 2006).

7. David S. Yeager, Ronald E. Dahl, and Carol S. Dweck, "Why Interventions to Influence Adolescent Behavior Often Fail but Could Succeed," *Perspectives on Psychological Science* 13, no. 1 (December 12, 2017): 101–22, https://doi.org/10.1177/1745691617722620.

8. Sarra Hayes, Colin MacLeod, and Geoff Hammond, "Anxiety-Linked Task Performance: Dissociating the Influence of Restricted Working Memory Capacity and Increased Investment of Effort," *Cognition and Emotion* 23, no. 4 (2009): 753–81, https://doi.org/10.1080/02699930802131078.

9. Hayes, MacLeod, and Hammond, "Anxiety-Linked Task Performance."

10. Melissa Isaacson, "How Serena Williams Has Mastered the Art of the Comeback," *ESPN*, June 26, 2015, https://www.espn.com/espnw/news-commentary/story/_/id/13142903/how-serena-williams-mastered-art-comeback.

11. Douglas Robson, "Mouratoglou: The Man Behind Serena's Latest Surge," *USA Today Sports*, September 2, 2013, https://www.usatoday.com/story/sports/tennis/2013/09/02/us-open-2013-serena-williams-patrick-mouratoglou-partnership/2755659/.

12. Danielle Rossigh, "Serena's Paris Failure Sparked Run Back to Top at 31," *Bloomberg*, May 23, 2013, https://www.bloomberg.com/news/articles/2013-05-23/serena-s-paris-failure-sparked-run-back-to-top-at-31.

13. For more on the notion of deliberate learning, see David A. Kolb and Bauback Yeganeh, "Deliberate Experiential Learning," in *Contemporary Organizational Behavior: From Ideas to Action*, ed. Kimberly D. Elsbach, Anna Kayes, and D. Christopher Kayes (Pearson, 2016).

14. Michael C. Sturman, "Searching for the Inverted U-Shaped Relationship Between Time and Performance: Meta-Analyses of the Experience/Performance, Tenure/Performance, and Age/Performance Relationships," *Journal of Management* 29 (2003):

609–40, https://doi.org/10.1016/S0149-2063(03)00028-X. See also W. J. Abernathy and K. Wayne, "Limits of the Learning Curve," *Harvard Business Review* 52 (September/October 1974), 109–19.

15. Ester Adi-Japha, Avi Karni, Ariel Parnes, Iris Loewenschuss, and Eli Vakil, "A Shift in Task Routines During the Learning of a Motor Skill: Group-Averaged Data May Mask Critical Phases in the Individuals' Acquisition of Skilled Performance," *Journal of Experimental Psychology: Learning, Memory, and Cognition* 34, no. 6 (2008): 1544–51, https://doi.org/10.1037/a0013217.

16. Jeffrey B. Vancouver, Charles M. Thompson, Casey E. Tischner, and Dan J. Putka, "Two Studies Examining the Negative Effect of Self-Efficacy on Performance," *Journal of Applied Psychology* 87, no. 3 (2002): 506–516: https://doi.org/10.1037/0021-9010.87.3.506.

17. Lauren C. Howe and Carol S. Dweck, "Changes in Self-Definition Impede Recovery from Rejection," *Personality and Social Psychology Bulletin* 42, no. 1 (2016): 54–71, doi: 10.1177/0146167215612743. David A. Nussbaum and Carol S. Dweck, "Defensiveness Versus Remediation: Self-Theories and Modes of Self-Esteem Maintenance," *Personality and Social Psychology Bulletin* 34, no. 5 (2008): 599–612, https://doiorg.proxygw.wrlc.org/10.1177/0146167207312960

18. Victor F. Sisk, Alexander P. Burgoyne, and Brooke N. Macnamara, "To What Extent and Under Which Circumstances Are Growth Mind-Sets Important to Academic Achievement? Two Meta-Analyses," *Psychological Science* 29, no. 4 (2018): 549–571, doi: 10.1177/0956797617739704.

19. D. Christopher Kayes, *Destructive Goal Pursuit: The Mt. Everest Disaster* (London: Palgrave Macmillan, 2006).

20. Barry J. Zimmerman, "Becoming a Self-Regulated Learner: An Overview," *Theory Into Practice* 41, no. 2 (2002): 64–70, http://www.jstor.org/stable/1477457.

21. The use of reframing unpleasant emotions and loss is discussed in cognitive behavioral therapy. For an explanation of the effects of reframing on teens as well as details on the mechanisms at work see: Elizabeth Svoboda, "Intervention at an Early Age May Hold Off the Onset of Depression," *Scientific American*, December 19, 2023. https://www.scientificamerican.com/article/intervention-at-an-early-age-may-hold-off-the-onset-of-depression.

Chapter 4

1. Geoffrey Skelley, "Biden Has Lost Support Across All Groups of Americans—but Especially Independents and Hispanics," *FiveThirtyEight*, October 21, 2021, https://fivethirtyeight.com/features/biden-has-lost-support-across-all-groups-of-americans-but-especially-independents-and-hispanics/?ex_cid=538fb.

2. Greg L. Stewart and Amit K. Nandkeolyar, "Exploring How Constraints Created by Other People Influence Intraindividual Variation in Objective Performance Measures," *Journal of Applied Psychology* 92, no. 4 (2007): 1149–58, https://doi.org/10.1037/0021-9010.92.4.1149.

3. Geir Jordet, Esther Hartman, Chris Visscher, and Koen A. P. M. Lemmink, "Kicks

from the Penalty Mark in Soccer: The Roles of Stress, Skill, and Fatigue for Kick Out-comes," *Journal of Sports Sciences* 5, no. 2 (2007): 121–29; Tjerk Moll, Geir Jorrdet, and Gert-Jan Pepping, "Emotional Contagion in Soccer Penalty Shootouts: Celebration of Individual Success Is Associated with Ultimate Team Success," *Journal of Sports Sciences* 28, no. 9 (2010): 983–92, https://doi.org/10.1080/02640414.2010.484068; also, Ben Cohen, "A Psychologist Spent Five Years Studying World Cup Penalty Shootouts," *Wall Street Journal*, December 9, 2022, https://www.wsj.com/articles/world-cup-penalty-kick -shootout-geir-jordet-11670449695.

4. For an interesting study on transitions see, Karalyn F. Enz, David B. Pillemer, and Kenneth M. Johnson, "The Relocation Bump: Memories of Middle Adulthood Are Or-ganized Around Residential Moves," *Journal of Experimental Psychology: General* 145, no. 8 (2016): 935–40, https://doi.org/10.1037/xge0000188.

5. David A. Kolb, *Experiential Learning* (Pearson FT Press, 2014).

6. Kolb, *Experiential Learning*.

7. NPR, "Tom Hanks Says Self-Doubt Is 'A High-Wire Act That We All Walk,'" April 26, 2016, http://wwno.org/post/tom-hanks-says-self-doubt-high-wire-act-we-all-walk-0.

8. For a detailed research review of the STOP method of mindfulness see, Yanhui Liao, Ling Wang, Tao Luo, Shiyou Wu, Zhenzhen Wu, Jianhua Chen, Chen Pan, et al., "Brief Mindfulness-Based Intervention of 'STOP (Stop, Take a Breath, Observe, Pro-ceed) Touching Your Face': A Study Protocol of a Randomised Controlled Trial," *BMJ Open* 10, no. 11 (2020), https://doi.org/10.1136/bmjopen-2020-041364.

9. For examples of Djokovic, see "Novak Djokovic: The 60 Minutes Interview." You-Tube, December 11, 2023, https://www.youtube.com/watch?v=iBxprBcvpSA; Jeff Haden, "Novak Djokovic (and Science) Says It Takes Just 5 Seconds to Decrease Stress, Boost Focus, and Be More Successful, Present, and Happy," *Inc.*, December 19, 2023, https:// www.inc.com/jeff-haden/novak-djokovic-and-science-says-it-takes-just-5-seconds-to -decrease-stress-boost-focus-be-more-successful-present-happy.html.

10. This exercise is based on: D. Scott DeRue and Ned Wellman, "Developing Lead-ers via Experience: The Role of Developmental Challenge, Learning Orientation, and Feedback Availability," *Journal of Applied Psychology* 94, no. 4 (2009): 859–75, https://doi .org/10.1037/a0015317; Kolb, *Experiential Learning*; and Cynthia D. McCauley, Marian N. Ruderman, Patricia J. Ohlott, and Jane E. Morrow, "Assessing the Developmental Com-ponents of Managerial Jobs," *Journal of Applied Psychology* 79, no. 4 (1994): 544–60.

Chapter 5

1. John Dewey, *Education and Experience* (New York: Simon and Schuster, 1938), 27.

2. Cynthia D. McCauley, Marian N. Ruderman, Patricia J. Ohlott, and Jane E. Morrow, "Assessing the Developmental Components of Managerial Jobs," *Journal of Ap-plied Psychology* 79, no. 4 (1994): 544–60, https://doi.org/10.1037/0021-9010.79.4.544.

3. D. Scott DeRue and Ned Wellman, "Developing Leaders via Experience: The Role of Developmental Challenge, Learning Orientation, and Feedback Availability," *Journal of Applied Psychology* 94, no. 4 (2009): 859–75, https://doi.org/10.1037/a0015317.

4. McCauley et al., "Assessing the Developmental Components of Managerial Jobs."

5. , Michael C. Sturman, "Searching for the Inverted U-Shaped Relationship between Time and Performance: Meta-Analyses of the Experience/Performance, Tenure/ Performance, and Age/Performance Relationships," *Journal of Management* 29 (2003): 609–40, https://doi.org/10.1016/S0149-2063(03)00028-X.

6. Gina Dokko, Steffanie L. Wilk, and Nancy P. Rothbard, "Unpacking Prior Experience: How Career History Affects Job Performance," *Organization Science* 20, no. 1 (2009): 51–68, https://doi.org/10.1287/orsc.1080.0357.

7. Matthew Fisher and Frank C. Keil, "The Curse of Expertise: When More Knowledge Leads to Miscalibrated Explanatory Insight," *Cognitive Science* 40 (2016): 1251–1269, https://doi.org/10.1111/cogs.12280.

8. Anders Ericsson, *The Cambridge Handbook of Expertise and Expert Performance* (Cambridge: Cambridge University Press, 2018); Malcolm Gladwell, *Outliers: The Story of Success* (New York: Little, Brown and Company, 2008).

9. Brooke N. Macnamara, David Z. Hambrick, and Frederick L. Oswald, "Deliberate Practice and Performance in Music, Games, Sports, Education, and Professions: A Meta-Analysis," *Psychological Science* 25, no. 8 (2014): 1608–18, https://doi.org/10.1177/095679 7614535810.

10. Giovanni B. Moneta, "Cognitive Flow," in *Encyclopedia of Animal Cognition and Behavior*, ed. J. Vonk and T. Shackelford, 1–5 (Cham: Springer, 2018), https://doi.org/10 .1007/978-3-319-47829-6_1587-2. See also Giovanni B. Moneta and Mihaly Csikszentmihalyi, "The Effect of Perceived Challenges and Skills on the Quality of Subjective Experience," *Journal of Personality* 64, no. 2 (1996): 275–310, https://doi.org/10.1111/j.1467-64 94.1996.tb00512.x.

11. "How Free Solo Climber Alex Honnold Faces Fear" (transcript), TED, accessed January 30, 2024, https://www.ted.com/podcasts/how-free-solo-climber-alex-honnold -faces-fear-transcript.

12. Moneta and Csikszentmihalyi, "The Effect of Perceived Challenges and Skills."

13. Moneta and Csikszentmihalyi, "The Effect of Perceived Challenges and Skills."

14. Todd Martens, "'Zelda' Keeps Things Wild at Gaming Expo," *Baltimore Sun and Tribune*, June 14, 2016, https://digitaledition.baltimoresun.com/tribune/article_ popover.aspx?guid=2d1a94d0-b7b3-49b6-80a1-a36e57f835db.

15. Suzy Fox and Paul E. Spector, "A Model of Work Frustration-Aggression," *Journal of Organizational Behavior* 20, no. 6 (1999): 915–31, https://doi.org/10.1002/(sici)1099-1379(19 9911)20:6<915::aid-job918>3.3.co;2-y; Birgit Abler, Henrik Walter, and Susanne Erk, "Neural Correlates of Frustration," *NeuroReport* 16, no. 7 (2005): 669–72, https://doi.org/ 10.1097/00001756-200505120-00003.

16. Joshua D. Berke, "What Does Dopamine Mean?" *Nature Neuroscience* 21, no. 6 (2018): 787–93, https://doi.org/10.1038/s41593-018-0152-y.

17. Martin Zack, Ross St. George, and Luke Clark, "Dopaminergic Signaling of Uncertainty and the Aetiology of Gambling Addiction," *Progress in Neuro-Psychopharma-*

cology and Biological Psychiatry 99 (2020): 109853, https://doi.org/10.1016/j.pnpbp.2019
.109853.

18. Iddo Mayan and Nachshon Meiran, "Anger and the Speed of Full-Body Approach
and Avoidance Reactions," *Frontiers in Psychology* 2 (2011), https://doi.org/10.3389/fpsyg
.2011.00022; R. James Blair, "Psychopathy, Frustration, and Reactive Aggression: The
Role of Ventromedial Prefrontal Cortex," *British Journal of Psychology* 101, no. 3 (2010):
383–99, https://doi.org/10.1348/000712609x418480.

19. Dustin Scheinost, Javid Dadashkarimi, Emily S. Finn, Caroline G. Wambach,
Caroline MacGillivray, Alexandra L. Roule, Tara A. Niendam, et al., "Functional Connectivity During Frustration: A Preliminary Study of Predictive Modeling of Irritability
in Youth," *Neuropsychopharmacology* 46, no. 7 (2021): 1300–1306, https://doi.org/10.1038
/s41386-020-00954-8.

20. Diogo S. Teixeira, Marlene N. Silva, and António L. Palmeira, "How Does Frustration Make You Feel? A Motivational Analysis in Exercise Context," *Motivation and
Emotion* 42, no. 3 (2018): 419–28, https://doi.org/10.1007/s11031-018-9690-6.

21. Kate Whalen, "Beginners 101: How to Confront and Overcome the Discomfort of
Starting Something New," The Conversation, October 20, 2023, https://theconversation
.com/beginners-101-how-to-confront-and-overcome-the-discomfort-of-starting
-something-new-157110; David M. Tokar, Taneisha S. Buchanan, Linda M. Subich, Rosa-
lie J. Hall, and Christine M. Williams, "A Structural Examination of the Learning Experiences Questionnaire," *Journal of Vocational Behavior* 80, no. 1 (2012): 50–66, https://doi
.org/10.1016/j.jvb.2011.08.003.

22. Moneta and Csikszentmihalyi, "The Effect of Perceived Challenges and Skills."

23. See Maxim Voronov and Russ Vince, "Integrating Emotions into the Analysis of
Institutional Work," *Academy of Management Review* 37, no. 1 (2012): 58–81, https://doi
.org/10.5465/amr.2010.0247; Diane Coutu, "The Anxiety of Learning," *Harvard Business
Review*, March 2002, https://hbr.org/2002/03/the-anxiety-of-learning.

24. Daniel J. Beal, Howard M. Weiss, Eduardo Barros, and Shelley M. MacDermid,
"An Episodic Process Model of Affective Influences on Performance," *Journal of Applied
Psychology* 90, no. 6 (2005), 1054–68, https://doi.org/10.1037/0021-9010.90.6.1054.

25. David Schwandt 2017 "Karl E. Weick: Departing from Traditional Rational
Models of Organizational Change," in *The Palgrave Handbook of Organizational Change
Thinkers*, ed. David B. Szabla, William A. Pasmore, Mary A. Barnes, and Asha N. Gipson,
1415–31.

26. https://www.npr.org/2018/03/05/590963450/u-god-pod. For a review of his autobiography, see: https://www.theguardian.com/books/2018/mar/17/raw-by-lamont-u-god
-hawkins-review-wu-tang-clan. See also: https://www.newyorker.com/books/page
-turner/the-unexpectedly-moving-story-of-u-god-the-least-loved-member-of-the-wu
-tang-clan.

27. This exercise is adopted from a variety of sources: Stephen Denning, *The Leader's
Guide to Storytelling: Mastering the Art and Discipline of Business Narrative* (San Fran-

cisco: Jossey-Bass, 2011) provides a comprehensive application of storytelling techniques to leaders. The *Harvard Business Review* provides regular articles on storytelling, including Bronwyn Fryer, "Storytelling That Moves People," *Harvard Business Review*, August 1, 2014, https://hbr.org/2003/06/storytelling-that-moves-people; and John Hamm, "The Five Messages Leaders Must Manage," *Harvard Business Review*, July 14, 2015, https://hbr.org/2006/05/the-five-messages-leaders-must-manage.

Chapter 6

1. See for more details, Leonard Mlodinow, "What We Get Wrong About Emotions," *The Atlantic*, January 4, 2022, https://www.theatlantic.com/family/archive/2022/01/emotion-isnt-the-enemy-of-reason/621148/.

2. Joseph E. LeDoux and Richard Brown, "A Higher-Order Theory of Emotional Consciousness," *Proceedings of the National Academy of Sciences of the United States of America* 114, no. 10 (2017): E2016–E2025.

3. Myeong-Gu Seo, Lisa Feldman Barrett, and Jean M. Bartunek, "The Role of Affective Experience in Work Motivation," *Academy of Management Review* 29, no. 3 (2004): 423–39, https://doi.org/10.5465/amr.2004.13670972.

4. Seo, Barrett, and, Bartunek, "The Role of Affective Experience in Work Motivation," 426.

5. Linguistic Inquiry and Word Count, LIWC-22, available at https://www.liwc.app.

6. Seo, Barrett, and, Bartunek, "The Role of Affective Experience in Work Motivation," 424.

7. Lisa Quadt, Sarah N. Garfinkel, James S. Mulcahy, Dennis E.O. Larsson, Marta Silva, Anna-Marie Jones, Clara Strauss, and Hugo D. Critchley, "Interoceptive Training to Target Anxiety in Autistic Adults (ADIE): A Single-Center, Superiority Randomized Controlled Trial," *EClinicalMedicine* 39 (2021): 101042. https://doi.org/10.1016/j.eclinm.2021.101042.

8. Fuli Li, Tingting Chen, Nancy Yi-Feng Chen, Yun Bai, and J. Michael Crant, "Proactive Yet Reflective? Materializing Proactive Personality into Creativity Through Job Reflective Learning and Activated Positive Affective States," *Personnel Psychology* 73, no. 3 (2019): 459–89, https://doi.org/10.1111/peps.12370; Wolf E. Mehling, Michael Acree, Anita Stewart, Jonathan Silas, and Alexander Jones, "The Multidimensional Assessment of Interoceptive Awareness, Version 2 (Maia-2)," *PLOS ONE*, accessed January 15, 2024, https://doi.org/10.1371/journal.pone.0208034; João Medeiros, "Listening to Your Heart Might Be the Key to Conquering Anxiety," *Wired*, October 20, 2020, https://www.wired.co.uk/article/sarah-garfinkel-interoception.

9. For intelligence: D. Goleman, R. E. Boyatzis, and A. McKee, *Primal Leadership: Unleashing the Power of Emotional Intelligence* (Boston: Harvard Business School Press, 2016); Yuntao Dong, Myeong-Gu Seo, and Kathryn M. Bartol, "No Pain, No Gain: An Affect-Based Model of Developmental Job Experience and the Buffering Effects of Emotional Intelligence," *Academy of Management Journal* 57, no. 4 (2014): 1056–77, https://doi.org/10.5465/amj.2011.0687.

10. Vivianna Fang He, Charlotta Sirén, Sheetal Singh, George Solomon, and Georg von Krogh, "Keep Calm and Carry On: Emotion Regulation in Entrepreneurs' Learning from Failure," *Entrepreneurship Theory and Practice* 42, no. 4 (2018): 605–30, https://doi .org/10.1177/1042258718783428; Dong, Seo, and Bartol, "No Pain, No Gain."

11. Jared B. Torre and Matthew D. Lieberman, "Putting Feelings into Words: Affect Labeling as Implicit Emotion Regulation," *Emotion Review* 10, no. 2 (2018): 116–24, https:// doi.org/10.1177/1754073917742706; Matthew D. Lieberman, Naomi I. Eisenberger, Molly J. Crockett, Sabrina M. Tom, Jennifer H. Pfeifer, and Baldwin M. Way, "Putting Feelings into Words," *Psychological Science* 18, no. 5 (2007): 421–28, https://doi.org/10.1111/j.1467-9280 .2007.01916.x; Daniel J. Beal, Howard M. Weiss, Eduardo Barros, and Shelley M. MacDer- mid, "An Episodic Process Model of Affective Influences on Performance," *Journal of Ap- plied Psychology* 90, no. 6 (2005): 1054–68, https://doi.org/10.1037/0021-9010.90.6.1054.

12. Vivian Kraaij and Nadia Garnefski, "The Behavioral Emotion Regulation Ques- tionnaire: Development, Psychometric Properties and Relationships with Emotional Problems and the Cognitive Emotion Regulation Questionnaire," *Personality and Indi- vidual Differences* 137 (January 2019): 56–61, https://doi.org/10.1016/j.paid.2018.07.036.

13. Barbara L. Fredrickson, "The Role of Positive in Positive Psychology: The Broaden-and-Build Theory of Positive Emotions," *American Psychologist* 54: no. 3 (2001), https://doi.org/10.1037%2F%2F0003-066x.56.3.218.

14. Ed Diener and Robert A. Emmons, "The Independence of Positive and Negative Affect," *Journal of Personality and Social Psychology* 47, no. 5 (1984): 1105–17, https://doi. org/10.1037//0022-3514.47.5.1105.

15. D. Christopher Kayes, Philip W. Wirtz, and Jing Burgi-Tian, "Overcoming Un- pleasant Affective Experiences While Learning: Latent Profiles of Resilience While Learning," *Journal of Management Development*, January 24, 2024, https://doi.org/10.11 08/jmd-05-2022-0121.

16. Kaplan, Van Damme, and Levine, "Motivation Matters."

17. Paul Bloom, "Hedonism Is Overrated—To Make the Best of Life There Must Be Pain, Says This Yale Professor," *The Guardian*, January 23, 2022, https://www.theguardian .com/lifeandstyle/2022/jan/23/hedonism-is-overrated-to-make-the-best-of-life-there -must-be-pain-says-yale-professor.

18. Sandra J. Langeslag and Michelle E. Sanchez, "Down-Regulation of Love Feel- ings After a Romantic Break-Up: Self-Report and Electrophysiological Data," *Journal of Experimental Psychology: General* 147, no. 5 (2018): 720–33, https://doi.org/10.1037/xge00 00360.

19. Eric N. Smith, Michael D. Young, and Alia J. Crum, "Stress, Mindsets, and Suc- cess in Navy Seals Special Warfare Training," *Frontiers in Psychology* 10 (2020), https:// doi.org/10.3389/fpsyg.2019.02962.

20. Jamie Waters, "How to Learn the Trick of Confidence" *The Guardian*, January 9, 2022, https://www.theguardian.com/lifeandstyle/2022/jan/09/how-to-learn-the-trick -of-confidence, based on Nathaniel Zinsser, *The Confident Mind: A Battle-Tested Guide to Unshakable Performance* (London: Penguin Books, 2023).

21. Matthew Eriksen, "On Facilitating the Development of Leaders' Ability to Exercise Good Judgment," in *Judgment and Leadership*, ed. A. Kayes and D. C. Kayes, 192–202 (Cheltenham, UK: Edward Elgar: 2021).

22. Dean A. Shepherd, Holger Patzelt, and Marcus Wolfe, "Moving Forward from Project Failure: Negative Emotions, Affective Commitment, and Learning from the Experience," *Academy of Management Journal* 54, no. 6 (2011): 1229–59, https://doi.org/10.5465/amj.2010.0102.

23. Michael Jarrett and Russ Vince, "Mitigating Anxiety: The Role of Strategic Leadership Groups During Radical Organisational Change," *Human Relations*, April 27, 2023, https://doi.org/10.1177/00187267231169143.

24. Jarrett and Vince, "Mitigating Anxiety."

25. Natalia Vuori, Timo O. Vuori, and Quy N. Huy, "Emotional Practices: How Masking Negative Emotions Impacts the Post-acquisition Integration Process," *Strategic Management Journal* 39, no. 3 (2017): 859–93, https://doi.org/10.1002/smj.2729; Joseph P. Forgas and Rebekah East, "On Being Happy and Gullible: Mood Effects on Skepticism and the Detection of Deception," *Journal of Experimental Social Psychology* 44, no. 5 (2008): 1362–67, https://doi.org/10.1016/j.jesp.2008.04.010.

26. For more on the role of negative emotions, see Lew Hardy and Andrew Hutchinson, "Effects of Performance Anxiety on Effort and Performance in Rock Climbing: A Test of Processing Efficiency Theory," *Anxiety, Stress, and Coping* 20, no. 2 (2007): 147–61, https://doi.org/10.1080/10615800701217035; Tori Rodriguez, "Negative Emotions Are Key to Well-Being," *Scientific American*, May 1, 2013, https://www.scientificamerican.com/article/negative-emotions-key-well-being; W. G. Parrott, ed., *The Positive Side of Negative Emotions* (New York: Guilford Press, 2014); for more on negative emotions related to stress, see Jiaxuan Du, Jiali Huang, Yuanyuan An, and Wei Xu, "The Relationship Between Stress and Negative Emotion: The Mediating Role of Rumination," *Clinical Research and Trials* 4, no. 1 (2018), https://doi.org/10.15761/crt.1000208.

27. Guy Winch, "How to Recover from Romantic Heartbreak," *Scientific American*, May 5, 2020, https://www.scientificamerican.com/article/how-to-recover-from-romantic-heartbreak/.

28. Kathleen A. Garrison, Dustin Scheinost, Patrick D. Worhunsky, Hani M. Elwafi, Thomas A. Thornhill, Evan Thompson, Clifford Saron, et al., "Real-Time fMRI Links Subjective Experience with Brain Activity During Focused Attention," *NeuroImage* 81 (2013): 110–18, https://doi.org/10.1016/j.neuroimage.2013.05.030; Shamani Joshi, "How to Not Be Boring, According to a Psychologist Who Researches Boredom," *Vice*, April 7, 2022, https://www.vice.com/en/article/z3n7w8/scientist-studies-boredom-boring-people-jobs-psychology; Todd B. Kashdan and Paul J. Silvia, "Curiosity and Interest: The Benefits of Thriving on Novelty and Challenge," in *The Oxford Handbook of Positive Psychology*, ed. C. R. Snyder, S. J. Lopez, L. M. Edwards, and S. C. Marques, 482–92 (Oxford: Oxford University Press, 2021).

29. Wijnand A. van Tilburg and Eric R. Igou, "Boredom Begs to Differ: Differentiation from Other Negative Emotions," *Emotion* 17, no. 2 (2017): 309–22, https://doi.org/10

.1037/emo0000233; Wijnand A. van Tilburg and Eric R. Igou, "Can Boredom Help? Increased Prosocial Intentions in Response to Boredom," *Self and Identity* 16, no. 1 (2016): 82–96, https://doi.org/10.1080/15298868.2016.1218925.

30. Parts of this exercise were adapted from Yuntao Dong, Myeong-Gu Seo, and Kathryn M. Bartol, "No Pain, No Gain: An Affect-Based Model of Developmental Job Experience and the Buffering Effects of Emotional Intelligence," *Academy of Management Journal* 57, no. 4 (2014): 1056–77, https://doi.org/10.5465/amj.2011.0687.

Chapter 7

1. These five strategies were first mentioned in D. Christopher Kayes, Jeewan Yoon, and Crystal H. H. Tsay, "Five Routines That Help Leaders Learn," *Organizational Dynamics* 52, no. 3 (2023): 100991, https://doi.org/10.1016/j.orgdyn.2023.100991. For theoretical and research support for these factors see, D. Christopher Kayes and Jeewan Yoon, "Learning Routines That Build Organizational Resilience, in *Handbook of Organizational Resilience*, ed. Ned Powley, Brianna Caza, and Arran Caza Edward, 203–13 (Elgar Press, 2020).

2. Ayelet Fishbach, *Get It Done* (New York: Little, Brown, 2012); A. Fishbach and J. Choi, "When Thinking About Goals Undermines Goal Pursuit," *Organizational Behavior and Human Decision Processes* 118 (2012): 99–107.

3. George Loewenstein, "The Psychology of Curiosity: A Review and Reinterpretation," *Psychological Bulletin* 116, no. 1 (1994): 75–98, https://doi.org/10.1037//0033-2909.116.1.75.

4. Alicea Lieberman, "Research: How to Power Through Boring Tasks," *Harvard Business Review*, April 28, 2022, https://hbr.org/2022/04/research-how-to-power-through-boring-tasks?utm_source=pocket-newtab; P. A. O'Keefe, C. S. Dweck, and G. M. Walton, "Implicit Theories of Interest: Finding Your Passion or Developing It," *Psychological Science* 29 (2018): 1653–64.

5. Reeve, Charlie L. Reeve, and Milton D. Hakel,. "Toward an Understanding of Adult Intellectual Development: Investigating Within-Individual Convergence of Interest and Knowledge Profiles,." *Journal of Applied Psychology* 85, no. 6 (2000): 897–908,. https://doi.org/10.1037//0021-9010.85.6.897

6. Kang, Min Jeong, Ming Hsu, Ian M. Krajbich, George Loewenstein, Samuel M. McClure, Joseph Tao-yi Wang, and Colin F. Camerer. "The Wick in the Candle of Learning." *Psychological Science* 20, no. 8 (August 2009): 963–73.

7. Tom Foster, "The Rewards of Risk: Mark Fitzloff, a Top Player in the Ad Game, Reveals His Secrets to Creativity and Connectivity," *Men's Health*, January/February 2017, 40–41, https://gshslinn.weebly.com/uploads/2/9/1/8/2918373/the_rewards_of_risk.pdf; see also Robert Siegel (host) and T. Frank, "Imagine This: A Super Bowl Ad for the Government," *All Things Considered*, February 4, 2011, https://www.npr.org/2011/02/04/133504071/Imagine-This-A-Super-Bowl-Ad-For-The-Government.

8. Francis Ford Coppola, "Francis Ford Coppola on Family, Fulfillment, and Breaking the Rules" [podcast], *Harvard Business Review*, 2011, https://hbr.org/podcast/2011/09/francis-ford-coppola-on-family.

9. Tammy Sihna and Manu Kapur, "When Problem-Solving Followed by Instruction Works: Evidence for Productive Failure," *Review of Educational Research* 91 no. 5 (2021): 761–98.

10. Robert S. Siegler, *Emerging Minds: The Process of Change in Children's Thinking* (New York: Oxford University Press, 2020).

11. Li et al., "Proactive yet Reflective?"

12. Mai Trinh, "Learning Identity, Flexibility, and Lifelong Experiential Learning," in *Oxford Research Encyclopedia of Business and Management* (New York: Oxford University Press, 2019).

13. Carol S. Dweck, "Motivational Processes Affecting Learning," *American Psychologist* 41 (1986): 1040–48.

14. Charalampos Mainemelis, Richard E. Boyatzis, and David A. Kolb. "Learning Styles and Adaptive Flexibility," *Management Learning* 33, no. 1 (March 2002): 5–33, https://doi.org/10.1177/1350507602331001.

15. D. Scott DeRue, Susan J. Ashforth, and Christopher G. Myers, "Learning Agility: In Search of Conceptual Clarity and Theoretical Grounding," *Industrial and Organizational Psychology* 5 (2012): 258–79.

16. George A. Bonanno, "The Resilience Paradox," *European Journal of Psychotraumatology* 12, no. 1 (2021), https://doi.org/10.1080/20008198.2021.1942642.

17. Yuen Lam Bavik, Jason D. Shaw, and Xiao-Hua (Frank) Wang, "Social Support: Multidisciplinary Review, Synthesis, and Future Agenda," *Academy of Management Annals* 14, no. 2 (July 2020): 726–58.

18. Ericsson, K. A. Ericsson, ed., *The Cambridge Handbook of Expertise and Expert Performance* (Cambridge, UK: Cambridge University Press, 2018); Ericsson, K. A. Ericsson, and A. C. Lehmann., "Expert and Exceptional Performance: Evidence of Maximal Adaptation to Task Constraints.," *Annual Review of Psychology* 47, no. 1 (February 1996): 273–305., https://doi.org/10.1146/annurev.psych.47.1.273. See also, Boyatzis, Richard E. Boyatzis, Melvin Smith, and Ellen Van Oosten, *Helping People Change: Coaching with Compassion for Lifelong Learning and Growth* (Cambridge, MA: Harvard University Press, 2019) and S. Cohen and T. A. Wills, "Stress, Social Support, and the Buffering Hypothesis," *Psychological Bulletin* 98 (1985): 310–57.

19. Katy Milkman, *How to Change* (New York: Portfolio, 2021); Wendy Wood, *Good Habits, Bad Habits: The Science of Making Positive Changes That Stick* (New York: Macmillan, 2019).

20. Aviva Romm, *The Adrenal Thyroid Revolution: A Proven 4-Week Program to Rescue Your Metabolism, Hormones, Mind and Mood* (HarperOne, 2017). Ellen J. Langer, *Mindfulness* (Boston: Da Capo Press, 1989).

21. Carol Dweck, *Mindset—Changing the Way You Think to Fulfill Your Potential,* updated ed. (Little, Brown Book Group, 2017).

22. K. Anders Ericsson and Kyle W. Harwell, "Deliberate Practice and Proposed Limits on the Effects of Practice on the Acquisition of Expert Performance: Why the

Original Definition Matters and Recommendations for Future Research," *Frontiers in Psychology* 10 (October 25, 2019), https://doi.org/10.3389/fpsyg.2019.02396.

23. Adapted from D. Christopher Kayes, Philip W. Wirtz, and Jing Burgi-Tian, "Overcoming Unpleasant Affective Experiences While Learning: Latent Profiles of Resilience While Learning," *Journal of Management Development*, January 24, 2024, https://doi.org/10.1108/jmd-05-2022-0121.

Chapter 8

1. Kay Peterson, "Leaders, Learn How to Learn Leadership," *Forbes Coaches Council,* February 25, 2019, https://www.forbes.com/sites/forbescoachescouncil/2019/02/25/leaders-learn-how-to-learn/?sh=e3ca060406d3.

2. See Scott Barry Kaufman, *Transcend: The New Science of Self-Actualization* (New York: TarcherPerigee, 2021). For self-determination theory see, R. M., Ryan and E. L. Deci, *Self-Determination Theory: Basic Psychological Needs in Motivation, Development, and Wellness* (Guilford Press, 2017), https://doi.org/10.1521/978.14625/28806; and Daniel Pink, *Drive* (New York: Riverhead, 2011).

3. James Zull, *From Brain to Mind*, 19th ed. (Sterling, VA: Stylus, 2011).

4. Brian Kolb, Grazyna Gorny, Yilin Li, Y., Anna-Noel Samaha, and Terry E. Robinson. (2003). Amphetamine or Cocaine Limits the Ability of Later Experience to Promote Structural Plasticity in the Neocortex and Nucleus Accumbens, *Proceedings of the National Academy of Sciences* 100, no. 18 (2003): 10523–28, https://doi.org/10.1073/pnas.1834271100, as recounted in Anna Lembke, *Dopamine Nation* (New York: Dutton, 2021).

5. Mary-Frances O'Connor, *The Grieving Brain: The Surprising Science of How We Learn from Love and Loss* (San Francisco: HarperCollins, 2023). Kristen Martin, "'The Body Keeps the Score' Offers Uncertain Science in the Name of Self-Help. It's Not Alone," *Washington Post*, August 2, 2023, https://www.washingtonpost.com/books/2023/08/02/body-keeps-score-grieving-brain-bessel-van-der-kolk-neuroscience-self-help/.

6. For the mechanisms of prediction error see, Joshua D. Berke, "What Does Dopamine Mean?" *Nature Neuroscience* 21, no. 6 (2018): 787–93, https://doi.org/10.1038/s41593-018-0152-y.

7. Robert M. Sapolsky, *Why Zebras Don't Get Ulcers: The Acclaimed Guide to Stress, Stress-Related Diseases, and Coping* (New York: Henry Holt and Co., 2004).

8. Teresa Amabile and Steven J. Kramer, *The Progress Principle* (Cambridge, MA: Harvard Business School Press, 2011).

9. Andrew Jenkins and Tarek Mostafa, "The Effects of Learning on Wellbeing for Older Adults in England," *Ageing and Society* 35, no. 10 (2014): 2053–70, https://doi.org/10.1017/s0144686x14000762.

10. Andrew Jenkins, "Participation in Learning and Wellbeing Among Older Adults," *International Journal of Lifelong Education* 30, no. 3 (2011): 403–20, https://doi.org/10.1080/02601370.2011.570876.

11. K. Anders Ericsson, Ralf T. Krampe, and Clemens Tesch-Römer, "The Role of De-

liberate Practice in the Acquisition of Expert Performance," *Psychological Review* 100, no. 3 (1993): 363–406, https://doi.org/10.1037//0033-295x.100.3.363. See also, R. E. Boyatzis, M. L. Smith, and E. B. Van Oosten, *Helping People Change: Coaching with Compassion for Lifelong Learning and Growth* (Cambridge, MA: Harvard Business Review Press, 2019).

12. George Loewenstein, "The Psychology of Curiosity: A Review and Reinterpretation," *Psychological Bulletin* 116, no. 1 (1994): 75–98, https://doi.org/10.1037//0033-2909.116.1.75.

13. Berke, "What Does Dopamine Mean?"

14. For adaptive adequacy and how the term is used in research see, Geoffrey L. Cohen and David K. Sherman, "The Psychology of Change: Self-Affirmation and Social Psychological Intervention," *Annual Review of Psychology* 65, no. 1 (2014): 333–71, https://doi.org/10.1146/annurev-psych-010213-115137.

15. Johannes H. Decker, Frederico S. Lourenco, Bradley B. Doll, and Catherine A. Hartley, "Experiential Reward Learning Outweighs Instruction Prior to Adulthood," *Cognitive, Affective, and Behavioral Neuroscience* 15, no. 2 (2015): 310–20, https://doi.org/10.3758/s13415-014-0332-5.

16. David A. Kolb, *Experiential Learning* (Pearson FT Press, 2014).

17. George A. Bonanno, "The Resilience Paradox," *European Journal of Psychotraumatology* 12, no. 1 (2021), https://doi.org/10.1080/20008198.2021.1942642.

18. Shanthi Rexaline, "Elon Musk vs. Tim Cook Feud Gets Over in a Heartbeat: Analyst Says We Were Just Served 'Masterclass in Crisis Management,'" Benzinga, December 2, 2022, https://www.benzinga.com/analyst-ratings/analyst-color/22/12/29935877/elon-musk-vs-tim-cook-feud-gets-over-in-a-heartbeat-analyst-says-we-were-just-serve. Bill Murphy, "Elon Musk Just Deleted His 'Go to War' Tweet About Apple. But the Battle Has Already Begun," *Inc.*, November 29, 2022, https://www.inc.com/bill-murphy-jr/elon-musk-just-deleted-his-go-to-war-tweet-about-apple-can-you-guess-1-thing-thats-missing.html. Patrick McGee, "Tim Cook Charm Resolves Twitter Spat Yet China Crisis Rumbles On," *Financial Times*, December 2, 2022, https://www.ft.com/content/c2a96807-f931-4c14-bd31-b213d9c41c45. Kate Conger and Tripp Mickle, "Elon Musk Says 'Misunderstanding' with Apple Is Resolved," *New York Times*, November 30, 2022, https://www.nytimes.com/2022/11/30/technology/elon-musk-apple-misunderstanding.html?action=click&module=RelatedLinks&pgtype=Article.

Chapter 9

1. Jaya Saxena, "No One Has What It Takes to Lead Margaritaville," Eater, December 13, 2023, https://www.eater.com/24000211/margaritaville-times-square-director-of-operations-job-description.

2. Jason Marsh, "Is Attention the Secret to Emotional Intelligence?" Greater Good, accessed January 14, 2024, https://greatergood.berkeley.edu/article/item/is_attention_the_secret_to_emotional_intelligence.

3. Lea Winerman, "Suppressing the 'White Bears,'" *APA Monitor*, October 2011, https://www.apa.org/monitor/2011/10/unwanted-thoughts.

4. Michael B. Reid and J. Timothy Lightfoot, "The Physiology of Auto Racing," *Medicine and Science in Sports and Exercise* 51, no. 12 (2019): 2548–62, https://doi.org/10.1249/mss.0000000000002070.

5. "Arie Crashes in Indy Finale." CBS News, December 13, 1999, https://www.cbsnews.com/news/arie-crashes-in-indy-finale/.

6. Zach Shipstead, Tyler L. Harrison, and Randall W. Engle, "Working Memory Capacity and Fluid Intelligence," *Perspectives on Psychological Science* 11, no. 6 (2016): 771–99, https://doi.org/10.1177/1745691616650647.

7. Cal Newport has a number of books and a popular blog on the topic of focus. See Cal Newport, *Deep Work: Rules for Focused Success in a Distracted World* (New York: Grand Central, 2023).

8. Allison Gabriel, Charles Calderwood, Andrew A. Bennett, Elena M. Wong, Jason J. Dahling, and John P. Trougakos, "Examining Recovery Experiences Among Working College Students: A Person-Centered Study," *Journal of Vocational Behavior* 115: 103329, https://doi.org/10.1016/j.jvb.2019.103329.

9. Selina Platte, Ulrich Wiesmann, Richard G. Tedeschi, and Doris Kehl, "Coping and Rumination as Predictors of Posttraumatic Growth and Depreciation," *Chinese Journal of Traumatology* 25, no. 5 (2022): 264–71, https://doi.org/10.1016/j.cjtee.2022.02.001.

10. Michael J. Kane, Georgina M. Gross, Charlotte A. Chun, Bridget A. Smeekens, Matt E. Meier, Paul J. Silvia, and Thomas R. Kwapil, "For Whom the Mind Wanders, and When, Varies Across Laboratory and Daily-Life Settings," *Psychological Science* 28, no. 9 (2017): 1271–89, https://doi.org/10.1177/0956797617706086.

11. Mitsue Nagamine, Hiroko Noguchi, Nobuaki Takahashi, Yoshiharu Kim, and Yutaka Matsuoka, "Effect of Cortisol Diurnal Rhythm on Emotional Memory in Healthy Young Adults," *Scientific Reports* 7, no. 1 (2017), https://doi.org/10.1038/s41598-017-10002-z; Katie O'Donnell, Ellena Badrick, Meena Kumari, and Andrew Steptoe, "Psychological Coping Styles and Cortisol over the Day in Healthy Older Adults," *Psychoneuroendocrinology* 33, no. 5 (June 2008): 601–11, https://doi.org/10.1016/j.psyneuen.2008.01.015.

12. Kierstan Boyd, "Computers, Digital Devices and Eye Strain," American Academy of Ophthalmology, August 8, 2023, https://www.aao.org/eye-health/tips-prevention/computer-usage.

13. D. Christopher Kayes and Jeewhan Yoon, "Cognitive Offloading Strategies and Decrements in Learning: Lessons from Aviation and Aerospace Crises," *Journal of Human Performance in Extreme Environments* 17, no. 1 (2022), https://doi.org/10.7771/2327-2937.1146.

14. Robert M. Sapolsky, *Why Zebras Don't Get Ulcers: The Acclaimed Guide to Stress, Stress-Related Diseases, and Coping* (New York: Henry Holt and Co., 2004).

15. Erin Westgate and Timothy D. Wilson, "Boring Thoughts and Bored Minds: The Mac Model of Boredom and Cognitive Engagement," *Psychological Review* 125, no. 5 (2018): 689–713, https://doi.org/10.1037/rev0000097.

16. I first heard about the ADHD study on the Andrew Huberman podcast: "ADHD and How Anyone Can Improve Their Focus," Huberman Lab Podcast #37, YouTube,

September 13, 2021, https://www.youtube.com/watch?v=hFL6qRIJZ_Y. The original study: Yi-Jung Lai and Kang-Ming Chang, "Improvement of Attention in Elementary School Students Through Fixation Focus Training Activity," *International Journal of Environmental Research and Public Health* 17, no. 13 (2020): 4780, https://doi.org/10.3390/ ijerph17134780.

17. Cal Newport was quoted in "Don't Quit Booze—Just Drink Differently: 15 Ways to Change Your Life without Trying All That Hard," *The Guardian*, December 30, 2023, https://www.theguardian.com/lifeandstyle/2023/dec/30/dont-quit-booze-just-drink -differently-15-ways-to-change-your-life-without-trying-all-that-hard?ref=mattruther ford.co.uk. Adapted from Cal Newport, *A World Without Email* (London: Penguin, 2021).

18. Robert Sutton, "This Is Why Your Job Is Becoming Impossible to Do," *The Ladders*, November 23, 2017, https://www.theladders.com/career-advice/tragedy-of-organi zational-overload.

19. Alexis B. Castorri and Jane Heller, *Exercise Your Mind: 36 Mental Workouts for Peak Performance* (New York: Citadel Press, 1992).

20. Kayes and Yoon, "Cognitive Offloading Strategies and Decrements in Learning: Lessons from Aviation and Aerospace Crisis."

21. Ingrid Fetell Lee, "Can't Seem to Meditate? 7 Joyful Activities for You to Try Instead," *Ideas.Ted.com*, January 11, 2022, https://ideas.ted.com/cant-seem-to-meditate-7-joy ful-activities-for-you-to-try-instead/?utm_source=pocket-newtab. Tara Swart Bieber and Contributor, "A Neuroscientist Shares the 3 Exercises She Does to Stop Stress and Anxiety-in 'Just a Few Minutes,'" CNBC, December 1, 2022, https://www.cnbc.com/2022/12/ 01/neuroscientist-shares-exercises-she-does-to-instantly-calm-stress-and-anxiety.html.

Chapter 10

1. As told to Walter Isaacson, *Steve Jobs* (New York: Simon & Schuster, 2022).

2. Sigal G. Barsade, "The Ripple Effect: Emotional Contagion and Its Influence on Group Behavior," *Administrative Science Quarterly* 47, no. 4 (2002): 644–75, https://doi. org/10.2307/3094912.

3. Carolina Herrando and Efthymios Constantinides, "Emotional Contagion: A Brief Overview and Future Direction," *Frontiers in Psychology* 12 (2021), https://doi.org/ 10.3389/fpsyg.2021.712606.

4. Emily Crockett, "The Woman Who Inspired Martin Luther King's 'I Have a Dream' Speech." *Vox*, January 18, 2016, https://www.vox.com/2016/1/18/10785882/ martin-luther-king-dream-mahalia-jackson.

Chapter 11

1. Tomi Laamanen, Juha-antti Lamberg, and Eero Vaara, "Explanations of Success and Failure in Management Learning: What Can We Learn from Nokia's Rise and Fall?" *Academy of Management Learning and Education* 15, no. 1 (2016): 2–25, https://doi.org/10 .5465/amle.2013.0177.

2. Based on Myeong-Gu Seo and Lisa Feldman Barrett, "Being Emotional During Decision Making—Good or Bad? An Empirical Investigation," *Academy of Management Journal* 50, no. 4 (August 2007): 923–40, https://doi.org/10.5465/amj.2007.26279217; adapted from Kimberly D. Elsbach, Anna Kayes, and D. Christopher Kayes, eds., *Contemporary Organizational Behavior: From Ideas to Action* (London: Pearson, 2016).

3. Christina Caron, "How to Feel Alive Again," *New York Times*, February 27, 2023, https://www.nytimes.com/2023/02/27/well/mind/katherine-may-enchantment.html?utm_source=pocket-newtab.

4. Johann Hari, "It's Not Your Fault You Can't Pay Attention," *The Ezra Klein Show*, February 11, 2022, https://www.nytimes.com/2022/02/11/opinion/ezra-klein-podcast-johann-hari.html?showTranscript=1.

5. Theodore Kinni, "Pay Attention to Your Attention," Strategy+business, February 10, 2022, https://www.strategy-business.com/blog/Pay-attention-to-your-attention.

6. Ashton Jackson, "Mark Cuban Says 'Good Businesses' Embrace Diversity: 'The Loss of DEI-Phobic Companies Is My Gain,'" CNBC, January 5, 2024, https://www.cnbc.com/2024/01/05/mark-cuban-on-diversity-the-loss-of-dei-phobic-companies-is-my-gain.html.

7. Rob Stumpf, "Elon Musk Wants Tesla Gigafactory Employees to Live on Site in Mobile Homes," The Drive, June 11, 2019, https://www.thedrive.com/news/24163/tesla-looks-to-expand-gigafactory-with-proposed-employee-housing-compound. https://www.travelandleisure.com/disney-affordable-housing-project-central-florida-7483253.

8. Pierre Gurdjian, Thomas Halbeisen, and Kevin Lane, "Why Leadership-Development Programs Fail," *McKinsey Quarterly*, 2014, https://www.mckinsey.com/featured-%20insights/leadership/why-leadership-development-programs-fail; Dennis Tourish, *Management Studies in Crisis: Fraud, Deception and Meaningless Research* (Cambridge: Cambridge University Press, 2019); Joshua Rothman, "Shut Up and Sit Down: Why the Leadership Industry Rules," *New Yorker*, 2016, https://www.newyorker.com/magazine/2016/02/29/our-dangerous-leadership-obsession.

9. Yuntao Dong, Myeong-Gu Seo, and Kathryn M. Bartol, "No Pain, No Gain: An Affect-Based Model of Developmental Job Experience and the Buffering Effects of Emotional Intelligence," *Academy of Management Journal* 57, no. 4 (August 2014): 1056–77, https://doi.org/10.5465/amj.2011.0687; Lisa Dragoni, Paul E. Tesluk, Joyce E. Russell, and In-Sue Oh, "Understanding Managerial Development: Integrating Developmental Assignments, Learning Orientation, and Access to Developmental Opportunities in Predicting Managerial Competencies," *Academy of Management Journal* 52, no. 4 (August 2009): 731–43, https://doi.org/10.5465/amj.2009.43669936; Eduardo Salas, Scott I. Tannenbaum, Kurt Kraiger, and Kimberly A. Smith-Jentsch, "The Science of Training and Development in Organizations," *Psychological Science in the Public Interest* 13, no. 2 (June 2012): 74–101, https://doi.org/10.1177/1529100612436661.

10. Susan Lucas, "Costco Employees Just Voted to Unionize. The Company's Response Is Remarkable," *Inc.*, January 4, 2024, https://www.inc.com/suzanne-lucas/costco-employees-vote-unionize-company-response-remarkable.html.

11. DJ Sixsmith and Alex Sherman, "Disney's Wildest Ride: Inside the Story," CNBC, October 25, 2023, https://www.cnbc.com/video/2023/09/08/disneys-wildest-ride-in side-the-story.html.

12. Nick Vega, "Disney's Bob Iger Says He's Bringing More 'Self-Awareness' in Return to CEO Role," CNBC, February 10, 2023, https://www.cnbc.com/2023/02/09/ disneys-bob-iger-says-success-made-him-dismissive-of-others-ideas.html.

13. Tchiki Davis, *Happiness Skills Workbook* (CreateSpace, 2016).

14. Anna B. Kayes and D. Christopher Kayes, *Judgment and Leadership: A Multidisciplinary Approach to Concepts, Practice, and Development* (Cheltenham, UK; Northampton, MA: Edward Elgar, 2021).

15. R. E. Boyatzis, M. L. Smith, and E. B. Van Oosten, *Helping People Change: Coaching with Compassion for Lifelong Learning and Growth* (Boston: Harvard Business Review Press, 2019).

16. James M. Kouzes and Barry Z. Posner, *The Leadership Challenge: How to Make Extraordinary Things Happen in Organizations* (Hoboken, NJ: Wiley, 2023).

17. David C. Stockwell, D. C. Kayes, and Eric. J. Thomas, "Patient Safety: Where to Aim When Zero Harm Is Not the Target–A Case for Learning and Resilience," *Journal of Patient Safety* 18, no. 5 (2022), https://doi.org/10.1097.

18. Peter Coy, "The Scariest Part About the Boeing 737 MAX 9 Blowout," *New York Times*, January 10, 2024, https://www.nytimes.com/2024/01/10/opinion/boeing-737 -max-alaska-japan-airlines.html; Douglas MacMillan and Michael Laris, "After Midair Failure, Critics Ask: Did Boeing Learn from Max Crashes?" *Washington Post*, January 12, 2024, https://www.washingtonpost.com/business/2024/01/12/boeing-max-safety -crashes/; " 'It Ain't Working': Boeing's Quality Pledges in Question After Max 9 Incident," *Financial Times*, accessed January 15, 2024, https://www.ft.com/content/233d6387 -ebof-4df1-b1e5-8ba3679fdb78.

Chapter 12

1. For the basis of the tiered approach see, Dick Moss, "Sport Psychology: Goal Setting—Try the Three-Tier System." Physical Education Update, April 18, 2011, https:// www.physicaleducationupdate.com/public/Sport_Psychology_Goal_SettingTry_the _ThreeTier_System.cfm. For the research basis to the need for better planning and goal-setting, see C. Townsend and W. Liu, "Is Planning Good for You? The Differential Impact of Planning on Self-Regulation," *Journal of Consumer Research* 39, no. 4 (2012): 688–703, https://doi.org/10.1086/665053.

2. Mark E. Bouton, "Why Behavior Change Is Difficult to Sustain," *Preventive Medicine* 68 (2014): 29–36, https://doi.org/10.1016/j.ypmed.2014.06.010.

3. Ian R. Gellatly and John P. Meyer, "The Effects of Goal Difficulty on Physiological Arousal, Cognition, and Task Performance," *Journal of Applied Psychology* 77, no. 5 (1992): 694–704, https://doi.org/10.1037/0021-9010.77.5.694.

4. I first heard about this study on the Andrew Huberman podcast. Aaron S. Andalman, Vanessa M. Burns, Matthew Lovett-Barron, Michael Broxton, Ben Poole, Samuel J.

Yang, Logan Grosenick, et al., "Neuronal Dynamics Regulating Brain and Behavioral State Transitions," *Cell* 177, no. 4 (2019), https://doi.org/10.1016/j.cell.2019.02.037. For a description of the process see, Yasemin Saplakoglu, "Scientists Watch a Memory Form in a Living Brain," *Quanta Magazine*, March 3, 2022, https://www.quantamagazine.org/scientists-watch-a-memory-form-in-a-living-brain-20220303/.

5. Robin L. Kaplan, Ilse Van Damme, and Linda J. Levine, "Motivation Matters: Differing Effects of Pre-Goal and Post-Goal Emotions on Attention and Memory," *Frontiers in Psychology* 3 (2012), https://doi.org/10.3389/fpsyg.2012.00404

6. Andrew P. Hill and Thomas Curran, "Multidimensional Perfectionism and Burnout: A Meta-Analysis," *Personality and Social Psychology Review* 20, no. 3 (2016): 269–288, https://doi-org.proxygw.wrlc.org/10.1177/1088868315596286.

7. Thomas Curran and Andrew P. Hill, "Perfectionism Is Increasing over Time: A Meta-Analysis of Birth Cohort Differences from 1989 to 2016," *Psychological Bulletin* 145, no. 4 (2019): 410–29, https://doi.org/10.1037/bul0000138.

8. Talya Minsberg and Kevin Quealy, "Why Are American Women Running Faster Than Ever? We Asked Them—Hundreds of Them," *New York Times*, February 28, 2020, https://www.nytimes.com/interactive/2020/02/28/sports/womens-olympic-marathon-trials.html.

9. B. Muniz-Pardos, S. Sutehall, K. Angeloudis, F. M. Guppy, A. Bosch, and Y. Pitsiladis, "Recent Improvements in Marathon Run Times Are Likely Technological, Not Physiological," *Sports Medicine* 51, no. 3 (2021): 371–78, https://doi.org/10.1007/s40279-020-01420-7.

10. Lindsay Crouse, "I Am 35 and Running Faster Than I Ever Thought Possible," *New York Times*, January 31, 2020, https://www.nytimes.com/2020/01/31/opinion/sunday/olympic-runners-women-qualifiers.html.

11. Lindsay Crouse, "How the 'Shalane Flanagan Effect' Works," *New York Times*, November 11, 2017, https://www.nytimes.com/2017/11/11/opinion/sunday/shalane-flanagan-marathon-running.html.

12. Muniz-Pardos et al., "Recent Improvements in Marathon Run Times Are Likely Technological."

13. Rachel Goldsmith Turow, "Five Ways to Feel like You're Doing Enough," Greater Good, accessed January 12, 2024, https://greatergood.berkeley.edu/article/item/five_ways_to_feel_like_youre_doing_enough; Pim Cuijpers, Annemieke van Straten, and Lisanne Warmerdam, "Behavioral Activation Treatments of Depression: A Meta-Analysis," *Clinical Psychology Review* 27, no. 3 (2007): 318–26, https://doi.org/10.1016/j.cpr.2006.11.001.

Conclusion

1. D. Christopher Kayes, Philip W. Wirtz, and Jing Burgi-Tian, "Overcoming Unpleasant Affective Experiences While Learning: Latent Profiles of Resilience While Learning," *Journal of Management Development*, January 24, 2024, https://doi.org/10.1108/jmd-05-2022-0121.

2. Montse C. Ruiz, Yuri Hanin, and Claudio Robazza, "Assessment of Performance-Related Experiences: An Individualized Approach," *Sport Psychologist* 30, no. 3 (2016): 201–18, https://doi.org/10.1123/tsp.2015-0035.

3. D. Christopher Kayes, Jing Bergi-Tian, and Phil W. Wirtz, "Resources for Self-Assessment and Development of Learning Routines and Resilience," Session 882, Academy of Management Annual Meeting, Professional Development Workshop, 2022.

4. Michael J .Wheeler, Daniel J. Green, Kathryn A. Ellis, Ester Cerin, Ilkka Heinonen, Louise H. Naylor, Robyn Larsen, et al., "Distinct Effects of Acute Exercise and Breaks in Sitting on Working Memory and Executive Function in Older Adults: A Three-Arm, Randomised Cross-Over Trial to Evaluate the Effects of Exercise with and without Breaks in Sitting on Cognition," *British Journal of Sports Medicine* 54, no. 13 (2019): 776–81, https://doi.org/10.1136/bjsports-2018-100168.

5. Linda Searing, "Every 2,000 Steps a Day Could Help Keep Premature Death at Bay," *Washington Post*, October 4, 2022, https://www.washingtonpost.com/wellness/2022/10/04/walk-more-steps-live-longer/.

6. Maria A. Åberg, Nancy L. Pedersen, Kjell Torén, Magnus Svartengren, Björn Bäckstrand, Tommy Johnsson, Christiana M. Cooper-Kuhn, N. David Åberg, Michael Nilsson, and H. Georg Kuhn. "Cardiovascular Fitness Is Associated with Cognition in Young Adulthood," *Proceedings of the National Academy of Sciences* 106, no. 49 (2009): 20906–11, https://doi.org/10.1073/pnas.0905307106.

7. Emily Pennington, "6 Ways to Level Up Your Daily Walk," *New York Times*, June 29, 2022, https://www.nytimes.com/2022/06/29/well/move/daily-walk-exercise-fun.html.

8. For a summary of Alistar Humphries, see "A single small map is enough for a lifetime." *Noema*, January 23, 2024. https://www.noemamag.com/a-single-small-map-is-enough-for-a-lifetime/

9. Stanford Medicine, Center on Stress and Health Publications, accessed April 26, 2023, https://med.stanford.edu/stresshealthcenter/publications.html.

Notes on Methods

1. Rebecca Willis, "The Use of Composite Narratives to Present Interview Findings," *Qualitative Research*, 19, no. 4 (2019): 471–80, https://doi-org.proxygw.wrlc.org/10.1177/1468794118787711.

INDEX

activation theory and behavioral
    activation, 182, 189
activity creep, 143
adaptive adequacy, 118–119, 121
ADHD (attention deficit hyperactivity
    disorder), 142–143
affect *see also* emotions, 36, 76, 87–88
Air France Flight 447, 140–141
Airbus, 140
Alcoholics Anonymous, 148
Amabile, Teresa, 118
Amazon, 16, 169
AMD, 25
anxiety: absent from flow, 76; accepting
    and reducing, 36, 38, 77, 144, 178, 186,
    201; essential for learning and growth,
    2, 15, 46, 97–98, 158, 164, 182; focus,
    and, 142; frustration, and, 77–79;
    leadership, as part of, 1, 23, 6, 20, 28, 33;
    Nokia, at, 162; recognizing, 88–93, 95,
    145; results in organizations, 168, 174,
    178; social problem, 24, 28; teams, 151;
    triggers, 64; zone, 2, 3, 5
Apocalypse Now (film), 106
App Store, 125–126

Apple, 16, 21, 125–126, 148, 162
Apple iPhone, 21, 148
Argyris, Chris, 45
auto racing, 134

Barsade, Segal, 149
baseball, 31, 39–41, 44
behavioral economics, 118
Better.com, 25
Big (film), 63
Big Five Personality, 133, 163
Blockbuster video, 16–17
Bloom, Paul, 94
Boeing, vii, viii, 174–175bo
Bonanno, George, 34, 35, 109
boredom, 76–77, 87, 93, 98, 119, 135, 142,
    184, 198
Boyatzis, Richard, 28, 45, 172
brain: focus, and the, 138, 141, 182;
    frustration, 78; goal setting, 182–183;
    hippocampus, 64; neurodiversity, 104;
    overload, 140; positive outlook, 54;
    pre-frontal cortex, 120; resilience, 117;
    response to triggers, 64–65; structure
    and learning, 116

Brooks, Heidi, 21
Burgi-Tian, Jing, 194
Burns, Ursula, 26
Bush, George W., US President, 58

Chapek, Bob, 25, 169
chronotype, 137–138
Circuit City, 174
coaching, viii, 28, 164–165
cognitive-offloading, 10, 140–141, 145
cognitive overload, 10, 135, 140, 143,145
Cohen, Geoffrey, 31–33, 42
comfort zone: definition of 2, 3f;
    developmental value of, 122; emotions
    in, 86, 95, 98; goals, and, 185; moving
    outside of, 83, 132; leading, steps for
    successfully, 7,8; readiness to lead
    outside of, 196–198; relationships, 118;
    stress, 117, 141–142; teams, 148; why
    leaders stay in the, 5, 118
competencies: cognitive, 170; developing,
    83; emotional intelligence as, 172;
    general; leadership, 6, 10, 73, 170–172;
    performance, as 46; relational, 172;
    resilience, 33, 38–39, 171, 170, 175;
    strategic, 172
conscientiousness, 37
Cook, Tim, 125–126,
Coppola, Frances Ford, 106
cortisol, 138–139, 139f
COVID–19, 16, 27, 30, 199
creative problem-solving and creativity:
    definition and role, 5, 6, 10, 102, 104,
    106–107; improving, 110–111; measur-
    ing, 113, 195f; organizations, in, 164;
    self-report, of, 113; teams, 151–152
Crouse, Lindsey, 187
Csikszentmihalyi, Mihaly, 76
Curtis-Wright curve, 51

DEI efforts, 167
DeSantis, Ron, 169

Dewey, John, 72–73, 83
Dickey, R.A., 39–41
Disney, 25, 169–170
Djokovic, Novak, 65
Dopamine, 78, 116–117, 182
Donkey Kong, 77
dopamine, 78, 116–117, 182
Dorsey, Jack, 22, 26
Duckworth, Angela, 36–37
Dwek, Carol, 46, 52, 107–108

emotional coalitions, 97
emotions: accepting, 7,8, 86–88; comfort
    zone, in the 2–3; expressing, 59–60, 149;
    improving, awareness of, 99–101;
    learning, role in, 8, 8f, 46, 74t, 75, 91–94,
    93t; leading through, 59, 89, 90–92;
    measuring with the Learning Strategies
    Questionnaire, 195–196; mental
    toughness, 36; moving outside the
    comfort zone, 28; positive engagement
    with, 102–105; recognition and
    engagement with, 87–89; self-
    awareness, of, 97–99; teams, in, 149;
    triggers, sensitivities, and transitions,
    of, 60–65, 91; unpleasant, 5–7, 8f, 20, 23,
    33–34, 39, 46, 73t, 79, 86–87
Enchantment: Awakening wonder in an
    anxious age, 163
Ericsson, Anders, 45–50, 75, 110
Eriksen, Matthew, 97
Everest, Mount, 53
experiences that support learning, 74t
experiential learning, 122–123
Experiential Learning, Institute for, 115
experiential learning cycle, 122, 123f

FAANG stocks (Facebook, Amazon,
    Apple, Netflix, Google), 16
Facebook, (Meta), 17
Fang He, Vivian, 90
Federer, Roger, 65

Fishbach, Ayelet, 102–103, 110
Flanagan, Shalane, 187
flexibility: competency, as a, 171: improving, 111; learning strategy, as a, 6, 102, 104, 108–109, 113, 195*f*; leadership, and, 37; measuring, 113; organizations, in, 165, 168; teams, in 153
flow, 76–77, 79, 91
focus, 91, 188–120, 131–140, 142–145
football (American and European), 57–60
Fortune 500 CEOs, 26, 126
French Open, 47–48
frustration 1, 4–5, 183, 194, 196–198; accepting of, 10, 21–22, 31, 53; leadership while feeling, 6, 49, 75*t*; neuroscience of, 78; role in learning and resilience, 77–79, 39, 46

General Electric, 8, 15–17
Gladwell, Malcolm, 75
goals: SMART, 178–182, 191; stretch, 177–178, 181–182; tiered, 187–189, 188*t*; tiered goals examples of, 190*t*; willpower, and, 103; zero-harm, 172–174
Goldman, Daniel, 131
Google, 16
grit, 36–37, 102
growth mindset *see also* Dweck, Carol, 107–108, and growth mindset

habits, vii, 20, 110, 181, 199
Hanks, Tom, 63–64
Harrison, Natasha, 27
Hastings, Reed, 17, 19
Hawkins, Lamont (pseud. U-God), 81–82,
healthcare, 34, 73, 168, 171–175
Honnold, Alex, 76
Howard, Ron, 63

Iger, Bob, 169–170
improving and improvement: creative problem solving, 164; emotions, and

the role of, 164, 186; focus, 139, 142–143, 166; goals, 177, 182, 202, 191; matrix, 48–51; optimizing, 50, 154, 188*t*, 197; teams, in, 154–159
Indianapolis 500, 134
Into Thin Air, 53

Jobs, Steve, 148
judgment: competency, as a, 4, 7, 171; decision making, 93; definition of 9, 15, 16, 22, 23, 23*f*, 24–25; grit, 37; improvement of, 110, 122, 164

King, Martin Luther, Jr., 155–156
Kolb, David, 45, 62, 111, 121–123
Krakauer, John, 53

Langer, Ellen, 110
LEAD Model of leadership in healthcare, 172–175
leadership, leader, leading: challenges and opportunities of, 23*t*; changing nature of, 16–18, 154, 177; Cold War versus contemporary, 18; competencies, 170–172; confidence, and, 52; demands of, 4, 7, 171, 152; developing, 65, 67, 72–78, 82–83, 115, 119, 123, 202; emotions, and, 64, 75, 87–99, 124; 'everyday', 21; focus, 131; focusing on positive emotions only, 98–99; goals, 177–178, 183, 186, 189; heroic, 22; learning and, 20; learning cycle and, 122; learning strategies as part of, 103–110, 193; moving outside the comfort zone, 28–32, 86–87; myths, 8, 18–28; need for new strategies, vii, 1, 8, 51; organizations, in 161, 168–171, 175; power and, 58; resilience, 34–38, 42*f*, 57; self-sacrifice and, 8; skills, 18; storytelling, 81, 83–85; teams, 147–149, 158; transitions, 61–63; values, 3

learning *see also* Experiential Learning: abilities, 62; benefits for leading, 4; brain, and the, 116–117; comfort zone, 1–3, 3*f*, 5–6; cycle, 123; deliberate, 49, 49*f*; emotions, and, 93; goal setting, 177, 189, *see also*, LEAD Model; identity, 6, 107–108; neurobiology of, 117; opportunities for, 33; optimized, 33*t*, 49*f*, 50; organizations, in, 164; overcoming loss, 117; performing, versus 2, 9, 47*t*, 76, 43–56; relationships, 118; resilience, as a form of, 1; self-confidence, 52–53; sleep, and, 139, 200–201; teams, in 154–159; zone, 2–5, 3*f*

learning strategies 7–8, 38, 71, 102–111, 124, 142, 193–195; implementation of, 115, 121, 150, 158, 200, 203; organizations, in, 161,163, 175, 189; well-being, and, 159

Learning Strategies Questionnaire, 193–195, 195*f*

Legend of Zelda, 77

Lovell, Jim, 63

Lowenstein, George, 118

Luyendyk, Arie. Sr., 134–135

Mainemelis, Charalampos, 108

march on Washington, 155

Marvel, 169

Maslow, Abraham, 116, 119

MBA students, 104–105, 109, 196

mental contrasting, 185

mental toughness, 31, 34–39

Milkman, Katy, 110

mindset *see also* Dweck, Carol, and growth mindset: viii, 44–46; changing of, 95–96, 99, 164; dual, 9, 45, 48, 54–55, 200; goal setting, 189; improvement, 62; resilience, 39

Miyamoto, Shigeru, 77

Morrissey, Helena, 27

Mouratoglou, Patrick, 48

Musk, Elon, 21–22, 26, 125–126,

Nadal, Raphael, 65

Navy SEALs, 95–96, 98

Netflix, 8, 15–17, 19–20, 169

neurodiversity, 104

New York City Marathon, 187

New York Times, 187

Newport, Cal, 143

Nike, 106

9/11, 35, 58

Nokia, 162

Oettingen, Gabriele, 185

Olympic athletes, 77

Olympics, 187

Outliers, (book), 75

patient safety, 173, 175

peer coaching, 28, 164,

perfectionism, 184,

Peterson, Kay, 115

Pink, Daniel, 116

Plateau: in teams, 154–155, 159; performance, 42, 49–50, 50*f*, 56

positive emotional engagement 5, 163, 196; improves focus, 142; learning strategy, as a, 104–106, 113; measuring, 113; organizations, in, 163; teams, in, 150–151

posttraumatic stress and growth, 34–35

power, 58, 126; emotions, 164; groups and teams, in, 148–150; heroic leadership, 22; learning, 5, 124; myth of leadership, 19–21; resource, as a, 9, 15–17, 20, 19*t*, 150; traditional leadership, 15, 17; university leaders and lack of, 26

Price, Terry, 25

procrastination, 5, 87, 93*f*, 178–180, 184, 191

productive failure, 107

productive well-being, 126, 205–206

resilience: adapting to adversity, 34–36; biology and neurobiology of, 78, 199–200; building blocks of, 38–42;

competencies, 8, 38, 170–172; definition of, 5, 16, 30–34, 115–117, 124; development of, 41–42, 62, 74, 96, 193; emotions related to, 5, 88, 90–91, 97–99; focusing for, 137–138, 140; goal setting, 182, 189; leading, as the basis for, 1, 22; learning, as the basis for, 17, 95, 201; mental toughness and grit, 36–37; myths about, 16, 19t, 21; need for, 24, 26, 175; organizational, 161–165, 167; performance, 78, 127; positive, 33, 54; returning to normal, 37–38; stories of, 79, 81; strategies for building, 102–110; teams, 148, 149, 159; training, 38

Samsung, 162

Sapolsky, Robert, 117–118, 141–142

Sarandos, Ted, 17, 19,

satisfaction, work, 1, 38, 93t, 116, 185

Segway, 166–167

Seidel, Molly, 187

self-confidence, 51–53, 107

Self-determination Theory, 116, 119

self-esteem, 22, 37, 48, 53–54, 103, 107, 111, 189

Sherman, David, 31–33, 42

Smith, Melvin, 172

soccer, 59–60

social support 7, 10, 28, 35, 39, 109–110; development of, 111, 113, 197; learning strategy, 102, 104, 105, 109–110, 118; organizations, 171; teams, 153–154

Solomon, George, 90

special forces (US) *see also* Navy SEALs, 36

Stockwell, David, 173

STOP technique, 65

stress: emotions, 89, 93t, 97; goal setting, 179, 184; grit, 36–37; hormones and biological mechanisms, 64, 118; leadership demands related to, 5; leading outside the comfort zone, and,

3, 4; learning, and its role in, 2, 117–118, 142; life transitions, and, 105, 109; management as a learning strategy, 103–104, 141–142, 197; millennial generation, 24; overcoming through training practices, 38; performing, while, 46, 195; reducing at the organizational level, 126; resilience and adapting to, 31, 34, 38–39, 54, 95–98, 144–146; short-term relief through self-care, 22; situations associated with, 134, 140; sleeping to reduce, 201; teams, in, 157–164, 195; work, at, 2, 168, 171, 174–175, 199

stressors, 26, 145, 134, 139, 179, 194

Super Mario Bros., 77

teams: balancing learning and performing, 154–155; conflict, 82; diverse workforce, 67, 73; emotions, 89, 147–150, 157–159; Everest Mount climbing, 53; football and soccer, 58–5; healthcare, 73; leadership teams, 17; leading outside the comfort zone, 147, 156–157; musical, 82; positive resilience and, 34; social change, 15; strategies for leading, 150–154

technology firms, 8, 16, 19, 20, 22, 61, 105, 119, 162

Tedeschi, Richard, 35

10,000-hour rule, 75

The Godfather, (film), 106

30 percent club, 27

Thomas, Eric, 173

Trinh, Aurora, 107

Tsay, Crystal, 105, 109

Twitter, (X), 22, 125–126,

U.S. Air Force Academy, 144

U.S. Naval Academy, 144

U.S. Surgeon General, 24

university presidents, 25

Van Oosten, Ellen, 172
Van Tilburg, 98
Vince, Russ, 23, 79, 97
visual shifting, 157
Vygotsky, Lev, 2

Wegner, Daniel, 133–134
Weick, Karl, 81
Welch, Jack, 8, 17–18
well-being: building blocks of, 199–201;
    careers, 27; competency models, 171;
    emotions, 71, 87–88, 91, 99; focus
    and, 143, 154; goal setting, 177; health
    care, in 174–175; judgment and, 25;
    leading for, 8f, 19t, 23f, 97; leadership
    role in, 171; learning, 57, 115–116,
    118–119, 20; learning strategies, 159;
    myths about, 21–22, organizational
    effectiveness, 24–27, 161, 17; persever-
    ance, 103; policies to support, 167,

16; rumination, 136; sleep, 138; stress,
    141
Wells Fargo, 174
WeWork, 174
white bears experiment, 133–134, 137, 143
Williams, Serena, 47–48
Winch, Guy, 98
Wirtz, Phil, 194
Wood, Wendy, 110
work-life balance, 24, 27, 187
World Health Organization, 24
World Trade Center, 58
Wu-Tang Clan, 81–82

Xerox, 26

yoga, 103, 144

zero-harm targets, 172–174
Zull, Jim, 116–118